论语辨正与美译

An Interpretation and Translation of the Analects of Confucius

侯长林　译注

辽宁人民出版社

图书在版编目（CIP）数据

《论语》辨正与英译 / 侯长林译注. —沈阳：辽宁人民出版社，2023.3

ISBN 978-7-205-10619-5

Ⅰ. ①论… Ⅱ. ①侯… Ⅲ. ①儒家 ②《论语》—研究 Ⅳ. ①B222.25

中国版本图书馆CIP数据核字（2022）第207860号

出版发行：辽宁人民出版社
　　　　　地址：沈阳市和平区十一纬路25号　邮编：110003
　　　　　电话：024-23284321（邮　购）　024-23284324（发行部）
　　　　　传真：024-23284191（发行部）　024-23284304（办公室）
　　　　　http://www.lnpph.com.cn
印　　刷：辽宁新华印务有限公司
幅面尺寸：145mm×210mm
印　　张：12
字　　数：300千字
出版时间：2023年3月第1版
印刷时间：2023年3月第1次印刷
责任编辑：顾　宸
封面设计：陈天艺
版式设计：姿　兰
责任校对：刘再升
书　　号：ISBN 978-7-205-10619-5

定　　价：58.00元

前　言

这本书的写作原属偶然。给学生上翻译课，时常用到《论语》的译例，后来专门开设了《论语》英译课。备课的需要，得以深入探究《论语》的词句理解及英语翻译。先贤严肃的探究有时也会错得很离谱，很乐人，于是萌生了一个念头：自己写一本"辨正与英译"的书。三年时间整理成书，虽始于偶然，却也水到渠成。

我的《察微治细》一书里有一辑"论语辨正"，那里的短文是就某一词句穷挖，语气也有畅所欲言的放肆。而现在这书的辨正则尽量简洁，芟尽枝蔓芜杂，庄重起来，趣味少了。

现代人解读古代经典，犹如考古。言者已作古，不能起而面谈，解惑答疑，然而文字犹在，沿文法训诂之道，迤逦探寻，再征之古籍，当能探得言者之旨。

探寻之路，多是踏着先贤的足迹。例如，《先进第十一》"颜路请子之车以为之椁"句，句中有"以车为椁"，却看不出"卖车买椁"的意思。宦懋庸《论语稽》中指出"卖车买椁之说有八不可解"。令人感到奇怪的是，就如白平《杨伯峻〈论语译注〉商榷》中所指出的，"这些分析都有理有据，被程树德誉为'发前人未发，确不可易'。程氏《论语集释》，大家都作为自己写书的参考，不知道为什么在这个'棹'的解释上置'八不可解'于不顾而不肯采纳宦懋庸的意见。"先贤溯流穷源，结论确不可易者，后来人就应沿袭，而不必再辟蹊径，别树一帜了。

解经释典，当于纷纭众说中判定正误，识别正途而趋近言者原意。徐晋如《晋如说儒》里提出了"三个原则"，值得遵循："解释经典，我觉得要符合三个原则：第一个原则，就是要符合小学的原则，就是你必须要在文字、音韵、训诂这些方面能够有一个比较直接的证据来证明；第二就是你必须要符合上下文的逻辑关系；第三个你要符合整个思想体系，你不能在整个思想体系之内，内在是矛盾的。因为一个思想体系，它的内在一定要是自洽的，一定不能是矛盾的。"

在纷纭聚讼中振叶寻根，探究最接近言者真意的解读，是极高的追求。就如杨逢彬在《论语新注新译》中所说，"著者的理想是，将词句考证做成环环相扣严丝合缝的艺术品"，或如李克曼在其《论语》译本里所说，"我的期望是学术与文学兼顾（My hope is to reconcile learning with literature）"，都是完美的、无可挑剔的理想。而实践起来则会发现，完美可望而难及。自以为寻得了孔子的真意，在他者看来或许只是自以为是。我们只求尽力探寻，贡献我们自以为是的见解。时光水逝，岁月浪淘，后来者不乏明眼人，他们自会从中识辨，在探寻真意的道路上更进一步，解读更臻完美。

我要感谢澳大利亚的罗斯·可胡恩（Ross Colquhoun）博士，他在中国生活工作多年，对中国文学和中国文化有着广博的了解，因此，他能对我的英译进行纠错、改进、润色，还提出了极有价值的建议。我还要感谢澳大利亚阿德莱德大学毕业的朱莹博士对我工作的支持，是她将罗斯·可胡恩博士介绍给我。

侯长林

二〇二二年三月于济南大学

目录

学而第一

1·1 子曰："学而时习之，不亦说①乎？有朋自远方来，不亦乐乎？人不知，而不愠②，不亦君子乎？"

【注释】
①说（yuè）：通"悦"，愉悦，高兴。
②愠（yùn）：恼怒，怨恨。

【今译】
夫子说："学了然后适时练习，不是很愉快吗？有朋友从远方来，不是很高兴吗？别人不了解自己而不愠怒，不是很（有）君子（的德行）吗？"

【英译】

The Master said: "Is it not pleasant to learn and then practice at the right time what one has learnt? Is it not delightful to receive like-minded friends who come from afar? Is it not gentlemanly to remain unoffended when not being understood?"

【辨正】
杨树达《论语疏证》："时习而说，学者自修之事也；朋来而乐，以文会友之事也；不知而不愠，则为德性坚定之人矣。孔子之言次第极分明也。"不无道理。但像南怀瑾《孔学新语自序》所说，"二十篇《论语》，每篇都条理井然，脉络一贯。而且二十篇的编排，都是首尾呼应，等于一篇天衣无缝的好文章"，就又走至极端了。牛泽群《论语札记》里说"坚确《论》虽杂排，'学而'居首不为随机，乃措意之为，何其迂拘也。"

1·2　有子曰："其为人也孝弟^①，而好^②犯上者，鲜^③矣；不好犯上，而好作乱者，未之有也。君子务本，本立而道生。孝弟也者，其为仁之本与！"

【注释】
①弟（tì）：同"悌"，弟弟敬爱兄长。
②好（hào）：喜爱。
③鲜（xiǎn）：寡，少。同"尠"。

【今译】
有子说："做人孝顺父母、敬爱兄长却好犯上的人，非常少见；不好犯上却好作乱的，从未有过。君子致力于根本，根本确立了，道就产生了。孝与悌，就是仁道的根本啊！"

【英译】
Master You said: "Among those who are filial and fraternal, few will be inclined to defy their superiors; among those who are not inclined to defy their superiors, no single one will foment a rebellion. A gentleman will commit himself to cultivate the roots, which, once firmly established, the principles will naturally sprout therefrom. Filial piety and fraternity are therefore the very roots of benevolence."

1·3 子曰:"巧言令色,鲜矣仁!"

【今译】

夫子说:"言语甜蜜动听,容色悦目谄媚,这种人很少有仁者。"

【英译】

The Master said, "Rarely is a man benevolent whose speech is cunning and whose countenance is ingratiating."

1·4 曾子曰:"吾日三省吾身①:为人谋而不忠乎?与朋友交而不信乎?传不习乎?"

【注释】

①三省(xǐng):参省,反省。"叁"通"参",比勘,验证。

【今译】

曾子说:"我每天都省察自己:为别人办事没有尽心竭力吗?与朋友交往没有信守诺言吗?老师传授的学业没有练习吗?"

【英译】

Master Zeng said, "Every day I examine myself on these counts: Was I dedicated to my duty when working for others? Was I trustworthy in dealing with friends? Was I well acquainted with what I was taught?"

《大戴礼记·曾子立事》说："日旦就业，夕而自省思，以
殁其身，亦可谓守业矣。"看来并非一天到晚地多次反思。

白平《杨伯峻〈论语译注〉商榷》说："这里的'三'当
通'参'，'参省'当为复语，'参'亦'省'义。《荀子·劝
学》：'君子博学而日参省乎已，则知明而行无过矣。'"

**1·5 子曰："道千乘之国①，敬事而信②，节用而爱人，
使民以时③。"**

【注释】

①道：同"导"，领导、治理。千乘（shèng）：方圆百里
之诸侯国。包咸曰："千乘之国者，百里之国也。古者井田，
方里为井，十井为乘；百里之国，适千乘也。"

②敬事：处理国家大事严肃谨慎。事，指国家大事，主要
是祭祀与军事（"国之大事，在祀与戎"）。

③使：役使，令百姓服徭役。以时：根据时令，不在耕种
或收割季节役使百姓。

【今译】

夫子说："治理一个诸侯国，行事要敬慎，有诚信，节省
财用，爱养人民，役使百姓要依据农时。"

【英译】

The Master said, "To govern a country of a hundred square
li, the ruler should: conduct state affairs with sincerity and punc-
tually observe his promises; be frugal in expenditure and preserve his people, employing them in public affairs only between

the intervals in farming."

【辨正】

方观旭《论语偶记》:"《先进篇》冉有曰:'方六七十如五六十,谦不敢当千乘之国。'则千乘之国为百里甚明。"《春秋》述三代之制:"大国地方百里,有万井。十井而赋一乘,故曰千乘。"

日本物茂卿《论语徵》:"万乘、千乘、百乘,古言也。谓天子为万乘,诸侯为千乘,大夫为百乘,语其富也。如千金之子,孰能计其囊之藏适若干而言之乎?古来注家布算求合,可谓'不解事子云'矣。"

1·6 子曰:"弟子,入则孝,出则弟,谨而信,泛爱众,而亲仁。行有余力,则以学文。"

【今译】

夫子说:"年轻人,回家就孝顺父母,出外就敬顺兄长,寡言而守信,普爱众人,亲近仁者。这样做还有余力,再学习文化。"

【英译】

The Master said, "A young man should be filial towards his parents at home and obedient to his elders when out. He should be reserved in speech and observe his words, overflow with love toward all people and befriend the virtuous. If he still has energy after performing all of these, he can go on to cultivate himself."

1·7 子夏曰："贤贤易色；事父母，能竭其力；事君，能致其身；与朋友交，言而有信。虽曰未学，吾必谓之学矣。"

【今译】

子夏说："崇尚内在贤德，不重表面容色；侍奉父母，能够尽心竭力；服侍君主，能够舍命；与朋友交往，能信守诺言。这样的人，即使说没有学习，我一定说他已学过了。"

【英译】

Zixia said, "A man should value virtues rather than outward appearance, do his utmost in serving his parents, be ready to give up his life in serving his lord, and be trustworthy in his relationships with friends. Such a man is, to me, certainly well-educated even if he is said to be ignorant."

【辨正】

杨伯峻《论语译注》里注曰："贤贤易色——这句话，一般的解释是：'用尊贵优秀品德的心来交换（或者改变）爱好美色的心。'照这种解释，这句话的意义就比较空泛。陈祖范的《经咫》、宋翔凤的《朴学斋札记》等书却说，以下三句，事父母、事君、交朋友，各指一定的人事关系；那么，'贤贤易色'也应该是指某一种人事关系而言，不能是一般的泛指。奴隶社会和封建社会把夫妻间关系看得极重，认为是'人伦之始'和'王化之基'，这里开始便谈到它，是不足为奇的。我认为这话很有道理。'易'有交换、改变的意义，也有轻视（如言'轻易'）、简慢的意义。因之我便用《汉书》卷七十五《李寻传》颜师古注的说法，把'易色'解为'不重容貌'。"赞同把"易"解成"不重"，这与"贤"字正相对。解作"交换"或"改变"都太滑稽，并非"以贤易色"，再说"用尊贵优秀品德的心来交换（或者改变）爱好美色的心"，何为？色不是美色，是容色。

事父母以孝，事君以忠，交朋友以信，贤贤易色却未必是事妻。若是，能解释清楚"事妻"二字为何省去不言吗？

1·8 子曰："君子不重则不威；学则不固。主忠信。无友不如己者；过，则勿惮改。"

【今译】

夫子说："君子不庄重就没有威严；学习就不会固陋；崇尚忠信。不与不如自己的人交朋友；有了过错，就不要怕改正。"

【英译】

The Master said, "A gentleman will not be dignified without being solemn. Study will keep him from being ignorant. He values highly devotion and trustworthiness. He will not make friends with those who are less virtuous. He will readily correct his mistakes if he makes any."

【辨正】

说"不重则不威"有道理，但若说"不庄重，学的东西就不稳固"就欠妥了。把"学"译为名词"所学"，不是译"学则不固"，而是在译"则学不固"。"学"应当是动词。

"无友不如己者"不是教人"势利""计量彼我之高下优劣，而定择交之条件"，而是以胜己者为榜样，见贤思齐，不断提高自己的道德。

1·9 曾子曰："慎终，追远①，民德归厚矣②。"

【注释】

①慎：诚敬，慎重。终：人死曰终，曰归。古者谓死人为归人。追：祭祀先人，永志不忘。远：时间久，代指远祖，先祖。

②归：逐渐地，最终变得……。厚：淳厚，忠厚，不偷薄。

【今译】

曾子说："诚敬对待丧葬，祭祀远代祖先，民风就会逐渐变得淳厚起来。"

【英译】

Master Zeng said, "Cultivate respect for the dead by conducting the funeral with piety, bring forth the memory of distant ancestors by offering them sacrifices, and the virtue of the people will come to be pure and honest."

1·10 子禽问于子贡曰：夫子至于是邦也，必闻其政，求之与？抑与之与？"子贡曰："夫子温、良、恭、俭、让以得之。夫子之求之也，其诸异乎人之求之与？"

【今译】

子禽问子贡说："老师到了一个国家，总能了解到这国的政事，是他自己要求的呢，还是人家主动给他的呢？"子贡说："老师温、良、恭、俭、让而得到的。老师的求法，大概与别人的求法不一样吧？"

【英译】

Ziqin asked Zigong, "When arriving in a state, the Master will invariably be consulted on its government affairs. Does he seek it? Or is it offered to him?" "The Master," replied Zigong, "gets it through being cordial, well- behaved, respectful, frugal and deferential. The way he seeks it is, perhaps, different from that of others?"

1 · 11　子曰："父在，观其志；父没，观其行①；三年无改于父之道，可谓孝矣。"

【注释】

①行（xìng）：指行为举止等。

【今译】

夫子说；"他父亲在世时，观察他的志向；他父亲去世后，观察他的行为；若是（守丧）三年不改变他父亲的行事原则，就可以说是孝了。"

【英译】

The Master said, "Observe a man's aspiration when his father is alive, and observe his actions after his father's death. If he does not alter the ways of his father in the three years of mourning, he can be counted as a filial son."

【辨正】

"其"指子，不指父。《十三经注疏》里邢昺说得很清楚："'父在观其志'者，在心为志。父在，子不得自专，故观其志而已。'父没观其行'者，父没可以自专，乃观其行也。'三年无改于父之道，可谓孝矣'者，言孝子在丧三年，哀慕犹若父存，无所改于父之道，可谓为孝也。"

把"其"解作"父"则滑稽不通。"杨循吉谓宜作人子之观其父解，父在时子当观父志之所在而曲体之，父没则父之志不可见，而其生平行事尚有可记者，则即其行事而取法之。"（赵翼《陔余丛考》）实是费力穿凿。首先，为何人一死，志就亡？"从其生平行事尚有可记者"观其志可否？其次，父行为何要在父没以后观？父在世，一举一动都在眼前可观，为何此时不观，偏要待父没以后从"尚有可记者"中观呢？

"父之道"不能强解为"父亲正确的方法或原则"，否则就有两点难以讲通。其一是"三年内不改父亲的正确原则，父亲错误的原则可以改"。即便是错误原则，父殁即改，也非孝子。其二是"三年内不改父亲的正确原则，三年后就可以改"。改变正确的原则，向哪个方向改？既是正确原则，就无需改动，那么，孔子所树的"三年"这个界限有何意义？其实"三年无改于父之道"是说，孝就是子承父志，即使父有错要改，也须在服丧三年之后。

这一章讲的是"如何判断一个人孝"，所以我们要观其志，观其行，还要观其守丧三年改不改父道。

1·12　有子曰："礼之用，和为贵。先王之道，斯为美。小大由之，有所不行。知和而和，不以礼节之，亦不可行也。"

【今译】

有子说："礼的应用，以和为贵。古代君主的治国方法，可贵的地方就在这点。大事小事都以和为贵，却行不通。为和而和，不以礼来节制，也不可行。"

Master You said, "In practicing the rites, harmony is most valued. It is the most excellent quality of the ways of the ancient kings. Yet it is not to be observed in all cases regardless of the particular situation. It is not desirable to achieve harmony for its own sake without being restrained by the rites."

【辨正】

"和"的含义很多，注家莫衷一是，时常前后抵牾，难得贯通。这里解作"和谐"，也就是双方相容相济，不冲突。与"君子和而不同"的"和"也一致。

"小大由之"的"之"，即"和为贵"，也就是"斯为美"的"斯"。

断句是这一节的问题所在。"先王之道，斯为美，小大由之。"就是称赞先王处理事情不论大小都追求和，这是"美"，而下面又说，只追求和，不以礼节之，也不可行。——这等于又把"大小事都追求和"给否了。"小大由之"，与前面对先王的赞美分开，连到下句"有所不行"。下面的"知和而和"是"有所不行"的例子。

1·13　有子曰："信近于义，言可复也。恭近于礼，远耻辱也。因不失其亲，亦可宗也。"

【今译】

有子说："信与义相近，诺言可以兑现。恭与礼相近，使人免于耻辱。信、恭因为与义、礼存在紧密关系，因此也可尊崇。"

Master You said, "Trustworthiness approximates to righteousness in that promises can be fulfilled. Respectfulness approximates to rites in that it can keep clear of disgrace and insults. Closely related to righteousness and rites, trustworthiness and respectfulness can therefore also be observed."

【辨正】

"信"是"信用""守信"之"信"，是"信""义""恭""礼"四种德性之一，即诚实不欺，不能具体解释成"诺言"；"近"即相近、接近，不要牵强讲成"符合"；"亲"是"关系（密切）"，不是"关系深的人"；"宗"不是形容词"可靠"，也不是名词"主"或"宗族"，而是动词"遵奉""尊崇"。

朱熹《论语集注》里说："复，践言也。"

"姻"从"因"来，也不能因此而证"因"即"姻"。古书古语里有"姻不失亲"的说法，也不能因此肯定此处就是指缔姻。"缔姻不失其可亲之人，则亦可等于同宗"何其悠谬且不说，只说，上面讲"信""义""恭""礼"的关系，何以突转到婚姻上去呢？

1·14 子曰："君子食无求饱，居无求安，敏于事而慎于言，就有道而正焉，可谓好学也已。"

【今译】

夫子说："君子，饮食不求饱足，居住不求舒适，做事勤勉，说话谨慎，请教有道者以匡正自己，就可以说是好学了。"

The Master said, "A gentleman may be said to love learning if he seeks no satiety in food, nor comfort in dwelling, being diligent in action and cautious in speech, and consults virtuous people to reform himself."

1·15　子贡曰："贫而无谄①，富而无骄，何如？"子曰："可也；未若贫而乐，富而好礼者也。"

　　子贡曰："《诗》云'如切如磋，如琢如磨②'，其斯之谓与？"子曰："赐也，始可与言《诗》已矣，告诸往而知来者③。"

【注释】

①谄（chǎn）：阿谀，奉承。

②如切如磋，如琢如磨：见《诗经·卫风·淇澳》。切：用刀切断。磋：用锉锉平。琢：用刀雕刻。磨：用物磨光。这两句以治骨角玉石等比喻君子努力修学进德。

③诸：之。往：过去。来：未来。而（néng）：能。

【今译】

　　子贡说："贫穷而不谄媚，富有而不傲慢，怎么样？"夫子说："这也不错了。但不如贫却快乐，富却好礼。"

　　子贡说："《诗经》上说，'如切如磋，如琢如磨'，讲的就是这个意思吧？"夫子说："赐呀，从此可以与你谈论《诗经》了。告诉你过去，你就能知道未来。"

【英译】

Zigong asked the Master, "What do you think of the people

who do not flatter when poor, and are not arrogant when rich?" "They are good enough," replied the Master, "but better still are those who are content when poor, and ready to abide by the rites when rich."

"Is this a case in point," Zigong proceeded, "spoken of in *The Book of Songs*— 'Cutting, filing, carving and polishing make a complete man.'" The Master said, "I can talk about *The Book of Songs* with you from now, Ci, as you can know the future when told about the past."

1·16　子曰："不患人之不己知，患不知人也。"

【今译】

夫子说："不必担心别人不了解自己，应担心自己不了解别人。"

【英译】

The Master said, "Worry not about whether people appreciate you, but whether you appreciate others."

为政第二

2 · 1 子曰："为政以德①，譬如北辰，居其所而众星共之②。"

【注释】

①为政以德：即"以德为政"，用道德教化来治理国家。

③所：位。共（gǒng）：同"拱"，捧，归向，拱卫。

【今译】

夫子说："以德治国，（百姓归心），就像北极星在其位，众星都归向它一样。"

【英译】

The Master said, "Governing a state with virtue makes the subjects comply willingly the same way the polestar, staying in its place, attracts other stars toward it."

【辨正】

这一篇的主旨是讲，以德治国能赢得民众归心、拥戴，就像众星捧北辰一样。是说民心归向如众星共（拱）北辰，并不强调众星是不是绕北辰一圈。

这一点也可以从"共"字的字形上得到佐证。

四手共力，是"共"。两手奉物，即是"供"，"供奉"；供奉要诚敬，那就是"恭"；两手上举，即"拱"手；一手不能完成，要两手一起，那就是"共"同。由"捧举"到"拱手"，再到"两手合围"，就是俗语里测量树的粗度，有"一搂""一抱"粗。但"共"并没有"环绕"义。

北辰居上，众星在下共之捧之。

2·2　子曰："《诗》三百，一言以蔽之，曰：'思无邪①'。"

【注释】

①思无邪：此为《诗经·鲁颂·駉》里的一句。思：句首词，无意义。无邪：纯正，情真。

【今译】

夫子说："《诗经》三百篇，用一句话来概括它，就是'（思想）纯正'。"

【英译】

The Master said, "The three hundred pieces of poetry in *The Book of Songs* can be summed up in one phrase—'They are unaffected.'"

2·3　子曰："道之以政，齐之以刑，民免而无耻；道之以德，齐之以礼，有耻且格。"

【今译】

夫子说："用政令教导百姓，用刑法来规矩他们，老百姓就放逸，没有羞耻之心；用道德教化百姓，用礼制去规矩他们，百姓就有羞耻之心，且能遵守法度。"

The Master said, "Guide the common people by edicts, regulate them with punishments, and they will try to stay out of trouble without developing the sense of shame. Guide them by virtue, regulate them with rites, and they will have the sense of shame and become disciplined."

【辨正】

《礼记·缁衣》："夫民，教之以德，齐之以礼，则民有格心；教之以政，齐之以刑，则民有遁心。"

"格"解释成"至""来"，引申为归服，不妥。来归之前，不是其民，如何道与齐？

2·4 子曰："吾十有五而志于学，三十而立，四十而不惑，五十而知天命，六十而耳顺，七十而从心所欲，不逾矩。"

【今译】

夫子说："我十五岁立志学习；三十岁自立；四十岁不再有疑惑；五十岁懂得了天命；六十岁正确对待各种言论；七十岁随心所欲而不越出规矩。"

【英译】

The Master said, "At the age of fifteen I set my mind on learning; at thirty I became established; at forty I became insightful; at fifty I came to know the mission I was endowed with; at sixty I became attuned to any comments; at seventy I follow my heart without violating the rites."

2 · 5　孟懿子问孝，子曰："无违。"

樊迟御，子告之曰："孟孙问孝于我，我对曰，无违。"

樊迟曰："何谓也？"子曰："生，事之以礼；死，葬之以礼，祭之以礼。"

【今译】

孟懿子请教孝道，夫子说："不要违背（礼）。"樊迟给夫子驾车，夫子对他说："孟孙问我什么是孝，我回答说，不要违背（礼）。"樊迟说："这是什么意思呢？"夫子说："父母活着，要按照礼侍奉他们；父母去世了，要按照礼安葬他们、祭祀他们。"

【英译】

Meng Yizi asked about filial piety. The Master answered, "Never go against the rites." Afterwards the Master said to Fan Chi, who was driving, "Mengsun asked me about filial piety, and I replied 'Never go against the rites.'" Fan Chi thereupon asked, "What did you mean by that?" The Master answered: "While parents live, serve them in accordance with the rites; after they pass away, bury them and offer sacrifice to them in accordance with the rites."

【辨正】

"无违"是"毋违父命"，还是"毋违礼"？"善事父母，旧时以尽心奉养和绝对服从为孝。"按照这种"孝"的定义，孟懿子既是问孝，作为回答的"无违"解释成"不违逆父母命"，可以说文从字顺。但是，接下来孔子自己对"无违"解释说，"生，事之以礼；死，葬之以礼，祭之以礼"，可见"无违"解作"毋违礼"更恰当。

孔子对孟懿子说，遵从父命，就是孝；对樊迟解释说，事亲以礼，就是孝。为何只说"无违"而不直说"无违父母命"或"无违礼"呢？《论语集解义疏》里说："不即告孟孙者，初时意在简略，欲使思而得之也。必告樊迟者，恐孟孙以为从父之令是无违，故既与别，后告于樊迟，将使复告孟孙也。"无违亲命之孝，亦当以礼节之，以礼衡之。

2·6　孟武伯问孝。子曰："父母唯其疾之忧。"

【今译】

孟武伯请教孝道。夫子说："父母（没有什么担心的，）只担心子女生病。"

【英译】

Meng Wubo asked about filial piety. The Master answered: "Do not make your parents worry about you except when you fall ill."

【辨正】

"父母唯其疾之忧。"这里的"其"指谁？换句话说，谁生病？谁担忧？

李零《丧家狗：我读〈论语〉》里说："'父母，唯其疾之忧'，是子女唯恐父母生病。《淮南子·说林》'忧父母之疾者子，治之者医'，是年代较早的证明。马融说，孝子从来不让父母操心，除了生病，说法太绕。朱注也绕。他们都说反了。"

毛子水《论语今注今译》里说："马曰：'言孝子不妄为非，唯疾病然后使父母忧。'马融以为孔子这话的意思是：一个人能够做到只有生病的时候才使父母担忧，便可以算是孝了。马氏这个解释，可以说是这一章古来最好的解释；实在，这一章亦只有这个解释讲得通。（'其'，指人子讲；以前学者有以为指父母讲的，大错！）"

两说一矛一盾，必不共存。既是问孝，子忧父母疾，似乎很自然。但是，句中还有一"唯"字需要解释。子只忧父母疾，不管其它，如何称孝子？况且，"'其'字与父母重复，终觉未安"（程树德《论语集释》）。即便"父母"后以逗号断开，重复的毛病依然未愈。为人子者，不使父母担心，即是孝，而疾病者，非人力所能止，是父母唯一需要担心的。这样解可能有点绕，"圣人之告人未有隐约其词若此者"，然而，文顺义洽，是毛子水所说的唯一"讲得通""古来最好的解释"。

2·7　子游问孝。子曰："今之孝者，是谓能养①。至于犬马，皆能有养；不敬，何以别乎？"

【注释】

①养（yàng）：供养。《玉篇·食部》："养，具珍馐以供养尊者也。"

【今译】

子游请教孝道。夫子说："如今所谓的孝，只叫供养。就是犬马，都能得到供养。如果没有敬意，何以区别于供养犬马呢？"

【英译】

Ziyou asked about filial piety. The Master said, "Being filial nowadays is merely being able to keep parents, which, in some ways, is similar to keeping hounds and horses. Without due reverence, in what way can it be different from keeping animals?"

2·8 子夏问孝。子曰："色难。有事，弟子服①其劳；有酒食，先生馔，曾②是以为孝乎?"

【注释】
①服：从事，担负。
②曾（zēng）：乃，竟。

【今译】
子夏请教孝道，夫子说："（孝），最不容易的就是事父母时和颜悦色。仅仅是有了事情，替先生去做，有了酒饭，让先生吃，难道这样就可以认为是孝了吗?"

【英译】
Zixia asked about filial piety. The Master said, "The most difficult thing to do is to serve their parents with a pleasant countenance. Do you think being filial is merely the same as serving a teacher—taking on the toil when there is work to do, or serving the teacher with wine and food when available?"

【辨正】
色，有两说，一说是侍奉父母时的容色，即和颜悦色。一说是承顺父母颜色。杨伯峻不取第二说，因为"若原意果如此的话，应该说为'侍色为难'，不该简单地说为'色难'。"
为什么这里不直接说父母与儿女，而说先生与弟子? 先生是否可指父兄？

　　刘沅《四书恒解》："称父母为先生，人子与父母前称弟子，自古无此理。此章言敬而不爱，亦不得为孝也。服劳奉养，凡弟子事尊长皆然。事父母则深爱，和气自心，即有他事，一见父母便欣然蔼然，凡忧闷之都忘却了，此为色难。子夏未知此，故夫子晓之，言弟子事先生亦不可例父母也。郑氏《述要》：集注以先生训父兄，家庭父子兄弟竟改称先生弟子，虽曰本于马注，而他外绝不经见，向甚疑之，及读《四书考异》云云，遂为恍然。事师事亲同一左右就养，虽为《内则》所载，然师者道之所在，严肃之意较多，事父母更当柔色以温之。夫子言此，用弟子事先生之礼不足以为孝也。"

　　2·9　子曰："吾与回言终日，不违，如愚。退而省其私，亦足以发，回也不愚。"

【今译】

　　夫子说："我给颜回讲学一整天，他也没有反对意见，像是很愚笨。他回去后，我考察他私下的言行，觉得他完全可以点拨指导，颜回并不愚笨。"

【英译】

The Master said, "I talked with Hui a whole day long and he did not raise any objection, as if he were stupid. But when I observe him when he is on his own, I knew for sure that he can be enlightened and was by no means stupid."

2·10　子曰：“视其所以①，观其所由②，察其所安③。人焉廋④哉？人焉廋哉？”

【注释】

①以：因，凭依。所以：行事所凭依的原则。
②由：从，行。所由：从何而来，所行之道。
③安：乐。所安：意气归向，喜欢所在。
④廋（sōu）：隐藏，掩饰。

【今译】

夫子说：“看看一个人所凭依的原则，观察他经由的道路，考察他心安的事情，他怎样能隐藏得了呢？他怎样能隐藏得了呢？”

【英译】

The Master said, "Look at what a man relies on, observe the course he takes, and examine what he rests content with, and then, how can he conceal himself? How can he conceal himself?"

2·11　子曰：“温故而知新，可以为师矣。”

【今译】

夫子说：“过去的事情温习不忘，就能由此知晓现在的事情，这样就可以做老师了。”

【英译】

The Master said, "A man is worthy of being a teacher if he

can keep fresh in mind what happened in the past and perceive clearly what happens later."

2·12 子曰："君子不器。"

【今译】

夫子说："君子不像器具那样（，只有某一方面的用途）。"

【英译】

The Master said, "A scholarly gentleman is not simply a vessel designed for a specific use."

2·13 子贡问君子。子曰："先行其言而后从之。"

【今译】

子贡问怎样做一个君子。夫子说："对于要说的话，先实践，然后再说出来。"

【英译】

Zigong asked about how to be a gentleman. The Master said, "He puts his ideas into action before speaking them out."

2·14 子曰："君子周^①而不比^②，小人比而不周。"

【注释】
①周：合群。
②比（bǐ）：勾结。

夫子说："君子团结众人而不拉帮结派，小人结党营私而不团结众人。"

【英译】

The Master said, "A gentleman associates with others for the benefit of all people whereas a petty man joins them for his own benefit."

2·15 子曰："学而不思则罔，思而不学则殆。"

【今译】

夫子说："只读书学习而不思考，就会茫然无知；只思考而不读书学习，就会疑惑不决。"

【英译】

The Master said, "He who learns without reflecting will be lost in a haze and he who reflects without learning will be baffled as if in a maze."

【辨正】

清王念孙："'思而不学则殆'，言无所依据则疑而不决也。又曰'多闻阙疑，慎言其余，则寡尤；多见阙殆，慎行其余，则寡悔。'殆，亦疑也。悔亦尤也，变文协韵耳。"

陆世仪《思辨录》："悟处皆出于思，不思无由得悟。思处皆缘于学，不学则无可思。学者，所以求悟也。悟者，思而得通也。"

王夫之《四书训义》："致知之道有二：曰学，曰思……学非有碍于思，而学愈博则思愈远；思正有功于学，而思之困则学必勤。"

2·16 子曰："攻乎异端，斯害也已。"

【今译】

夫子说："专攻他技小道，这就成祸害了。"

【英译】

The Master said, "To devote oneself to the study of heterodoxy is indeed harmful."

【辨正】

程树德《论语集释》按云："此章诸说纷纭，莫衷一是，此当以本经用语例决之。《论语》中凡用攻字均作攻伐解，如'小子鸣鼓而攻之'，'攻其恶，毋攻人之恶'，不应此处独训为治，则何晏、朱子之说非也。"杨伯峻先生的《论语译注》："《论语》共用四次'攻'字，像《先进篇》的'小子鸣鼓而攻之'、《颜渊篇》的'攻其恶，毋攻人之恶'的三个'攻'字都当'攻击'解，这里也不应例外。"何以这里就不应例外？对于一字一词究竟何义，不看句义语境等，而"以本经用语例决之"，终究难免武断而荒唐。实际上，无论一个字在前面出现过多少次，都无法确定下一次出现时必定是某一含义。"不应例外"的规则，本质上是以不完全归纳、数字统计的形式来确定词义，"不准新义产生"。

若按照"以本经用语例决之"，这句里的"也已"应当释为表肯定的语气词，因为多处"也已"都释为语气词。为何这里又把"也"释为语气停顿，把"已"释作动词"止"了呢？

"不应例外"为何此处不适用了呢?

2·17　子曰:"由,诲女知之乎? 知之为知之,不知为不知,是知也。"

【今译】

夫子说:"由,我教你的,你记下了吗? 知道就是知道,不知道就是不知道,这才是知(智)。

【英译】

The Master said, "Zilu, have you learnt by heart what I taught you? It is really wise to realize the limits of one's knowledge as well as knowing what one already knows."

2·18　子张学干禄①。子曰:"多闻阙②疑,慎言其余,则寡尤;多见阙殆③,慎行其余,则寡悔。言寡尤,行寡悔,禄在其中矣。"

【注释】

①干(gān):求也。禄:福也。
②阙:同"缺"。
③殆:同"疑"。

【今译】

子张问如何求得福禄。夫子说:"对于疑惑的地方,要多听,没有疑惑之处表达时要谨慎,说话过失就会减少;对于疑惑之事要多观察,不疑惑的事做时要谨慎,后悔的事就会减少。说话少过失,行事少后悔,福禄就在其中了。"

【英译】

Zizhang asked about how to obtain blessings. The Master said, "Listen more for what you are ignorant or in doubt about, and talk with caution about what you are confident with, then you will make fewer mistakes; watch more for what you are ignorant or in doubt about, and be cautious doing what you are confident with, then you will have less regrets. Fewer mistakes in speech and fewer regrets in actions—therein lies the way of obtaining blessings."

【辨正】

"阙"是动词，形容词，还是名词？如果把"阙疑"解释成"把有疑的地方留在一旁"，那么它就是动词，等于"（多）闻""阙（疑）""（慎）言"三个动作并列。如果把"阙疑"解释为"减少（或去除）疑惑"，那么"阙疑"即"多闻"的结果。如果把"阙疑"当作"多闻"的宾语，多听"阙"与"疑"的事，那么"阙"与"疑"就是名词，这样，"多闻"与"慎言"两个动作相并列。

黄怀信《论语新校释》："'禄'，《说文》：'福也。'谓福禄、福祉。旧释俸禄，非是，言寡尤行寡悔，何得就有俸禄？"

2·19 哀公问曰："何为则民服？"孔子对曰："举直错诸枉，则民服；举枉错诸直，则民不服。"

【今译】

鲁哀公问："怎样才能使百姓顺从呢？"孔子回答说："把正直者提拔起来，放在邪曲者之上，老百姓就会顺服；把邪曲者提拔起来，放在正直者之上，老百姓就不会顺服。"

【英译】

Duke Ai of the State of Lu asked how to make people convinced. The Master answered, "Promote the upright over the crooked, and the people will be readily convinced; promote the crooked over the upright, and the people will not be readily convinced."

2·20　季康子问："使民敬、忠以劝，如之何？"子曰："临之以庄，则敬；孝慈，则忠；举善而教不能，则劝。"

【今译】

季康子问："使老百姓对当政的人尊敬、忠心且尽力，该怎么样做？"夫子说："待百姓态度庄重，他们就会尊敬你；对父母孝顺、对子弟慈祥，百姓就会忠心；重用善良的人，又教育能力差的人，百姓就会努力做事。"

【英译】

Ji Kangzi asked, "What should be done to make people respectful, faithful and diligent?" The Master said, "Approach them with dignity, and they will be respectful. Be filial to your parents and be kind to the young, and they will be faithful. Promote the capable and instruct the incompetent, and they will be diligent."

2·21　或谓孔子曰："子奚不为政？"子曰："《书》云：'孝乎惟孝，友于兄弟。'施于有政，是亦为政，奚其为为政？"

【今译】

有人对孔子说："您怎么不出仕为政呢？"夫子回答说：

"《尚书》上说，'孝敬父母，友爱兄弟。'以孝悌处理家事，这也是为政，为什么一定要出仕为政呢？"

【英译】

When asked "Why don't you engage in the administration of government?" The Master replied, "As it is said in *The Book of Documents*, be filial to your parents and be fraternal to your brothers. Administrating family affairs this way is therefore virtually the same as administering the affairs of state. Why do I have to serve in the government?"

2·22　子曰："人而无信，不知其可也。大车无輗①，小车无軏②，其何以行之哉？"

【注释】
①輗（ní）：古代大车车辕前面横木上的木销子。
②軏（yuè）：古代小车车辕前面横木上的木销子。

【今译】
夫子说："做人不讲信用，不知道那怎么可以。大车没有輗、小车没有軏，怎么能（让它）行进呢？"

【英译】

The Master said, "I don't think a man can get anywhere if he cannot keep his word. How can a carriage keep moving without pins to secure its crossbar?"

2·23　子张问：“十世可知也?”子曰：殷因于夏，礼所损益，可知也；周因于殷，礼所损益可知也。其或继周者，虽百世，亦可知也。”

【今译】

子张问夫子：“十世以后的情况能知道吗？”夫子回答说：“商朝沿袭了夏朝，礼仪制度的增减可以知道；周朝沿袭了商朝，礼仪制度的增减可以知道。将来周朝之后若有继承者，就算百世以后的情况，也可以知道。”

【英译】

Zizhang asked whether we can know about the rites ten generations later. The Master replied, "We can know the modification of Yin's rites as it developed from Xia's. We can know the modification of Zhou's rites as it developed from Yin's. And hence we can know the rites of the successor's even a hundred generations later as it will develop from Zhou."

【辨正】

刘宝楠《论语正义》：“《汉书·杜周传》：‘钦对策曰：“殷因于夏，尚质；周因于殷，尚文。”’此读以夏、殷绝句。《汉书董仲舒传》有‘夏因于虞’之文，《史记集解》引《乐记》郑注：‘殷因于夏，周因于殷。’与杜读同。则知今人以‘礼’字断句者，误也。”

2·24　子曰："非其鬼而祭之，谄也。见义不为，无勇也。"

【今译】

夫子说："不是自己的祖先，却去祭祀它，是谄媚。见到正义的事却不挺身而出，是怯懦。"

【英译】

The Master said, "He is a flatterer who offers sacrifices to the spirit of other clans rather than his own ancestors; he is cowardly who, seeing what is righteous to do, fails to act boldly."

八佾第三

3·1　孔子谓季氏，"八佾①舞于庭，是可忍也，孰不可忍也？"

【注释】

①八佾（yì）：佾，古代奏乐舞蹈的行列，一行八人。八佾，即六十四人，是天子规格。八佾就是六十四人。马融曰："天子八佾，诸侯六、卿大夫四、士二。"四佾是季氏应该用的。

【今译】

孔子评论季氏说："他在庭上奏乐舞蹈用八佾规格，这种事情如果可以容忍，（还有）什么不能容忍？"

【英译】

Confucius remarked about Jisun, "He had eight rows of dancers perform for him in his courtyard. If this can be tolerated, what else cannot be?"

【辨正】

杨伯峻《论语译注》："一般人把它解为'容忍''忍耐'，不好；因为孔子当时并没有讨伐季氏的条件和意志，而且季平子削弱鲁公室，鲁昭公不能忍，出走到齐，又到晋，终于死在晋国之乾侯。这可能就是孔子所'孰不可忍'的事。《贾子·

道术篇》：'恻隐怜人谓之慈，反慈为忍。'这'忍'字正是此意。"

杨逢彬《论语新注新译》对"忍"字有详细考证，结论为："忍"是"忍耐"而不是"忍心"。从"可"字的"能被……"义，等于英语里的"can be...ed"的被动，或-able后缀，也可知"忍"字当为及物动词，进而排除"忍心"一说。

3·2 三家①者以《雍》彻②。子曰："'相维辟公③，天子穆穆'，奚取于三家之堂？"

【注释】

①三家：春秋后期掌握鲁国政权的三家贵族，仲孙、叔孙、季孙，他们是鲁桓公之后，也称"三桓"。

②《雍》：《诗经·周颂》中的一篇。是天子祭祖完毕撤去祭品时唱的乐歌。彻：同"撤"，撤掉。

③相（xiàng）：助祭者。维：语助词，无实义。辟（bì）公：诸侯。

【今译】

那三家大夫，在祭祖时，唱着《雍》乐撤去祭品。夫子说："'诸侯公卿助祭，天子庄严肃穆（地在那里主祭）。'为何在三家的庙堂上唱《雍》乐呢？

【英译】

The three families played *The Yung Ode* at the removal of the sacrifices. The Master said, "'Assisted by dukes and noblemen, there solemnly stands the son of Heaven'—Why is this ode with these words played in the hall of the three families?"

3·3　子曰："人而不仁，如礼何？人而不仁，如乐何？"

【今译】

做人却没有仁心，礼法又能怎样（他）？做人却没有仁心，音乐又能怎样（他）？

【英译】

The Master said, "To a man without the virtue of being benevolent, what good can the rites do? And to him, what good can music do?"

3·4　林放问礼之本。子曰："大哉问！礼，与其奢也，宁俭；丧，与其易也，宁戚。"

【今译】

林放问礼的根本。夫子说："这个问题问得大啊！礼，与其奢侈，宁肯简陋；丧，与其和悦，宁肯悲戚。"

【英译】

Lin Fang asked what the essence of rites was. The Master said, "A great question indeed! With rites, it is better to be sparing than extravagant. With the mourning-formalities, it is better to be grief-stricken than slack-minded."

【辨正】

邢昺疏："奢与俭、易与戚等，俱不合礼，但礼不欲失于奢，宁失于俭；丧不欲失于易，宁失于戚。言礼之本意，礼失于奢不如俭，丧失于和易不如哀戚。"

3·5　子曰："夷狄①之有君，不如诸夏②之亡也。"

【注释】

①夷：我国古代东方少数民族。狄：我国古代北方少数民族。夷狄：古代中原地区的人对周边地区的贬称，谓之不开化，缺乏教养，不知书达礼。

②诸夏：古代中原地区华夏族各诸侯国。

【今译】

夫子说："夷狄有君主，还不如中原诸国没有君主。"

【英译】

The Master said, "The barbarian states with monarchs cannot match the central Chinese states without monarchs."

【辨正】

"亡"，通"无"，与前面的"有"对照，不可解作"灭亡"。

"之"字的作用，使句子"夷狄有君"成为短语"夷狄的有君"。句子结构是"A不如B"。

"不如"不能解作"不像"。"不像"是介词unlike，若解释成"不像诸夏无君那样"，那么，前面就应当是主句，而"诸夏之有君"却不是句子。"不如"意思是"比不上"。句义是"夷狄有君主，不如诸夏没有君主。""鲁国的昭公、哀公，都曾逃往国外，形成某一时期内鲁国无国君的现象。由此，孔子发出感叹。"（徐志刚《论语通译》）三年无君，国照样国，三家不篡位，靠的正是"礼"。

释惠琳云："有君无礼，不如有礼无君。刺时季氏有君无礼也。"程子曰"夷狄有君长，不如诸夏之僭越，反无上下之分也。"这种解法虽"用意新颖"却置句子"A不如B"结构于不顾，只求义通而解反了。

3·6　季氏旅①于泰山。子谓冉有②曰："女弗能救③与？"对曰："不能。"子曰："呜呼！曾谓④泰山不如林放乎？"

【注释】

①旅：祭山曰旅。按周礼，天子祭天地及天下名山大川，诸侯祭其封地内山川。季氏只是鲁国大夫，祭祀泰山，属僭礼行为。

②冉有：姓冉，名求，字子有。当时是季氏的家臣，所以孔子责备他。

③救：劝阻，谏止。

④曾（zēng）谓：难道说。

【今译】

季孙氏去祭祀泰山。夫子对冉有说："你不能劝阻他吗？"冉有说："不能。"夫子说："唉！竟然认为泰山之神还不如林放（知礼吗）？"

【英译】

Jisun was about to offer a sacrifice to Mount Tai. The Master said to Ranyou, "Cannot you save him from this?" He answered, "I cannot." Confucius then sighed, "Alas! Do you really believe that the God of Mount Tai is not as discerning as Lin Fang?"

3·7　子曰："君子无所争。必也射乎！揖让而升，下而饮。其争也君子。"

【今译】

夫子说："君子之间没有可争的事。如果有所争，那一定是射箭比赛吧。比赛之前互相作揖礼让，然后登堂。比赛之后走下堂来，又互相敬酒。这种争也是君子之争。"

【英译】

The Master said, "A gentleman contends for nothing. The only occasion, if there is, when he contends, it must be in archery where he bows pleasantly to his opponents before ascending to the shooting-ground, and drinks to them after descending. So, gentlemanliness is the way he contends."

3·8　子夏问曰："'巧笑倩兮，美目盼兮，素以为绚兮。'①何谓也？"子曰："绘事后素②。"
曰："礼后乎？"子曰："起予者商也！始可与言《诗》已矣。"

【注释】

①巧笑倩兮，美目盼兮，素以为绚兮：前两句见《诗经·卫风·硕人》。巧：美好。倩：口角处好看。盼：眼睛黑白分明。绚：文采成章。

②绘：画。素：白色。绘事后素：绘画时，最后才使用素色。

【今译】

子夏问夫子:"'嫣然一笑那嘴角多么妩媚啊,明眸忽闪多么清澈明亮啊,以素色映出绚丽啊。'这是什么意思呢?"夫子说:"这是说绘画时,最后才使用素色。"子夏又问:"那么,礼放后吗?"夫子说:"能启发我的就是你卜商啊,现在就可与你讨论《诗经》了。"

【英译】

Zixia asked, saying, " 'Her mouth corners are so charming when she smiles,

And shinning while glancing are her eyes,

Like a gorgeous painting with white interspersing.'

What is the meaning of these lines?"

The Master said, "A painting is finished by white interspersing at the end." "Do rites likewise come afterwards?" he then asked. The Master said, "It is you, Shang, who can offer me illumination. Only with such a man like you should I talk about *The Book of Songs*."

【辨正】

"绘事后素"如何解?素在先,还是在后?

"先君后身""先国家之急而后私仇","后"是动词,"把⋯⋯放后"。郑玄注:"绘,画文也。凡绘画先布众色,然后以素分布其间,以成其文。喻美女虽有倩盼美质,亦须礼以成之也。"《周礼·考工记》:"杂四时五色之位以章之,谓之巧。凡画缋之事后素功。"《论语集释》:"云'素以为绚兮'者,言五采待素而始成文也。今时画者尚如此,先布众色毕,后以粉勾勒之,则众色始绚然分明。"

3·9　子曰："夏礼，吾能言之，杞不足征也；殷礼，吾能言之，宋不足征也。文献不足故也。足，则吾能征之矣。"

【今译】

夫子说："夏朝的礼制，我能讲，（而）杞国（的礼法制度）不足以证明；殷朝的礼制，我能讲，宋国（的礼制）不足以证明，因为历史文献不足。如果足够，我就能证明夏朝殷朝的礼制了。"

【英译】

The Master said, "I could talk about the rites of the Xia Dynasty, for which the State of Qi cannot furnish sufficient supporting evidence. I could talk about the rites of the Yin Dynasty, for which the State of Song cannot furnish sufficient supporting evidence. This is because there are not enough records and documentation. Otherwise, I could have proved the rites of the Xia and Yin Dynasty."

3·10　子曰："禘自既灌而往者①，吾不欲观之矣。"

【注释】

①禘（dì）：古代天子祭祀祖先的大礼，参与祭祀的人必须斋戒沐浴，一片至诚。灌：礼刚开始时即举行的献酒降神仪式。而往：指以下的礼仪节目。

【今译】

夫子说："举行禘祭典礼时，从第一次献酒之后，我就不想看下去了。"

The Master said, "At the great Di sacrifice, after the pouring of the libation on the ground, I have no wish to watch further."

3 · 11　或问禘之说①。子曰："不知也；知其说者之于天下也，其如示诸斯乎！"指其掌。

【注释】

①说：周代祭祀名。"掌六祈以同鬼神示，一曰类，二曰造，三曰禬（guì），四曰禜（yíng），五曰攻，六曰说。"

【今译】

有人问夫子关于禘祭的"说"。夫子说："我不知道。知道"说"的人看天下，大概就像看这里一样（清楚）吧！"指了指自己的手掌。

【英译】

Someone asked about the Shuo, one part of the great Di sacrifice. The Master said, "I do not know. He who knows it would know the things under the sun as clearly as this." He then pointed to his palm.

3 · 12　祭如在，祭神如神在。子曰："吾不与祭，如不祭。"

【今译】

祭祀就像真在一样，祭神就如同神在眼前一样。夫子说："我不能感觉与受祭的神祇同在，那么祭祀就像不祭一样。"

Sacrifice as if present. Sacrifice to the spirits as if the spirits were present. The Master said, "Sacrifices without the feeling of being with the spirits amounts to no sacrifice."

【辨正】

这一节是讲祭祀之礼，重在虔诚，就像鬼神真得就在跟前一样。"与祭"不只是"参与祭祀"，还是如《礼记》所言"凡祭，容貌颜色，如见所祭者""事死者如事生"。如果人与祭而心不诚，则祭如不祭。"与祭"就是"在"，只是角度不同，从受祭者的角度是"在"，从祭者的角度就是"与祭"，即与受祭的神灵同在。

3·13 王孙贾问曰："与其媚于奥，宁媚于灶^①，何谓也？"子曰："不然；获罪于天，无所祷也。"

【注释】

①媚：谄媚，巴结，奉承。奥：本义指室内的西南角。古时尊长居西南，故以奥为尊。灶：烧火做饭的土台，古人以灶为神，即"灶君"。"与其媚于奥，宁媚于灶"是当时俗语，近似"县官不如现管"。这里以奥喻君，以灶喻权臣，王孙贾想让孔子依附权臣，故意这么问孔子。

【今译】

王孙贾问道："'与其讨好奥神，不如讨好灶神。'这句话是什么意思？"夫子说："不是这样。如果得罪了天，就无处可祈祷了。"

【英译】

Wangsun Jia asked Confucius, saying, "What is the meaning of the saying, 'It is better to pay court to the god of the hearth than to the god of the hall'?" The Master said, "Not so. He who offends against Heaven has none to whom he can pray."

3·14　子曰："周监于二代，郁郁乎文哉！吾从周。"

【今译】

夫子说："周朝借鉴于夏、商两代，文采明著，蔚然辉煌啊！我尊从周朝（的礼）。"

【英译】

The Master said, "The Zhou Dynasty drew on the experience of the two past dynasties, Xia and Yin. How resplendently civilized it is! I favour the rites of the Zhou Dynasty."

3·15　子入太庙，每事问。或曰："孰谓鄹人之子知礼乎？入太庙，每事问。"子闻之，曰："是礼也。"

【今译】

夫子进入太庙助祭，对每件事都询问。有人说："谁说鄹人的儿子知道礼呢？进入太庙，每件事都要问一问。"夫子听到以后，说："这正是礼啊！"

【英译】

Confucius enquired about everything when he entered the Grand Temple. Someone said, "Who says that the son of the man of Zou knows the rites! He entered the Grand Temple and enquired about everything." Hearing this remark, the Master said, "This itself is a rite."

3·16　子曰：“射不主皮，为力不同科，古之道也。”

【今译】

夫子说：“（礼）射不以射穿皮靶子为要，因为各人的力气不同，这是昔时的做法。”

【英译】

The Master said, "Ceremonial Archery puts stress on hitting the target, not on piercing the hide, as the archers are different in physical strength. This was the practice of the ancients."

【辨正】

礼射与力射不同，力射主皮，礼射不主皮。程树德《论语集释》：“礼射二番不胜，仍待后番复升射。主皮之射则胜者复射，不胜者不复射，是尚力也。……乡射所以不用主皮之礼者，取其比于礼乐，不胜许其复射，不尚力也，为力不同等也。”

3·17　子贡欲去告朔①之饩羊②。子曰：“赐也！尔爱其羊，我爱其礼。”

【注释】

①告（gù）朔：阴历的每月初一，叫“朔”。古代制度，每年秋冬之交，周天子把第二年的历书颁发给诸侯。诸侯接受历书，藏之祖庙。每月初一杀一只羊祭于庙，表示每月“听

政"的开始，叫"告朔"。当时，鲁君主已不亲自到祖庙"告朔"，只杀羊。子贡认为不如干脆连羊也不杀。

②饩（xì）：活的牲畜。

【今译】

子贡想去掉每月初一告祭祖庙要杀一只羊的做法。夫子说："赐啊！你爱惜的是那只羊，我爱惜的是那种礼仪。"

【英译】

Zigong wanted to dispense with the sacrificial sheep at the monthly proclamation ceremony. The Master said, "Ci! You care for the sheep; I care for the ceremony."

3·18 子曰："事君尽礼，人以为谄也。"

【今译】

夫子说："侍奉国君，一切按照周礼要求的礼节去做，别人就认为你对国君谄媚。"

【英译】

The Master said, "One might be deemed to be obedient if he serves his ruler fully in accordance with the rites."

3·19 定公问："君使臣，臣事君，如之何？"孔子对曰："君使臣以礼，臣事君以忠。"

【今译】

鲁定公问："君主使用臣，臣事奉君主，应该怎么做？"孔子回答："君主应该按照礼法使用臣子，臣子应该以忠心侍奉君主。"

【英译】

Duke Ding asked how a ruler should employ his ministers, and how ministers should serve their ruler. Confucius replied, "A ruler should employ his ministers according to the rites; ministers should serve their ruler with loyalty."

3·20　子曰："《关雎》，乐而不淫①，哀而不伤。"

【注释】

①《关雎》（jū）：《诗经·周南》中的第一篇。淫（yín）：过分（快乐）而失当。

【今译】

夫子说："《关雎》篇，快乐而不放荡；忧愁而不悲伤。"

【英译】

The Master said, "The sentiment of *The Guanju* is joyful without being overindulgent, and sad without being excessively sorrowful."

3·21　哀公问社于宰我。宰我对曰："夏后氏以松，殷人以柏，周人以栗，曰，使民战栗。"子闻之，曰："成事不说，遂事不谏，既往不咎。"

【今译】

鲁哀公问宰我，土神的牌位（用什么木头做）。宰我回答说："夏朝人用松木，殷朝人用柏木，周朝人用栗木，意思是使老百姓战栗。"夫子听了后说："已经做成的事，不必再解释了；已经做完的事，不必再劝谏了；已经过去的事，不必再追究了。"

【英译】

Duke Ai asked Zaiwo about the wood used to make the altar to the God of Earth. Zaiwo replied, "Pinewood was used in the Xia Dynasty; cypress in the Yin Dynasty, and the wood of chestnut tree（li）in the Zhou Dynasty. It is said that using of the wood of chestnut tree was intended to cause the common people to tremble（li）in awe."

The Master, on hearing of this reply, commented, "Do not explain what is already done; do not advise against what is already accomplished; do not dwell on what has already gone by."

3·22　子曰："管仲之器小哉！"

或曰："管仲俭乎？"曰："管氏有三归，官事不摄①，焉得俭？"

"然则管仲知礼乎？"曰："邦君树塞门②，管氏亦树塞门。邦君为两君之好，有反坫③，管氏亦有反坫。管氏而知礼，孰不知礼？"

【注释】

①摄：兼职。

②邦君：国君。树：建立，动词。塞门：影壁，筑在大门外的矮墙，阻止外人探视。

③反坫（diàn）：用土堆成的土墩，类似茶几，上面可以放东西。

【今译】

夫子说："管仲的器量小啊！"有人问："管仲节俭吗？"夫子说："管仲家有三处采邑，为他家管事的官员是一人一职而不兼任，哪能说节俭呢？"那人又问："那么，管仲知礼吗？"夫子说："国君在宫殿大门前树立一道影壁短墙，管仲家门口也树立影壁短墙。国君设宴招待别国的君主，举行友好会见时，在堂上专门设置献过酒后放空杯子的土台，管仲家也设置这样的土台。倘若管仲知礼，那谁不知礼呢？"

【英译】

The Master said, "Guan Zhong was, indeed, a vessel of small capacity." Someone asked, "Was Guan Zhong thrifty, then?" The Master replied, "Guan kept three fiefs, each with a separate staff. How can he be considered thrifty?" Then they enquired, "Did Guan Zhong know the rites?" The Master said, "Only the ruler of the state may build a screen-wall to mask his gate, and Guan also built one at his. Only the ruler of the state may have a cup-stand in his hall for entertaining the ruler of another state, and Guan also had one. If Guan knew the rites, who else might not?"

3·23　子语鲁大师乐①，曰："乐其可知也：始作，翕如也②；从之，纯如也，皦如也，绎如也，以成。"

【注释】

①语（yù）：告诉。鲁大（tài）师：鲁国的乐官之长，负责诗教和乐教。

②翕（xì）：突起。如：助词，用作形容词后缀，相当于

"然"，表示"样子"。

【今译】

夫子告诉鲁国乐官乐理，说："奏乐的道理是可以知道的：开始时，有突起之感；接下来，有清纯之感，然后有明快之感，然后有延绵之感，然后结束。"

【英译】

The Master talked to the Grand Musician of Lu, saying, "This much can be known about music. It first rises vigorously, then sounds are pure, then bright, and then lengthening before coming to a close."

3·24　仪封人①请见，曰："君子之至于斯也，吾未尝不得见也。"从者见之②。出曰："二三子何患于丧乎③？天下之无道也久矣，天将以夫子为木铎④。"

【注释】

①仪：地名。封人：春秋时镇守边疆的官员。

②见（xiàn）：荐达，引见。

③二三子：这里是称呼孔子的弟子。二三：表示约数，犹言"各位"。丧：失去，这里指孔子失掉官位，没有官职。

④木铎（duó）：一种金口木舌的大铜铃。古时摇木铎以召集人民，宣布政令。

【今译】

仪地的边界官请求见夫子。他说："凡是到这个地方来的君子，我没有不得见的。"随从弟子引他见夫子。他出来后说：

"你们几位何必担心夫子失去官职呢？天下失去正道已经很长久了，上天将要以你们的老师为木铎（，让他四处宣扬教化）。"

【英译】

The border official of Yi requested an audience, saying, "I have never been denied an audience by any gentleman who came to this place." The attendant disciples presented him. When he came out, he said, "Why do you worry about your Master's loss of office? The world has long been off the right track; Heaven is going to make your Master an arousing Tocsin (to awaken people)."

3·25　子谓《韶》，"尽美矣，又尽善也"。谓《武》，"尽美矣，未尽善也"。

【今译】

夫子评价《韶》乐说：音律美极了，内容也好极了。而评价《武》乐时却说：音律美极了，内容却不够好。

【英译】

The Master spoke of the music *Shao*, "It was both perfectly beautiful and perfectly good." He spoke of the music *Wu*, "It was perfectly beautiful, yet not perfectly good.

3·26　子曰："居上不宽，为礼不敬，临丧不哀，吾何以观之哉！"

【今译】

夫子说："居上位不宽厚，举行仪式时不严肃恭敬，参加丧礼时不悲伤，对这种情况，我如何看得下去呢?"

【英译】

The Master said, "How could I bear to see a man in high position who is not generous, a man who is not respectful at ceremonies, and a man who does not grieve at a funeral?"

里仁第四

4·1　子曰："里^①仁为美，择不处^②仁，焉得知^③?"

【注释】

①里：居，处，动词。

②处（chǔ）：在一起居住。

③知（zhì）：同"智"。

【今译】

夫子说："与仁德者住在一起是美好的。居处不选择有仁德者为邻，怎么能说得上明智呢?"

【英译】

The Master said, "It is the benevolent people in the neighborhood that constitutes the excellence of a dwelling place; how can a man be considered wise if he does not choose to dwell amidst benevolent people?"

4·2　子曰："不仁者不可以久处约，不可以长处乐。仁者安仁，知者利仁。"

【今译】

夫子说："不仁的人不能长久处于贫困中，不能长久处于安乐中。有仁德的人安于仁；聪明的人顺守仁。"

【英译】

The Master said, "Those who are not benevolent cannot long live consistently in poverty, nor long in prosperity. In practicing benevolence, the benevolent man finds contentment while the wise man finds profits."

4·3　子曰："唯仁者能好人，能恶人。"

【今译】

夫子说："只有仁者能（恰当地）喜好人，能（恰当地）憎恶人。"

【英译】

The Master said, "Only the benevolent man knows how to love and how to hate."

【辨正】

朱熹《论语集注》："盖无私心，然后好恶当于理，程子所谓'得其公正'是也。游氏曰：'好善而恶恶，天下之同情，然人每失其正者，心有所系而不能自克也。惟仁者无私心，所以能好恶也。'"

4·4　子曰："苟志于仁矣，无恶也。"

【今译】

夫子说："假若立志实行仁德，就不会有恶行了。"

The Master said, "If a man is determined to practice benevolence, he will be free from evil-doing."

4·5 子曰："富与贵，是人之所欲也；不以其道得之，不处也。贫与贱，是人之所恶也；不以其道得之，不去也。君子去仁，恶乎成名？君子无终食之间违仁，造次必于是，颠沛必于是。"

【今译】

夫子说："富有和高贵，是人人所盼望的；不以正当方式得到，就不接受。贫困和卑贱，是人人所厌恶的；不以正当方式摆脱，就不摆脱。君子离了仁德，怎么成就自己的君子之名？君子没有哪怕一顿饭的时间背离仁德，仓卒匆忙时，他一定与仁同在；颠沛流离时，他也一定与仁同在。"

【英译】

The Master said, "Wealth and nobleness are what people desire. Unless obtained in the right way, they are not to be enjoyed. Poverty and humbleness are what people dislike. Unless getting rid of them in the right way, they are not to be evaded. Without being benevolent, how can a gentleman fulfill his reputation? A gentleman never, even for the span of a single meal, abandons his benevolence. In moments of haste, he cleaves to it. In times of adversity, he cleaves to it."

【辨正】

毛子水《论语今注今译》：王充《论衡·问孔篇》："贫贱

何故当言'得之'？顾当言贫与贱是人之所恶也，不以其道去之，则不去也。"按：王充于"得之"绝句，所以疑孔子说话不当，而要改第二"得之"为"去之"。若记《论语》这章的人本来于"得之"绝句的，则王充的修改亦颇有理。但"去之"写作"得之"，不是孔子说错，亦不是记的人记错。王充所以误解，乃是因为他不明白之字所代的字：上"得之"犹言"得处"，下"得之"犹言"得去"。经意：不由正道，则得处而不处，得去而不去的。

4·6　子曰："我未见好仁者，恶不仁者。好仁者，无以尚之；恶不仁者，其为仁矣，不使不仁者加乎其身。有能一日用其力于仁矣乎？我未见力不足者。盖有之矣，我未之见也。"

【今译】

夫子说："我未曾见过喜好仁德的人，未曾见过憎恶不仁的人。喜好仁德的人，无法超越了；厌恶不仁的人，践行仁道，不让自己陷于不仁。有谁能一整天致力于仁道吗？我未见过力不足的。这样的人大概有吧，但我并没见过。"

【英译】

The Master said, "I have never met a man who loves benevolence, or one who detests anyone who is malevolent. He who loves benevolence cannot be surpassed. He who detests malevolence would practice benevolence by keeping himself away from anything malevolent. Is there anyone who, for a single day, can devote all his effort toward benevolence, as everyone I met is capable of doing? Should there possibly be such a person, I have not yet met one."

4·7 子曰："人之过也，各于其党。观过，斯知仁矣。"

【今译】

夫子说："人的错误，带着其同类人的特点。看一个人的错误，就可了解一个人的仁德。"

【英译】

The Master said, "A man's mistakes are similar to those committed by the class of people he associates with. Analyzing his mistakes can tell how benevolent he is."

4·8 子曰："朝闻道，夕死可矣。"

【今译】

夫子说："早上听说道已行世，晚上死去也可以。"

【英译】

The Master said: "If I were told one morning that the right principles had prevailed in the world, I would be content to die even on that evening."

【辨正】

邢昺疏："此章疾世无道也。设若早闻世有道，暮夕而死，可无恨矣。言将至死不闻世之有道也。"皇侃疏："叹世无道，故言。设使朝闻世有道，则夕死无恨，故云'可矣'。栾肇曰：'道所以济民。圣人存身，为行道也。济民以道，非为济身也。故云诚令道朝闻于世，虽夕死可也。伤道不行，且明己忧世，不为身也。'"

4·9　子曰："士①志于道，而耻恶衣恶食②者，未足与议也。"

【注释】

①士：习学文武者为士。

②恶（è）衣恶食：粗衣粗粮。

【今译】

夫子说："志在追求真理却以粗衣粗食为耻的士人，不值得与他论道。"

【英译】

The Master said, "A gentleman, who is determined to pursue the truth, yet ashamed of wearing ragged clothes and eating coarse food, is not worthy to share your pursuit with."

4·10　子曰："君子之于天下也，无适①也，无莫②也，义之与比③。"

【注释】

①适（dí）：通"敌"，敌对。

②莫："慕"，向往，歆慕。

③义之与比：义与之相伴。比：并列，挨着，亲近。

【今译】

夫子说："君子行于天下，没有什么要敌对的，也没有什么要羡慕的，他与义同行。"

The Master said, "A gentleman has nothing to resist or to strive for in the world. He stays with righteousness."

【辨正】

《经典释文》："适，郑本作'敌'；莫，郑音'慕'，无所贪慕也。"《李杜列传》："爕并交二子，情无适莫，世称其平正。"《白虎通德论·谏诤》："君所以不为臣隐何？以为君之与臣无适无莫，义之与比，赏一善而众臣劝，罚一恶而众臣惧。""适""莫"相对明显。"言君子之于天下无所敌牾，无所贪慕，惟义是亲而已。""匹敌"之"敌"，无法与"（羡）慕"相对。

4·11 子曰："君子怀德，小人怀土；君子怀刑，小人怀惠。"

【今译】

夫子说："君子如果心里想着道德，小人就心里想着乡土；君子如果心里想着刑罚，小人就心里想着恩惠。"

【英译】

The Master said, "If a ruler keeps his mind on governing the state with morality, his people will keep their minds on their land; if a ruler keeps his mind on employing punishments, his people will think of moving to the states where the rulers are lenient."

4·12 子曰："放①于利而行，多怨。"

【注释】

①放（fǎng）：依。

【今译】

夫子说："行事依凭利益，就会招致很多怨恨。"

【英译】

The Master said, "Indulging oneself in seeking for personal profit will incur much ill-will."

4·13　子曰："能以礼让为国，于从政乎何有？不能以礼让为国，如礼何？"

【今译】

夫子说："如果能够用礼让来治理国家，那么从政有什么难的呢？如果不能用礼让来治理国家，那么有礼法又能怎样呢？"

【英译】

The Master said, "What difficulty can one have if he can govern the state with the rites and being considerate and courteous? If he cannot, of what use are rites?"

【辨正】

黄怀信《论语新校释》："按：'于从政'三字旧脱，从《后汉书·刘般传》贾逵上书及《列女传》曹世叔上疏所引补，而'从'又疑当作'行'。"加"于从政"三字，文从字顺；不加，"乎"字属前，"能以礼让为国乎"成了问句，设问没有回答，也不能与接下来"不能以礼让为国"形成对照，"何有"也少了话题。

4·14 子曰："不患无位，患所以立。不患莫己知，求为可知也。"

【今译】

夫子说："不要担心没有职位，要担心能否胜任。不要担心没有人欣赏，追求可以使人知道的本领。"

【英译】

The Master said, "Do not worry about not having an official position. Worry about whether you are qualified for such a position. Do not worry about failing to get recognition. Rather, seek to be worthy of being recognized."

4·15 子曰："参乎！吾道一以贯之。"曾子曰："唯。"

子出，门人问曰："何谓也？"曾子曰："夫子之道，忠恕而已矣。"

【今译】

夫子说："曾参啊！我的道有一思想贯穿始终。"曾参说："是的。"夫子离开了，其他弟子问道："这话是什么意思？"曾参说："夫子之道，讲的就是忠恕啊。"

【英译】

The Master said, "Shen, my teachings are united with one principle from the beginning to the end." Master Zeng replied, "Yes." The Master went out, and the other disciples asked, saying, "What did he mean?" Master Zeng said, "The essence of our Master's teachings has consistently been nothing but faithfulness and forgiveness."

4·16　子曰："君子喻于义，小人喻于利。"

【今译】

夫子说："君子明白在义，小人明白在利。"

【英译】

The Master said, "A gentleman is conversant with justice; a petty man is conversant with gain."

4·17　子曰："见贤思齐焉，见不贤而内自省也。"

【今译】

夫子说："见到贤人要想着向他看齐，见到不贤的人要在心里反省自己。"

【英译】

The Master said, "When you meet a man of virtue, think of emulating him; when you meet an unworthy man, turn inwards and examine yourself."

4·18　子曰："事父母几①谏，见志不从，又敬不违，劳而不怨。"

【注释】

①几（jī）：轻微，委婉。

【今译】

夫子说："事奉父母,(看到他们有过错时)要委婉地劝谏,见到自己的意见不被听从,仍然恭敬而不违拗,忧心但不怨恨。"

【英译】

The Master said, "In serving your parents, remonstrate with them in a tactful way when they are wrong; when you see your advice is not taken, remain respectful and obedient, worried yet not bitter."

4·19　子曰:"父母在,不远游,游必有方。"

【今译】

夫子说:"父母在世时,不出远门;如果要出远门,一定要有(确定的)地方。"

【英译】

The Master said, "While your parents are alive, do not travel afar; if you have to do so, you must let them know your particular destination."

4·20　子曰:"三年无改于父之道,可谓孝矣①。"

【注释】

①见《学而第一》1·11。

【今译】

夫子说：“三年不改变父亲的行事原则，就可以说是孝子了。”

【英译】

The Master said, "If he does not alter the ways of his father in the three years of mourning, he can be counted as a filial son."

4·21 子曰：“父母之年，不可不知也。一则以喜，一则以惧。”

【今译】

夫子说：“父母的年纪不可不记住！一方面因（他们长寿）而欢喜，一方面因（他们年迈）而忧惧。”

【英译】

The Master said, "You should always keep in mind the age of your parents so as to, on the one hand, feel happy for their longevity and, on the other, feel dread for their growing age."

4·22 子曰：“古者言之不出，耻躬之不逮也。”

【今译】

夫子说：“古代的人，诺言不轻易说出口，因为他们认为自己不能实现诺言是耻辱。”

The Master said, "The ancient people were loath to make a promise, for they considered it shameful to fail to live up to it."

4·23　子曰："以约失之者鲜矣。"

【今译】

夫子说："因为说话谨慎而未实现诺言的人很少。"

【英译】

The Master said, "It is rare for one who is prudent in speech to fail to keep his words."

4·24　子曰："君子欲讷①于言而敏于行。"

【注释】

①讷（nè）：语言迟钝，不善于表达。

【今译】

夫子说："君子要说话谨慎，行动迅速。"

【英译】

The Master said, "A gentleman wishes to be slow in speech and quick in action."

4·25　子曰:"德不孤，必有邻。"

【今译】

夫子说:"有德行的人并不孤单，一定有志同道合的人为邻。"

【英译】

The Master said, "A man of virtue is never isolated. He is sure to attract people to him."

4·26　子游曰:"事君数①，斯辱矣；朋友数，斯疏矣。"

【注释】

①数（shuò）：亲近，亲密。

【今译】

子游说:"侍奉君主，如果过于亲密，就会招致侮辱；对待朋友，如果过于亲密，就会被朋友疏远。"

【英译】

Ziyou said, "In serving a ruler, being too intimate will bring disgrace. Between friends, being too intimate will bring estrangement."

公冶长第五

5·1　子谓公冶长，"可妻①也。虽在缧绁②之中，非其罪也。"以其子③妻之。

【注释】

①妻（qì）：嫁，名词用作动词。

②缧绁（léi xiè）：缚犯人的绳索，这里指代监狱。

③子：儿女，古代儿子、女儿通称子。这里专指女儿。

【今译】

夫子谈到公冶长，说："这个人值得嫁。他虽被关押在监狱，但这不是他的过错。"于是把自己的女儿嫁给他为妻。

【英译】

The Master said of Gongye Chang, "He would make a good husband. It was not his fault although he was put in prison." He then married his daughter to Gongye Chang.

5·2　子谓南容，"邦有道，不废；邦无道，免于刑戮。"以其兄之子妻之。

【今译】

夫子谈到南容："国家政治清明时，（他）能做官不被废弃；

国家政治黑暗时，能免遭刑杀。"于是把哥哥的女儿嫁给了他。

【英译】

The Master said of Nan Rong, "When the state is well-governed, he will not be cast aside. When the state is ill-governed, he will manage to stay away from being penalized" He then married his elder brother's daughter to him.

5·3 子谓子贱①，"君子哉若人！鲁无君子者，斯焉取斯？"

【注释】

①子贱：鲁国人，姓宓（fú），名不齐，字子贱。宓，即"虙"之俗字，通"伏"。伏羲或谓之宓羲。

【今译】

夫子谈到宓子贱，说："这个人真是君子啊！鲁国如果没有君子，这个人从哪里学得这样好的品德呢？"

【英译】

The Master said of Zijian, "What a gentleman this man is! If there were no gentlemen in the state of Lu, how could this man have acquired such virtue?"

5·4 子贡问曰："赐也何如？"子曰："女，器也。"曰："何器也？"曰："瑚琏也。"

【今译】

子贡问道："我是一个怎样的人？"夫子说："你是一个有

用的器具。"子贡又问："什么器具?"夫子说："（是宗庙祭祀时盛黍稷的玉制）瑚琏。"

【英译】

Zigong asked, "What do you think of me?" The Master said, "You are a vessel." "What kind of vessel?" he asked. "A gemmed sacrificial vessel."

5·5　或曰："雍也仁而不佞①。"子曰："焉用佞? 御人以口给②，屡憎于人。不知其仁，焉用佞?"

【注释】

①佞（nìng）：口才捷利。

②御：对待。口给（jǐ）：口才敏捷。

【今译】

有人说："冉雍有仁德而没有口才"。夫子说："要口才干什么呢? 以善辩口才来待人，常常被人憎恶。不能了解他的仁，要口才干什么呢?"

【英译】

Someone said, "Yong is benevolent but not eloquent." The Master said, "What is the use of eloquence? An agile tongue will incur the hatred of others. What is the use of eloquence when his benevolence is not recognized by others?"

5·6 子使漆雕开仕。对曰："吾斯之未能信。"子说。

【今译】

夫子让漆雕开去做官。他回答说："我对这事还没有信心。"夫子听了很高兴。

【英译】

The Master told Qidiao Kai to take office. But Qidiao Kai said, "I am not yet confident about it." The Master was pleased to hear the reply.

5·7 子曰："道①不行，乘桴②浮于海。从我者，其由与?"子路闻之喜。子曰："由也好勇过我，无所取材③。"

【注释】

①道：学说，治国主张。
②桴（fú）：小木筏。
③材：通"裁"，取裁，裁夺。

【今译】

夫子说："（如果）道不能行，我乘木筏在海上漂流，那么跟随我的人，可能只有仲由吧?"子路听了这话很高兴。夫子说："仲由这个人啊，好勇超过我，只是不能裁夺事理。"

【英译】

The Master said, "If the Way fails to prevail, I shall drift on the sea on a raft. It must be Zilu who would follow me." Zilu, on hearing this, was overjoyed. The Master then said, "Zilu has more courage than I have, but he did not exercise his judgement when using it."

【辨正】

"无所取材"不宜解作"无处找做筏子的材料"。"由也好勇过我，无所取材"是完整的一句话，都是说仲由的，不能前半句说他好勇，后半句突然转到做木筏子上去了。

5·8　孟武伯问："子路仁乎？"子曰："不知也。"又问，子曰："由也，千乘之国，可使治其赋也，不知其仁也。"

"求也何如？"子曰："求也，千室之邑，百乘之家，可使为之宰也，不知其仁也。"

"赤也何如？"子曰："赤也，束带立于朝，可使与宾客言也，不知其仁也。"

【今译】

孟武伯问道："子路仁吗？"夫子说："不知道。"又问。夫子说："仲由这个人，在一个方圆百里的国家里，可以让他负责军政事务，他是否有仁德不知道。"

"冉求这个人怎么样？"夫子说："冉求这个人，在有一千户人口的城镇或有方圆三十多里的大夫之家，可以让他担任总管，他是否有仁德不知道。"

"公西赤这个人怎么样？"夫子说："公西赤这个人，穿上礼服，立于朝廷之上，可以让他接待外宾，他是否有仁德不知道。"

【英译】

Meng Wubo asked whether Zilu was benevolent. The Master said, "I do not know." Meng Wubo repeated the question. The Master replied, "Zilu can be given the responsibility of managing the military levies in a state of a hundred square *li*, but whether he is benevolent or not, I do not know."

"What about Qiu?" The Master replied, "Qiu can be given the responsibility of steward in a town with a thousand households or in a noble fief of more than thirty square *li*, but whether he is benevolent or not, I do not know."

"What about Chi?" The Master replied, "Chi can be given the responsibility of conversing with the guests when he takes his place at court, wearing his sash, but whether he is benevolent or not, I do not know."

5·9 子谓子贡曰："女与回也孰愈？"对曰："赐也何敢望回？回也闻一以知十，赐也闻一以知二。"子曰："弗如也；吾与女弗如也。"

【今译】

夫子问子贡："你与颜回相比，谁更强些？"子贡回答："我哪里敢与颜回相比呢？颜回听到一件事可以推知十件事，我听到一件事只能推知两件事。"夫子说："不如啊！我和你都不如他。"

【英译】

The Master said to Zigong, "Who is better, you or Hui?" Zigong answered, "How dare I compare myself with Hui? When he is told one thing, he understands ten. When I am told one thing, I understand two." The Master said, "You are not as good as him. You and I are no match for Hui."

【辨正】

"吾与女弗如也"的"与"字，是动词"赞同"，还是连词"和"？

杨逢彬《论语新注新译》："《论衡·问孔》引作'弗如也，吾与汝俱不如也'。《后汉书·桥玄传》'仲尼称不如颜渊'，李贤注引《论语》作：'赐也何敢望回？子曰："吾与汝俱不如也。"'汉代以来旧注大率如此。更重要的是，在《论语》时代以迄后来很长一段时间，"与"为动词表"赞同"义时，它后面的宾语都很简单，如"与其进也，不与其退也……与其洁也"（《述而》）"吾与点也"（《先进》），从未见"女弗如也"这样结构复杂的宾语。而在战国时期，连词'与'连接'吾'和'女''汝'，后面再接上一个谓语性质的结构，是很普遍的。如《左传·成公十三年》'吾与女同好弃恶''吾与女伐狄'，《庄子·大宗师》'吾与汝共之'，《应帝王》'吾与汝既其文，未既其实'。因此这一句的'与'还是视为连词为妥。"

5·10 宰予昼寝。子曰："朽木不可雕也，粪土之墙不可杇^①也；于予与何诛？"子曰："始吾于人也，听其言而信其行；今吾于人也，听其言而观其行。于予与改是。"

【注释】

①杇（wū）：同"圬"，名词，本义是刷墙工具。这里作动词用，指涂饰墙壁。

【今译】

宰予大白天睡觉。夫子说："腐朽的木头不能雕刻，粪土的墙壁不能涂饰，对于宰予还责备什么呢？"

夫子说："最初我对于人，是听了他的话便相信他的行为；现在，我对于人，是听了他的话还要观察他的行为。从宰予这开始我改变了观察人的方法。"

【英译】

Zai Yu was caught asleep during the daytime. The Master said, "Rotten wood cannot be carved; a wall of dirty earth cannot be trowelled. As for Zai Yu, what is the use of reproving him?"

The Master added, "I used to trust a man after listening to him. Now after listening to a man's words I will observe his deeds. It is from Zai Yu that I have learned to make this change."

5·11 子曰："吾未见刚者。"或对曰："申枨①。"子曰："枨也欲，焉得刚?"

【注释】

①申枨（chéng）：姓申，名枨，字周，鲁国人。

【今译】

夫子说："我未曾见过刚强的人。"有人答道："申枨。"夫子说："枨这个人私欲太多，怎么能刚强呢？"

【英译】

The Master said, "I have never met anyone who is truly unbending." Someone said, "Shen Cheng is." The Master said, "Cheng is full of desires. How could he be unbending?"

5·12　子贡曰："我不欲人之加诸我也，我亦欲无加诸人。"子曰："赐也，非尔所及也。"

【今译】

子贡说："我不愿他人强加于我，我也希望自己不强加于人。"夫子说："赐啊，这不是你能做到的。"

【英译】

Zigong said, "I do not wish to be imposed on, and I also wish I will not impose on others." The Master said, "Oh, Ci, that's a goal you cannot fully attain."

5·13　子贡曰："夫子之文章，可得而闻也；夫子之言性与天道，不可得而闻也。"

【今译】

子贡说："老师的文献，我们能得见；老师对人性与天道的谈论，我们无法得见了。"

【英译】

Zigong said, "Our Master's documents and writings are still available; his teachings on human nature and the Way of Heaven cannot be obtained now."

5·14　子路有闻，未之能行，唯恐有闻。

【今译】

子路听到某一道理，在还没有能够去实行的时候，唯恐又听到另外的道理。

【英译】

Zilu was afraid of hearing something new when he could not find time to put into practice what he had already heard.

5·15　子贡问曰："孔文子何以谓之'文'也?"子曰："敏而好学，不耻下问，是以谓之'文'也。"

【今译】

子贡问夫子："孔文子为什么被谥为'文'呢?"夫子说："他聪明又好学，肯向地位低下的人学习而不以为耻，所以得到'文'的谥号。"

【英译】

Zigong asked, "Why was Kong Wenzi honored as 'Wen' (after his death)?" The Master said, "He was quick and eager to learn, and not ashamed to seek the advice from those below his rank. This is why he was honored as 'Wen'."

5·16　子谓子产："有君子之道四焉：其行己也恭，其事上也敬，其养民也惠，其使民也义。"

【今译】

夫子说到子产："他合于君子之道的有四项：自身行为谦恭庄重，事奉君主认真负责，教化民众使民受惠，使役民众合乎道义。"

The Master said of Zichan, "He had the virtues of a gentleman in four counts: he was humble in conducting himself; respectful in serving his lord; beneficent in nourishing the people; and just in employing the people."

5·17　子曰："晏平仲善与人交，久而敬之。"

【今译】

夫子说："晏平仲善于与别人交朋友，时间长了，人都很敬重他。"

【英译】

The Master said, "Yan Pingzhong excels in making good friends with others. Over time, they all come to respect him."

5·18　子曰："臧文仲居蔡^①，山节藻棁^②，何如其知也?"

【注释】

①居蔡：指为大乌龟盖上房子藏起来以备占卜用。蔡：春秋时蔡国，在今河南省。蔡国出产大乌龟，这里用"蔡"代指大乌龟。居：房子，这里作动词用。

②山节藻棁（zhuō）：节，房柱子头上的斗拱；山节是把斗拱雕刻成山的形状。藻，水草；棁，房子大梁上的短柱；藻棁，在短柱上画上花草图案。山节藻棁，即俗说"雕梁画栋"，是古代建筑物的豪华装饰，只有天子才能把大乌龟壳藏在如此豪华的房屋里，臧文仲也这样做，显然是"越礼"行为。

【今译】

夫子说："臧文仲为大龟盖房子，房子的斗拱雕成山形，房梁短柱上画着水草。他的智慧如何？"

【英译】

The Master said, "Zang Wenzhong built a house for his giant tortoise, carving the ends of pillars in the shape of hills, painting duckweeds on the raft posts. Was it wise for him to do so?"

5·19　子张问曰："令尹子文①三仕为令尹，无喜色；三已之，无愠色，旧令尹之政，必以告新令尹。何如？"子曰："忠矣。"曰："仁矣乎?"曰："未知②；——焉得仁?"

"崔子弑齐君，陈文子有马十乘，弃而违之，至于他邦，则曰'犹吾大夫崔子也。'违之。之一邦，则又曰'犹吾大夫崔子也。'违之。何如？"子曰："清矣。"曰："仁矣乎?"曰："未知；——焉得仁?"

【注释】

①令尹子文：令尹，楚国的官职名，相当于宰相；子文：姓斗，名谷于菟，字子文，古文作"鬬穀於菟（dòu gòu wū tú）"，是楚国著名的贤相。

②未知：不明智。

【今译】

子张问道："令尹子文三次做令尹，没有喜悦的表情；三次被罢免，没有怨恨的表情。（每次去职）必定把自己的政事告知新令尹。他怎么样？"夫子说："很忠诚啊。"子张道："算不算是仁呢?"夫子道:"不明智,哪里算得上仁呢?"

　　子张又问:"崔杼弑杀齐庄公,陈文子有马四十匹,舍弃不要,离开齐国。到了外国,却说:'(这里掌权的)和我们的崔子一样。'离开。又到了一国,又说:'(这里掌权的)和我们的崔子一样。'又离开。他怎么样?"夫子道:"很清白啊。"子张道:"算不算仁呢?"夫子道:"不明智,哪里算得上仁呢?"

【英译】

Zizhang asked, "Ziwen showed no sign of elation three times when appointed as a Minister, and no sign of displeasure three times when dismissed from office. He always informed the new minister of the way in which he conducted government— what do you think of him?"

"He was loyal to his state," replied the Master.

"Can he be counted as benevolent?"

"If not wise, how can he be benevolent?"

"When Cui Zi killed the Duke of Qi, Chen Wenzi abandoned his fief with forty horses and left Qi. After he arrived in another state, he said 'The officials here are no better than our Minister Cui Zi.' When he arrived in yet another state, he once more said 'The officials here are no better than our Minister Cui Zi.' What do you think of him?"

The Master replied, "He was a man of integrity."

"Can he be counted as benevolent?"

"If not wise, how can he be benevolent?"

5·20　季文子三思而后行。子闻之，曰："再，斯可矣。"

【今译】

季文子这个人，每遇一件事都要反复思索之后才去做，夫子听到后说："想两次，就可以了。"

【英译】

Ji Wenzi always thought thrice before taking action. When the Master heard this, he said, "Twice will do."

【辨正】

孙钦善《论语新注》："季文子素以谨慎多虑著称，《左传》文公六年记有这样一件事：'秋，季文子将聘于晋，使求遭（遇）丧之礼以行。其人（指随从）曰："将焉用之？"文子曰："备豫（预备，事先准备）不虞（料想），古之善教也。求而无之，实难。过求，何害？"'由此可见，其有备无患的思想是可取的，但过于谨小慎微就会走向反面。孔子的纠偏，正是针对他的弱点而发的。"

"三思，言思之多，能审慎也。"这种"非确指"的解法通常是正确的，"三思而行"不是让人恰好想三次，不多也不少。然而，在这里我们又不能说"三"字是虚指，原因是下文有个"再"字。说孔子故意理解为实指"三"也可，说"再"字影响了前面的"三"字也可，总之，这"三"字不再是虚指了。孔子说，不用三次，考虑两次就行了。

5·21　子曰："宁武子，邦有道，则知；邦无道，则愚。其知可及也，其愚不可及也。"

【今译】

夫子说："宁武子在国家政治清明时，便聪明；在国家政治昏暗时，便愚傻。他的聪明，别人赶得上；他的愚傻，没人能赶得上。"

【英译】

The Master said, "Ning Wuzi displayed great wisdom when the state was well-governed; he acted like a fool when the state was ill-governed. His intelligence was within reach of others, yet his foolishness cannot be equaled by others."

5·22　子在陈，曰："归与！归与！吾党之小子狂简，斐然成章，不知所以裁之。"

【今译】

夫子在陈国，说："回去吧！回去吧！我家乡的年轻人，志向高大，文采富丽，却不知怎样裁制它。"

【英译】

While staying in the State of Chen, the Master said, "Let us go back home! Let us go back home! The youngsters at home are ambitious, and gorgeous like a piece of brocade, yet they do not know how to tailor it."

5·23　子曰：“伯夷、叔齐不念旧恶^①，怨是用希^②。”

【注释】

①伯夷、叔齐：商代孤竹国国君的两个儿子。相传其父要立次子叔齐作继位人，叔齐不从。孤竹君死后，兄弟想谦让而逃到周国。周武王伐纣，两人曾叩马谏阻。周灭商后，兄弟两人隐居首阳山，“义不食周粟”而饿死。旧恶：过去的仇恨。

②是用：因此，相当于“是以”。希：稀少。

【今译】

夫子说：“伯夷，叔齐不念旧恶，怨恨因此就少。”

【英译】

The Master said, "Bo Yi and Shu Qi did not keep in mind the past wrongs others did to them, and that's why they rarely incurred ill will."

5·24　子曰：“孰谓微生高直^①？或乞醯焉^②，乞诸其邻而与之。”

【注释】

①微生高：春秋时代鲁国人，姓微生，名高，以守信名于当时。

②或乞醯（xī）：有人向他讨醋。醯：醋。

【今译】

夫子说：“谁说微生高这个人性直？有人向他讨醋，他去邻居家讨了，给与那人。”

The Master said, "Who said Weisheng Gao was straight? Once when someone asked him for vinegar, he borrowed some from his neighbor and gave it to the man."

5·25　子曰：“巧言、令色、足恭①，左丘明耻之，丘亦耻之。匿怨而友其人，左丘明耻之，丘亦耻之。”

【注释】

①足（jù）恭：过度的谦恭。足，过分。

【今译】

夫子说：“花言巧语，面貌伪善，过分谦恭，左丘认为可耻，我也认为可耻。把怨恨藏匿在心而与人交友，左丘明认为可耻，我也认为可耻。”

【英译】

The Master said, "Cunning words, an ingratiating countenance, and obsequious conduct—these things Zuoqiu Ming found shameful. So do I. To pretend to be friendly toward someone while concealing resentment against him, this Zuoqiu Ming found shameful. So do I."

5·26　颜渊、季路侍。子曰："盍各言尔志？"

子路曰："愿车马衣（轻）裘①与朋友共，敝之②而无憾。"

颜渊曰："愿无伐善③，无施劳。"

子路曰："愿闻子之志。"

子曰："老者安之，朋友信之，少者怀之④。"

【注释】

①裘（qiú）：皮衣。"轻"字为衍文。

②敝之：把车马衣裘用破。

③伐善：夸耀功劳。伐，夸耀。

④怀：关怀，照顾。安之，信之，怀之，三个词组都是使动用法。

【今译】

颜渊、季路站夫子身边。夫子说："你们何不谈谈各自的志向呢？"子路说："我愿把车马、穿的衣服，与朋友共同使用，即使用坏了也不遗憾。"颜渊说："我愿不夸耀自己，不劳烦他人。"子路说："我们想听听老师的志向。"夫子说："使老年人安心，使朋友信任，使少年得到关怀。"

【英译】

Yan Yuan and Jilu were in attendance. The Master said, "Why not each of you talk about your ambition?

Zilu said, "I should like to share with my friends my carriage, horses and clothes, and have no regrets even if they get spoiled."

Yan Yuan said, "I should like never to boast of my merits and never to trouble others with labor."

Zilu said, "I should like, sir, to hear your ambition."

The Master said, "For the old, make them live in peace; for friends, make them trust others; for the young, make them cherished."

5 · 27　子曰："已矣乎，吾未见能见其过而内自讼者也。"

【今译】

夫子说："算了吧，我还没有见过发现了自己错误便自我批评的人呢。"

【英译】

The Master said, "Alas! I have not yet seen one who could blame himself inwardly when perceiving his faults."

5 · 28　子曰："十室之邑，必有忠信如丘者焉，不如丘之好学也。"

【今译】

夫子说："就是十户人家的小村邑里，也一定有像我这样既忠心又信实的人，只是不如我这样爱好学习。"

【英译】

The Master said, "In a village of ten families, there must be a man as honorable and sincere as I am, but not as fond of learning as I am."

雍也第六

6·1　子曰:"雍也,可使南面①。"

【注释】

①南面:即脸朝南。古代以坐北朝南为尊位。

【今译】

夫子说:"冉雍呀,可以让他做君主。"

【英译】

The Master said, "Yong（has in him the making of a prince and）can be made facing south."

6·2　仲弓问子桑伯子。子曰:"可也,简。"

仲弓曰:"居敬而行简,以临其民,不亦可乎?居简而行简,无乃大简乎?"子曰:"雍之言然。"

【今译】

仲弓问子桑伯子这个人。夫子说:"这人可以,他简而不繁。"仲弓说:"平时严肃慎重,施政简易,这样治理百姓,不是很可以吗?平时简慢而施政又简易,岂不太简了吗?"夫子说:"冉雍说得对。"

Zhonggong asked Zisang about Bozi. The Master said, "He is quite alright, as he acts in a simple way."

Zhonggong said, "Is it not acceptable to remain meticulous in daily life and simple in ruling the people? However, isn't it oversimplified when one remains indifferent in daily life and rules the people in a simple way?"

The Master said, "Yong is right in saying so."

6·3　哀公问：“弟子孰为好学?”孔子对曰：“有颜回者好学，不迁怒，不贰过。不幸短命死矣，今也则亡，未闻好学者也。”

【今译】

哀公问：“你的学生中谁最好学?”孔子回答：“有一个叫颜回的，很好学。自己的怒气不迁移到他人身上，自己犯的错误也不推诿成别人的。不幸短命死了。现在没有这样的人了，没有听说过好学的人。”

【英译】

Duke Ai asked Confucius, "Who among your disciples truly loves learning?" The Master answered, "There was one Yan Hui who loved learning. He never vents his anger nor shuffles his faults onto others. Unfortunately, he died young and now there is not such man. At least, I have not yet heard of anyone as fond of learning."

【辨正】

朱熹《论语集注》中说"怒于甲者，不移于乙，过于前者，不复于后。"然而，这种"气当拿甲不拿乙出，错当日日新而不重"解法走错了方向。

与"不迁怒"结构相同，"不贰过"中"贰"是动词，"过"是名词。"贰"，不是"再一次""重复"，而是"变易、更动"。"不贰过"是指自己出了过失，不推诿于人。孔子说："功不独居，过不推诿"。"不迁怒，不贰过"，这里的"迁""贰"都有"改变"的意思。自己的怒与过都不影响或牵及他人，即"怒不迁，过不诿"才是孔子对颜回真正的赞誉。

"贰"义的确定，可与"一""三"相比较。"一"是始终不变，如"其仪一兮""用心一也"；"贰"是"改变"，如"国不堪贰""士贰其行"；"三"是多次改变，反复无常，如"二三其德"。

6·4　子华使于齐，冉子为其母请粟。子曰："与之釜①。"
请益。曰："与之庾②。"
冉子与之粟五秉③。
子曰："赤之适④齐也，乘肥马，衣轻裘⑤。吾闻之也：君子周急不继富⑥。"

【注释】
①釜（fǔ）：古代量词，约合当时6斗4升。
②庾（yǔ）：古代量词，约合当时的2斗4升。
③秉：古代量词，合16斛（hú），160斗。五秉即800斗。
④适：往，到。
⑤衣（yì）轻裘：穿着又轻又暖的皮袍子。
⑥周急不继富：周济急需的人，不接济富有者。周：同

"週"，给，救济。继：增益。

【今译】

公西赤出使到齐国去，冉有替他母亲请求发放小米。夫子说："给他一釜。"冉求请求增加些。夫子说："（再）给他一庾。"冉求却给了他五秉。

夫子说："公西赤到齐国去，坐着由肥马拉的车，穿着轻暖的皮衣。我听说：君子周济贫穷的人，而不使富人更富。"

【英译】

Ranzi asked for grain for the mother of Zihua who was away on a mission to the State of Qi. The Master said, "Give her a *Fu* (equals 6.4 Chinese bushels)." Ran requested more. "Give her another *Yu* (equals 16 Chinese bushels)," said the Master. Ran gave her five *Bings* (equals 800 Chinese bushels).

The Master said, "Chi went off to the State of Qi in a carriage drawn by well-fed horses and was wearing light furs. I have heard it said, 'A gentleman helps meet an urgent need, but not to help add to the wealth of the rich.'"

6·5 原思为之宰，与之粟九百，辞。子曰："毋！以与尔邻里乡党乎！"

【今译】

原思为夫子做总管，夫子给他小米九百斗，原思推辞不要。夫子说："不要推辞！拿去给你的邻里乡亲吧！"

【英译】

When Yuan Si became Confucius' steward, he was given nine hundred measures of grain as his emolument. Yuan Si declined. The Master said, "Do not decline. You can give it to the people in your hometown."

6·6 子谓仲弓，曰："犁牛之子骍且角①，虽欲勿用，山川其舍诸？"

【注释】

①犁牛：即耕牛。骍（xīng）：牛马等毛色为红色。角：牛角长得好，长得端正。

【今译】

夫子谈到仲弓时说："耕牛生的小牛长着赤色的毛和端正的角，虽然不想用它作为牺牲来祭祀，山川之神难道会舍弃它吗？"

【英译】

The Master said of Zhonggong, "Should there be a bull born of plough oxen having a coat of red hair and well-formed horns, would the God of Mountains and Rivers let it be cast aside, even if people feel it is not good enough for ceremonial sacrifice?"

6·7　子曰：“回也，其心三月不违仁，其余则日月至焉而已矣。”

【今译】

夫子说：“颜回啊，他的心能连续三个月不离仁德，其他的学生则像日月到来一样，时而想起罢了。”

【英译】

The Master said, "For three months at a time Hui did not lapse from benevolence in his heart. Others attain benevolence intermittently, like the presence of the sun and the moon."

6·8　季康子问：“仲由可使从政也与？”子曰：“由也果，于从政乎何有？”

曰：“赐也可使从政也与？”曰：“赐也达，于从政乎何有？”

曰：“求也可使从政也与？”曰：“求也艺，于从政乎何有？”

【今译】

季康子问道：“仲由能去从政吗？”夫子说：“由果断，从政有何困难呢？”

季康子问道：“赐能去从政吗？”夫子说：“赐通达，从政有何困难呢？”

季康子问道：“求能去从政吗？”夫子说：“求多才多艺，从政有何困难呢？”

Ji Kangzi asked, "Could Zhong You be made an official?"

The Master said, "(Zhong) You is resolute. What difficulty is there for him to become an official?"

Ji Kangzi asked, "Could Ci be made an official?"

The Master said, "Ci is sagacious. What difficulty is there for him to become an official?"

Ji Kangzi asked, "Could Qiu be made an official?"

The Master said, "Qiu is versatile. What difficulty is there for him to become an official?"

6·9 季氏使闵子骞为费宰①。闵子骞曰："善为我辞焉②！如有复我③者，则吾必在汶上④矣。"

【注释】

①费（bì）：邑名，在今山东省费县，曾为季孙氏的采邑。宰：城邑的地方官。

②善：好，引申为委婉地。辞：推辞。

③复我：再来找我。复：再。

④汶上：在今山东大汶河之北。这里指齐国。

【今译】

季氏让闵子骞当费邑的长官，闵子骞对使者说："好好地替我辞掉吧。如果有人再来找我，那我一定会避居到汶水北边去。"

【英译】

The chief of the Ji family wanted to make Min Ziqian the steward of Bi. Min Zijian said, "Decline the offer for me tactfully. If anyone comes back for me, he would find me on the other side of the Wen River."

6·10　伯牛有疾，子问之，自牖执其手，曰："亡之，命矣夫！斯人也而有斯疾也！斯人也而有斯疾也！"

【今译】

舟伯牛生病，夫子去看望他，从窗口握着他的手说："将要失去他了，这是命运啊！这样的好人竟也会得这样的恶病啊！这样的好人竟也会得这样的恶病啊！"

【英译】

Boniu was ill. The Master visited him, holding his hand through the window, and said, "We are going to lose him. It must be destiny. Why else should such a man be stricken with such a disease? Why else should such a man be stricken with such a disease?"

6·11　子曰："贤哉，回也！一箪食，一瓢饮，在陋巷，人不堪其忧，回也不改其乐。贤哉，回也！"

【今译】

夫子说："颜回品德多么高尚啊！一篮饭、一瓢水，住在简陋的居室里，别人忍受不了那困厄，颜回却照样快乐。颜回品德多么高尚啊！"

【英译】

The Master said, "How admirable Hui is! Living in a mean

dwelling on a bowlful of rice and a ladleful of water is a hard life most people would find intolerable, but Hui has always enjoyed it. How admirable Hui is!"

6·12 冉求曰：“非不说子之道，力不足也。”子曰：“力不足者，中道而废。今女画^①。”

【注释】

①画：停止。能够前进而不坚持。

【今译】

冉求说：“我不是不喜欢老师的学说，是能力不足。”夫子说：“能力不够的人中途停顿下来。而现在是你还未开始就停下了。”

【英译】

Ran Qiu said, "It is not that I am not pleased with your teachings but rather that I've run out of strength." The Master said, "Those who run out of strength give up half way, but now you give up before starting."

6·13 子谓子夏曰：“女为君子儒，无为小人儒。”

【今译】

夫子对子夏说：“你要做君子式的学者，不要做小人式的学者。”

The Master said to Zixia, "Be a gentleman scholar, not a petty scholar."

6·14 子游为武城宰。子曰："女得人焉耳乎?"曰："有澹台灭明者^①，行不由径，非公事，未尝至于偃之室也。"

【注释】

①澹（tán）台灭明：复姓澹台，名灭明，字子羽，鲁国武城人。

【今译】

子游担任武城的长官。夫子说："你在那儿得到人才了吗?"子游说："有一个叫澹台灭明的人，行路不走小道；不是公事，从不到我的住所来。"

【英译】

Ziyou was the steward of Wucheng. The Master said, "Have you discovered any talented people there?" He answered, "There is a Dantai Mieming, who never takes shortcuts, and never comes to my house except on official business."

6·15 子曰："孟之反不伐，奔而殿，将入门，策其马，曰：'非敢后也，马不进也。'"

【今译】

夫子说："孟之反不夸耀功劳。军队败退时，他行在队伍后面掩护；将要进城门时，他又策马向队伍前面，说：'（刚才）不是我敢于殿后，是马不向前啊！'"

【英译】

The Master said, "Meng Zhifan does not boast to his credit. When the troops were retreating in defeat, he brought up the rear; when they were about to enter the city gate, he whipped up his horse, saying, 'It is not that I dared to be the rearguard, but that my horse simply refused to advance.'"

6·16　子曰："不有祝鮀之佞①，而有宋朝②之美，难乎免于今之世矣。"

【注释】

①不有：假如没有。祝鮀（tuó）：卫国大夫，字子鱼。佞：能言善辩，口才出众。

②宋朝（zhāo）：宋国的公子朝，以貌美闻名。

【今译】

夫子说："没有祝鮀的口才，而有宋朝的美貌，在现今的世上很难不遭灾祸。"

【英译】

The Master said, "If a man has the good looks of Song Zhao without the eloquence of Zhu Tuo, it is difficult for him to escape mishaps in the present world."

6 · 17 子曰：“谁能出不由户？何莫由斯道也？”

【今译】

夫子说：“谁能走出房子而不通过房门呢？什么事情能不由这个道呢？”

【英译】

The Master said, "Who can go out of a house except by the door? What can be achieved except by following the Way?"

6 · 18 子曰：“质胜文则野①，文胜质则史②。文质彬彬③，然后君子。”

【注释】

①质：朴质，指人的品行、知识等内在的品质。文：文采，指人的风采、言谈等外在的表现。野：山野村民，喻指过于质朴。

②史：本义是宗庙里掌礼义的祝官，官府里掌文书的史官。这里指像“史”那样，言词华丽，虚浮铺陈，心里并无诚意。含有浮夸虚伪的贬义。

③彬彬：文质兼备相称；文与质互相融和，配合得当。

【今译】

夫子说：“朴质胜过文饰，就会显得粗野；文饰胜过朴质，就会显得浮华。文饰与朴质配合得当，然后方为君子。”

【英译】

The Master said, "When one's natural talent prevails over

refinement, he will appear savage; when one's refinement pre-vails over natural talent, he will appear artificial; when natural talent and refinement are well-blended in one's character, he will appear graceful, and then a gentleman comes into being."

6·19　子曰："人之生也直^①，罔^②之生也幸而免。"

【注释】
①直：正直。
②罔（wǎng）：诬罔，虚妄。指不正直的人。

【今译】
夫子说："一个人活着，是由于正直；不正直的人活着，是由于侥幸而避免了灾祸。"

【英译】
The Master said, "Man is born to be upright. He who is not upright survives by mere chance."

6·20　子曰："知之者不如好之者，好之者不如乐之者。"

【今译】
夫子说："做一件事，了解的不如喜爱的，喜爱的不如以之为乐的。"

【英译】
The Master said, "In doing something honestly, knowing it is not as good as loving it; loving it is not as good as delighting

in it."

6·21　子曰：“中人以上，可以语上也；中人以下，不可以语上也。”

【今译】

夫子说：“中等水平以上的人，可以与他谈论高深的东西；中等水平以下的人，不可以与他谈论高深的东西。”

【英译】

The Master said, "You can discuss something profoundly only with those above average, but not with those below average."

6·22　樊迟问知。子曰：“务民之义，敬鬼神而远之，可谓知矣。”

问仁。曰：“仁者先难而后获，可谓仁矣。”

【今译】

樊迟问，怎样才是“智”。夫子说：“致力于百姓称“义”的事，尊敬鬼神而远离它，就可以说是‘智’了。”

樊迟问怎样才是“仁”。夫子说；“有仁德的人，遇到困难行在前，遇到好处行在后。就可以说是‘仁’了。”

【英译】

Fan Chi asked about wisdom. The Master said, "To devote oneself to what ought to be done for the people and staying aloof from ghosts and spirits while respecting them; that is wisdom."

He asked about benevolence. The Master said, "The benevolent man will be the first to tackle difficulties and the last to gain benefits. That is benevolence."

6·23　子曰："知者乐①水，仁者乐山。知者动，仁者静。知者乐，仁者寿。"

【注释】

①乐（yào）：喜爱。

【今译】

夫子说："智者喜爱水，仁者喜爱山。智者爱动，仁者爱静。智者快乐，仁者长寿。"

【英译】

The Master said, "The wise find joy in waters; the benevolent find joy in mountains. The wise are active; the benevolent are tranquil. The wise enjoy life; the benevolent are blessed with longevity."

6·24　子曰："齐一变，至于鲁；鲁一变，至于道。"

【今译】

夫子说："齐国（的政治）一经改革，便能达到鲁国的水平；鲁国（的政治）一经改革，便能合乎大道了。"

【英译】

The Master said, "The State of Qi, with a reform carried

out in its politics, can reach the level of the State of Lu; the State of Lu, with a reform carried out in its politics, can conform itself to the Way."

6·25 子曰："觚不觚①，觚哉！觚哉！"

【注释】

①觚（gū）：古代盛酒器具，上圆下方，容积约2升。

【今译】

夫子说："（现在）觚不像觚。觚啊！觚啊！"

【英译】

The Master said, "A cornered vessel without corners. What cornered vessel is this! What cornered vessel is this!"

【辨正】

孔子为何有"觚不觚"之叹，有两种说法，都可见于《论语集释》：（一）"古人制器尚象，以一觚言之，上圆象天，下方象地，且取其置顿之安稳焉。春秋之世，已有破觚为圆者。孔子于献酬之际，见而叹之，其事虽小而轻变古制，已有秦人开阡陌、废井田、焚诗书、尚法律之渐矣。"（二）"觚，酒器名。量可容二升者，其义寡也。古量酒以三升为当。五升为过，二升为寡，而制器者即因之。故凡设器命名，义各有取。君子顾其名当而思其义，所谓名以实称也。今名虽为觚，而饮常不寡。实则不副，何以称名？故曰'觚哉觚哉'。……王肃云：'当时沉湎于酒，故曰不觚。'王意盖谓古器各有取义，觚之为言寡，不寡则谓之不觚也。第一种解释是说，觚本当上圆下方，破觚为圆改了古制，变得觚不像觚了。第二种解释说，酒器名觚，"其义寡也"，就是为了戒酗酒，今名虽为觚，却不能限制人饮酒，觚还是觚吗？

孔子言"觚不觚"，实是对事物有所改变、有名无实、名实不副的感叹，表达了对当时"君不君，臣不臣，父不父，子不子"等社会现象的不满。

6·26　宰我问曰："仁者，虽告之曰，'井有仁焉。'其从之也？"子曰："何为其然也？君子可逝也，不可陷也；可欺也，不可罔也。"

【今译】

宰我问道："追求仁德的人，如果告诉他：'井里有仁德！'他会去追求吗？"夫子说："为什么要那样做呢？君子可以让他死，但不可陷害他；可以欺负他，但不可罔诬他。"

【英译】

Zaiwo asked, "When a benevolent man is told, 'Benevolence can be found in the well', will he follow it there?" Confucius said, "Why do so? A gentleman can be made to die, but not be framed; he can be bullied, but not be hoodwinked."

6·27　子曰："君子博学于文，约之以礼^①，亦可以弗畔^②矣夫！"

【注释】

①礼：社会道德伦理规范和生活准则。
②畔（pàn）：同"叛"，背离。

【今译】

夫子说：“君子广泛地学习文献典籍，用礼仪规范来约束自己，也就可以不背离（道义）了。”

【英译】

The Master said, "A gentleman, who is widely versed in literature and historical records and regulates himself with rites, can be relied upon not to go astray."

6·28 子见南子，子路不说。夫子矢之曰：“予所否者，天厌之！天厌之！”

【今译】

夫子会见南子，子路不高兴。夫子发誓说：“假如我做了什么不正当的事，就让上天厌弃我吧！就让上天厌弃我吧！”

【英译】

The Master went to see Nanzi. Zilu was displeased. The Master swore, "If I have done anything wrong, may Heaven detest me! May Heaven detest me!"

6·29 子曰：“中庸之为德也，其至矣乎！民鲜久矣。”

【今译】

夫子说：“中庸之道作为一种德行，该是最高的了，百姓缺乏这种德行已经很久了。”

The Master said, "Supreme indeed is the Constant Mean as a moral virtue! It has long been rare among the common people."

6·30　子贡曰:"如有博施于民而能济众,何如? 可谓仁乎?"子曰:"何事于仁! 必也圣乎! 尧舜其犹病诸! 夫仁者,己欲立而立人,己欲达而达人。能近取譬,可谓仁之方也已。"

【今译】

子贡说:"假如一个人广泛施惠于民并且能救助大众,怎么样啊? 能称为仁人吗?"夫子说:"岂止是仁人,该是圣人了! 尧、舜还恐怕做不到这样呢。仁人啊,自己要立身,也帮助别人立身;自己要通达,也帮助别人通达。能够就近作比,(推己及人),可以说是实行仁的方法啊。"

【英译】

Zigong said, "If there were a man who showers the people with blessings and is able to assist all, what do you think of him? Can he be considered benevolent?"

The Master said, "He is far more than being benevolent. He must have the qualities of a sage. Even Yao and Shun would have been solicitous about accomplishing as much. A benevolent man, wishing to establish himself, will help others get established; wishing to be illustrious himself, will help others become illustrious. To be able to regulate one's feelings to be in tune with those of others may be the best way to practice benevolence."

述而第七

7·1　子曰："述而不作，信而好古，窃比于我老彭①。"

【注释】

①老彭：指彭祖。传说是颛顼（zhuān xū，五帝之一）的玄孙陆终氏的第三个儿子，姓钱，名铿（kēng），尧封之于彭城。彭祖善养生，活到800岁。

【今译】

夫子说："只传述（旧的文化典籍）而不创作（新的），相信而且喜爱古代的（文化），我私下把自己比作老彭。"

【英译】

The Master said, "As I transmit the old literature and do not create new ones and believe in and admire the antiquities, I venture to compare myself to Old Peng."

7·2　子曰："默而识之，学而不厌，诲人不倦，何有于我哉？"

【今译】

夫子说："默默地记在心里，努力学习而不厌弃，教导别人而不疲倦，这对我来说算什么呢？"

【英译】

The Master said, "To quietly remember what is learned, to learn without satiety and to teach without weariness—what difficulty is there for me to do so?"

7·3 子曰："德之不修，学之不讲，闻义不能徙①，不善不能改，是吾忧也。"

【注释】

①徙：本义是迁移。这里指徙而从之，使自己的所作所为靠近义。

【今译】

夫子说："品德不修养，学业不讲习；知道了义之所在，却不能去做；有错误不去改正，这些是我所忧虑的啊！"

【英译】

The Master said, "It is these things that cause me concern: failure to cultivate virtue, failure to practice what is learned, inability to turn to righteousness when informed, and inability to correct wrongdoings."

7·4 子之燕①居，申申如也，夭夭如也。

【注释】

①燕：通"宴"，安闲。

【今译】

夫子闲居时，仪态舒缓，神色和悦。

【英译】

During his leisure moments, the Master was at ease in manner and looked pleased.

7·5　子曰：“甚矣，吾衰也！久矣，吾不复梦见周公！”

【今译】

夫子说：“我衰老得太厉害了！我很久没有梦见周公了！”

【英译】

The Master said, "How I have aged! It has been such a long time since I dreamed of the Duke of Zhou."

7·6　子曰：“志于道，据于德，依于仁，游于艺。”

【今译】

夫子说：“立志于道，据守于德，依赖于仁，优游于艺。”

【英译】

The Master said, "Be resolved to seek the Way, based on virtue, rely on benevolence and enjoy the Six Arts."

7·7 子曰:"自行束修以上,吾未尝无诲焉。"

【今译】

夫子说:"自十五岁(行束修)以上的,我从来没有不教诲的。

【英译】

The Master said, "To those who have reached the age of fifteen, I have never refused to give my instruction."

【辨正】

黄式三《论语后案》:"自行束修以上,谓年十五以上能行束带修饰之礼。郑君注如此,汉时相传之师说也。《后汉·伏湛传》'杜诗荐湛自行束修,迄无毁玷',注:'自行束修,谓年十五以上。'《延笃传》笃曰'吾自束修以来',注:'束修,谓束带修饰。郑玄注《论语》曰"谓年十五以上也。"'今疏本申孔注,异于郑君。然《尚书·泰誓》孔疏引孔注《论语》,以束修为束带修饰,为某传束修一介臣之证,是孔、郑注同。盖年十五以上,束带修饰以就外傅,郑君与孔义可合也。《曲礼》'童子委挚而退',疏曰:'童子之挚悉用束修。故《论语》孔子云:"自行束修以上,则吾未尝无诲焉。"是谓童子也。'"

张良皋《匠学七说》:"着深衣在室内行动,有履絇约束,可以见雍容揖让之态。但若到户外,显然不便,所以人们不能不在腰际束带,这应该是'束修'的来源。……把束修解释成'十条干肉',仿佛夫子只搞'有偿服务'。这里'行'不训'给予',而是'行年'之'行'。也就是孔子只教13-15岁以上的学生,'开蒙'不是他的事。对孔子的这一条言论,多少存在争议，但人们若懂得筵席，了解深衣，就不会产生误解。"

如果把"束修"释为"一束干肉""十挺干肉"，句子译成"只要自愿拿着十条干肉为礼来见我的人，我从来没有不给他教诲的。"那就是说：孔子教授弟子要收礼，没有见面礼者不教；见面礼有最低限度，低于十挺干肉的求学者不教；送礼必须"自行"，即不亲自送来，或送而不自愿者不教。这些可是主张有教无类、因材施教的教育家孔子的原意？

7·8 子曰："不愤不启①，不悱②不发。举一隅不以三隅反③，则不复也。"

【注释】

①愤：郁结于心。朱熹注："愤者，心求通而未得之意。"启：启发，开导。

②悱（fěi）：口欲言而未能。

③隅：角。反：类推。

【今译】

夫子说："教导学生，不到他有问题想问的时候，不去开导他；不到他想表达却表达不出的时候，不去启发他。讲了一方面却不能联想到其他方面，就不再教导他了。"

【英译】

The Master said, "Do not enlighten the disciple until he feels puzzled by the problem, or lost in expressing himself. Do not instruct him any longer if he cannot draw inferences after one instance is given."

7·9　子食于有丧者之侧，未尝饱也。

【今译】

夫子在有丧事的人旁边吃饭，未曾吃饱过。

【英译】

When eating in the presence of the bereaved, the Master never ate his fill.

7·10　子于是日哭，则不歌。

【今译】

夫子这天哭泣过，就不再唱歌。

【英译】

The Master would not sing for the rest of the day if he had wept（at a funeral）.

7·11　子谓颜渊曰："用之则行①，舍②之则藏，惟我与尔有是夫！"

子路曰："子行三军③，则谁与④？"

子曰："暴虎冯河⑤，死尔无悔者，吾不与也。必也临事而惧，好谋而成者也。"

【注释】

①行：实施，有所作为。

②舍：舍弃，此指不用。

③行：统率，指挥。三军：古代大国有上、中、下三军。

这里泛指军队。

④与：在一起，共事。

⑤暴虎冯（píng）河：高诱注："无兵搏虎曰暴，无舟渡河曰冯。"赤手与老虎搏斗，赤足淌水过河。

【今译】

夫子对颜渊说："得到任用，就去做事；不得任用，就隐藏起来。只有我和你能这样啊！"子路说："您若统帅三军，您会与谁共事呢？"夫子说："徒手与老虎搏斗，赤脚淌水过河，死了都不后悔的人，我是不会与他共事的。（我愿与之共事的），一定是处理事情小心谨慎，善于谋略而能成事的人！"

【英译】

The Master said to Yan Yuan, "Only you and I are able to go ahead when employed and remain reclusive when not employed."

Zilu said, "If you were to command the whole army, whom would you like to take along with you?"

The Master said, "I would not take along with me someone who would attack a tiger with bare hands or ford a river with bear feet and die without regret. It should be one who can act cautiously when confronting ordeals; one who can realize his goals by careful planning."

7·12　子曰：“富而可求也，虽执鞭之士，吾亦为之。如不可求，从吾所好。”

【今译】

夫子说：“如果财富可以求得，就是手执皮鞭（的低贱职业）我也愿做。如果求它不到，我还是做我爱好的事。”

【英译】

The Master said, "If wealth can be obtained by effort, then I wouldn't mind being a whip-holding guard. If it cannot, I'd rather follow my own inclination."

7·13　子之所慎：齐①，战，疾。

【注释】

①齐：同“斋”。指古代在祭祀之前虔诚的斋戒。

【今译】

夫子谨慎对待的是：斋戒，战争，疾病。

【英译】

The things the Master was cautious dealing with were—fasting, war, and sickness.

7·14　子在齐闻《韶》，三月不知肉味，曰："不图为乐之至于斯也。"

【今译】

夫子在齐国，听到《韶》乐，很长时间不觉得肉的美味，说："真想不到创作音乐能达到如此的水平。"

【英译】

The Master heard the *Shao* in the State of Qi and for a few months did not notice the taste of the meat he ate. "I never dreamt," he said, "that music could be made so wonderful."

7·15　冉有曰："夫子为卫君乎？"子贡曰："诺；吾将问之。"

入，曰："伯夷、叔齐何人也？"曰："古之贤人也。"曰："怨乎？"曰："求仁而得仁，又何怨？"

出，曰："夫子不为也。"

【今译】

冉有问道："老师会帮助卫国的国君吗？"子贡说："好的，我去问问老师。"子贡进到夫子屋里，问道："伯夷、叔齐是什么样的人呢？"夫子说："是古代的贤人。"子贡又问道："他们有怨恨吗？"夫子说："他们追求仁而得到了仁，又有什么怨恨呢？"子贡出来，对冉求说："老师不会帮助卫国的国君。"

【英译】

Ran You said, "Will our Master help the Lord of Wei?"

Zigong said, "Well! I shall put the question to him."

He went in and asked, "What sort of men were Bo Yi and Shu Qi?"

"Men of virtue in ancient times," said the Master.

"Were they regretful for what they had done?"

The Master again replied, "They sought benevolence and got it. What should they regret?"

Zigong went out and said, "Our Master will not help the Lord of Wei."

7·16　子曰："饭疏食^①，饮水^②，曲肱^③而枕之，乐亦在其中矣。不义而富且贵，于我如浮云。"

【注释】

①饭：作动词用，作"吃"解。疏食：粗粮。

②水：冷水，与"汤（热水）"相对。

③肱（gōng）：胳膊。

【今译】

夫子说："吃粗粮，喝白水，弯着胳膊作枕头睡，乐趣也就在其中了。用不正当的手段获得财富和尊贵，这对我来说，就像浮云一样。"

【英译】

The Master said, "Joy can be found in eating coarse grain, in drinking plain water and in a bent arm for a pillow to rest my head. To me, riches and honors attained immorally are mere drifting clouds."

7·17 子曰："加我数年，五十以学《易》，可以无大过矣。"

【今译】

夫子说："如果增加我几年寿命，五十岁开始学习《易经》，这样就不会有大过了。"

【英译】

The Master said, "If I were granted a few more years and started to learn *The Book of Changes* at the age of fifty, I will be free from making serious mistakes."

7·18 子所雅言，《诗》、《书》、执礼，皆雅言也。

【今译】

夫子讲标准语：读《诗》、《书》，主持礼仪，都讲标准语。

【英译】

Occasions when the Master uses standard language: When he reads aloud from *The Book of Songs* or *The Book of Documents*, or when performing ceremonies.

7·19 叶公问孔子于子路，子路不对。子曰："女奚不曰，'其为人也，发愤忘食，乐以忘忧，不知老之将至'云尔?"

【今译】

叶公向子路了解孔子，子路不回答。夫子（听说后，）说："你为什么不说：他这个人呀，发愤用功而忘记了吃饭，乐在其中而忘记了忧愁，不知道老年就要到来，如此而已？"

【英译】

Duke of She asked Zilu about Confucius. Zilu did not answer. The Master said, "Why did you not say something to this effect: 'He is a man who is so immersed in his studies that he forgets his meals, who is so happy that he forgets his worries, and who does not notice that old age is approaching?'"

7·20　子曰："我非生而知之者，好古，敏以求之者也。"

【今译】

夫子说："我不是生来就（什么都）知道的人，而是好古、勤奋而求得知识的人。"

【英译】

The Master said, "I was not born learned. I simply love ancient things and diligently seek for them."

7·21　子不语怪，力，乱，神。

【今译】

夫子不谈论怪异、暴力、叛乱和鬼神。

【英译】

The Master did not talk of the supernatural, violence, disorders or gods.

7·22 子曰："三人行，必有我师焉。择其善者而从之，其不善者而改之。"

【今译】

夫子说："三人一起做事，其中一定有值得我效法的人。选择他们好的地方效法，他们不好的地方就改掉。"

【英译】

The Master said, "Working in a party of three, I am bound to find one I can learn from. For the good traits I will follow; for the bad ones, I will correct in myself."

【辨正】

"三人行"的"三"，是虚指"很多"，还是实指"三个人"？这要看孔子强调人多还是人少，可作老师者难找还是易找，是不谦虚地说"很多人里才能找到一个可作我老师的！"还是谦虚地说"三个人里就能找到可作我老师的！"

不能既说"三"是虚指，又译成强调少的"几个人"。

陈天祥《四书辨疑》："果言善恶皆我师，则天下之人皆我师矣，何必专指三人？亦不须更言必有也。三人取其数少而言，必有二字于三人中又有所择也。三人行必有我师焉者，言其只三人行其间，亦必有可为师法者，择其善者而从之，其不善处改之者，非谓择其一人全善者从之，一人全恶者改之也。但就各人行事中择其事之善处从之，其不善处改之，不求备于一人也。全德之人世不常有，若直须择定事事全善之人然后从之，于普天下终身求之未必可得，三人中岂能必有也？止当随其各有之善从而师之，甲有一善则从甲之一善，乙有一善则从乙之一善，舜取诸人以为善，亦此道也。由是言之，三人行必有我师，信不诬矣。"

7·23 子曰："天生德于予，桓魋①其如予何?"

【注释】

①桓魋（tuí）：宋国的司马向氏，为宋桓公的后代。孔子
周游列国，经过宋国，与弟子在大树下习礼，桓魋欲杀孔子而
拔其树，弟子劝孔子快走，孔子因此说了这番话。

【今译】

夫子说："上天赋予我仁德，桓魋能把我怎么样?"

【英译】

The Master said, "Heaven bestowed virtue on me, so what
could Huan Tui do to me?"

**7·24 子曰："二三子以我为隐乎? 吾无隐乎尔。吾无行
而不与二三子者，是丘也。"**

【今译】

夫子说："你们几位以为我有什么隐瞒吗? 我没有隐瞒
啊。我没有什么行为不能告诉你们，这就是我孔丘。"

【英译】

The Master said, "Do you think, my disciples, that I am concealing anything from you? But I conceal nothing. There is nothing I do that I cannot share with you; that is my way."

7·25 子以四教：文、行、忠、信。

【今译】

夫子以四项内容教育学生，即文献，做事，忠诚，守信。

【英译】

The Master taught these four things: literature, ethical conduct, faithfulness and credability.

7·26 子曰："圣人，吾不得而见之矣；得见君子者，斯可矣。"

子曰："善人，吾不得而见之矣；得见有恒者，斯可矣。亡而为有，虚而为盈，约而为泰，难乎有恒矣。"

【今译】

夫子说："圣人，我见不到他们了；能够见到君子，就可以了。"夫子（又）说："善人，我见不到他们了；能够见到恒久向善的人，就可以了。没有却装作有，空虚却装作充实，贫穷却装作豪华，恒久向善就很难做到了。"

【英译】

The Master said, "I have no hope of meeting a sage. I would be content if I could meet someone who is a gentleman."

The Master said, "I have no hope of meeting a well-doer. I would be content if I could meet someone who has constancy. It is hard for those to have constancy who claim to be wealthy when they are actually needy, to be affluent when they are actually empty and to be prosperous when they are actually straitened."

7·27　子钓而不纲①，弋不射宿②。

【注释】

①钓：钓鱼。纲：网上大绳，这里作动词，撒网捕鱼。

②弋（yì）：带丝绳的箭，以便回收猎，这里用作动词，用带绳的箭射。宿：在巢内歇宿的鸟。

【今译】

夫子用鱼竿钓鱼，但不撒网捕鱼；用箭射鸟，但不射归巢歇宿的鸟。

【英译】

The Master angled, but did not use a net. He shot, but not at birds roosting.

7·28　子曰：“盖有不知而作之者，我无是也。多闻，择其善者而从之；多见而识之；知之次也。”

【今译】

夫子说：“大概有不懂得却做事的人，我不这么做。多了解，选择其中好的学着做；多经历，从而认识它，这是获取知识的次等方法。”

【英译】

The Master said, "There may be those who start doing something without fully knowing it, but I am not one of them.

Learning widely and choosing what is good to follow; experiencing much and then getting to know it—this is the second-best way of acquiring knowledge."

7·29 互乡难与言^①童子见，门人惑。子曰："与^②其进也，不与其退也，唯何甚？人洁己以进，与其洁也，不保其往也。"

【注释】

①互乡：地名。难与言：难于交谈。与（yú）：介词，跟。
②与（yǔ）：赞许，帮助。

【今译】

互乡有一难以交谈的少年去见夫子，弟子感到疑惑。夫子说："赞许他进步，不赞许他退步，有什么过分的？人家洁身以求进步，我们赞许他洁身，不固守他的过去。"

【英译】

A youngster of Huxiang, who was difficult to communicate with, got access to the Master. The disciples were puzzled by the interview.

The Master said, "I approve of his effort to progress, but not his reverse. Is this going too far? When he comes for progress by purifying himself, approve of his intent to do so and never be constrained by his past."

7·30　子曰：“仁远乎哉？我欲仁，斯仁至矣。”

【今译】

夫子说：“仁离我们很远吗？我想要仁，仁就来到了。”

【英译】

The Master said, "Is benevolence ever very far away? No sooner do I desire it than it is here."

7·31　陈司败问：“昭公知礼乎？”孔子曰：“知礼。”
孔子退，揖巫马期而进之，曰：“吾闻君子不党，君子亦党乎？君取于吴，为同姓，谓之吴孟子。君而知礼，孰不知礼？”
巫马期以告。子曰：“丘也幸，苟有过，人必知之。”

【今译】

陈国的司败问：“鲁昭公知礼吗？”孔子说：“知礼。”孔子退出，陈司败向巫马期作了个揖，请他上前，说：“我听说君子是不偏袒别人的，难道君子也偏袒别人吗？鲁君娶了一个吴国女子，是同姓，称她为‘吴孟子’。如果说鲁君知礼，还有谁不知礼呢？”巫马期把这些话告诉夫子。夫子说：“我真幸运，如果有过错，人家一定会知道。”

【英译】

The Minister of Justice of Chen, asked whether Duke Zhao of Lu knew the rites. Confucius answered, "Yes, he does."

After Confucius had left, the Minister bowed to Wuma Qi and had him come closer, saying, "I heard that a gentleman is never partial. Can a gentleman also be partial? Duke Zhao took from the State of Wu a lady with the same clan name as his own and renamed her Wu Mengzi. If the Duke knew the rites, who else doesn't?"

When Wuma Qi recounted this to him, the Master said, "I am a fortunate man! Whenever I make a mistake, there are always people who can detect it."

【辨正】

孙钦善《论语新注》："陈司败明知鲁昭公娶同姓为非礼，但不明言，只是笼统问鲁昭公是否知礼。孔子明知其意，但根据'《春秋》为尊者讳，为亲者讳，为贤者讳'（《公羊传》闵公元年）的原则，妄答为'知礼'。陈司败碍于礼道，不当面举鲁昭公娶同姓实例以驳孔子，而是向巫马期吐露实情，并怀疑孔子偏私。当巫马期把陈司败的话原原本本告知孔子后，孔子则以别人知其过为幸。如《论语集解》引孔安国曰：'以司败之言告也。讳国恶，礼也。圣人道弘，故受以为过。'如《论语集注》曰'孔子不可自谓讳君之恶，又不可以取同姓为知礼，故受以为过而不辞。'又，巫马期之所以要把陈司败的话明告孔子，孔子之所以闻过而喜，这是因为孔门有一个共识：君子于其过不加文饰，故人能知之，而小人则相反，参见19·8，19·21。"

7·32 子与人歌而善，必使反之，而后和之。

【今译】

夫子和别人一起唱歌，如果别人唱得好，就一定请他再唱一遍，然后自己再与他一起和唱。

【英译】

When the Master sang along with other people and found a good singer among them, he would always ask him to sing again and then sing together with him.

7·33 子曰："文莫①吾犹人也。躬行君子，则吾未之有得。"

【注释】

①文莫：努力。栾肇《论语驳》："燕齐谓勉强为文莫。"

【今译】

夫子说："在勤奋学习上，我大概和别人差不多。至于身体力行的君子，我还没有做到。"

【英译】

The Master said, "As far as effort is concerned, I might be equal to others, but as for becoming a gentleman who practices what he has learned, I have not yet attained it."

【辨正】

程树德《论语集释》："《方言》曰：'侔莫，强也。北燕之外郊凡劳而相勉，若言努力者，谓之侔莫。'案《说文》：'忞，强也。慔，勉也。''忞'读若旻，'文莫'即'忞慔'假借字也。"

7·34 子曰："若圣与仁，则吾岂敢？抑为之不厌，诲人不倦，则可谓云尔已矣。"公西华曰："正唯弟子不能学也。"

【今译】

夫子说："如果说'圣'与'仁'，那我怎么敢当！要是说"学之不厌，诲人不倦"则可以说做到了。"公西华说："这正是弟子无法学到的。"

【英译】

The Master said, "A sage and a benevolent man—how dare I claim to be! Or described as 'never bored with teaching and never tired at enlightening people', I almost deserve it." Gongxi Hua said, "This is precisely what we are unable to emulate."

7·35 子疾病①，子路请祷。子曰："有诸?"子路对曰："有之。《讄》②曰：'祷尔于上下神祇③。'"子曰："丘之祷久矣。"

【注释】

①疾病：病重。

②《讄》（lěi）：祈福的祷文。段玉裁注："讄，施于生者以求福；诔，施于死者以作谥。"

③上下神祇（qí）：天神和地神。祇：神。

【今译】

夫子病重，子路请求（为他）祈祷。夫子说："有这个道理吗？"子路回答说："有的。《讄》文上说'为您向天地上下的神祈祷。'"夫子说："那我的祈祷已经很久了。"

The Master was seriously ill. Zilu asked for permission to pray for him. The Master said, "Was this ever done before?" Zilu replied, "Yes. *The Book of Prayer* says, 'We pray for you to the gods above and below.'" The Master said, "In that case, I have long been offering my prayers."

7·36 子曰:"奢则不孙①,俭则固②。与其不孙也,宁固。"

【注释】

①孙:同"逊",恭顺,谦让。
②固:寒伧(chen),破败。

【今译】

夫子说:"奢侈了就会倨傲,节省了就会寒伧。与其倨傲,宁可寒伧。"

【英译】

The Master said, "Extravagance leads to arrogance, and frugality to shabbiness. I would rather be shabby than arrogant."

7·37 子曰:"君子坦荡荡,小人长戚戚。"

【今译】

夫子说:"君子胸怀坦荡,小人总是忧虑哀伤。"

【英译】

The Master said, "A gentleman is broad-minded and free of

worries, while a petty man is constantly troubled by anxiety."

7·38　子温而厉，威而不猛，恭而安。

【今译】

夫子温厚而又严厉，有威严而不凶猛，庄重而又安详。

【英译】

The Master was cordial yet stern, awe-inspiring yet not fierce, and dignified yet easy to approach.

泰伯第八

8·1　子曰："泰伯①，其可谓至德也已矣。三以天下让②，民无得而称焉③。"

【注释】

①泰伯：亦作"太伯"，周朝祖先古公亶（dǎn）父（周太王）的长子。《史记·吴太伯世家》："吴太伯、太伯弟仲雍，皆周太王之子，而王季历之兄也。季历贤而有圣子昌，太王欲立季历以及昌，于是太伯、仲雍二人乃奔荆蛮，文身断发，示不可用，以避季历。季历果立，是为王季，而昌为文王。"

②三以天下让：泰伯曾经三次把自己当继承的君位让于季历。刘宝楠《论语正义》引郑玄注曰："太王疾，泰伯因适吴越采药，太王殁而不返，季历为丧主，一让也。季历赴之，不来奔丧，二让也。免丧之后，遂断发文身，三让也。"

③民无得而称焉：民众不知怎样称颂他好了。

【今译】

夫子说："泰伯可以称得上是品德最高尚的人了，三次以天下相让，百姓不知道怎样称颂他好了。"

【英译】

The Master said, "Surely Taibo can be said to be of the highest virtue. Three times he renounced dominion over the entire empire and people could not find an adequate expression to praise him."

8·2　子曰：“恭而无礼则劳，慎而无礼则葸①，勇而无礼则乱，直而无礼则绞②。君子笃于亲，则民兴于仁；故旧不遗，则民不偷③。”

【注释】
①葸（xǐ）：胆小，畏缩。
②绞：尖酸刻薄。
③偷：感情淡泊。

【今译】
夫子说：“恭敬而不守礼就会疲惫；谨慎而不守礼就会怯惧；勇敢而不守礼就会作乱；直率而不守礼就会急躁。君子如果厚待父母，百姓就会喜爱仁德；君子如果不忘故旧，百姓就不会薄情寡义。”

【英译】
The Master said, "Without observing the rites, a courteous man will become weary, a cautious man will become timid, a brave man will become rebellious, and a straight-forward man will become impatient. If a ruler harbours a profound love for his parents, the common people will love virtue. If a ruler does not forsake his old friends, the common people will value friendship."

8·3　曾子有疾，召门弟子曰："启予足！启予手！《诗》云：'战战兢兢，如临深渊，如履薄冰。'而今而后，吾知免夫！小子！"

【今译】

曾参病重，召集弟子说："看看我的脚！看看我的手！《诗经》上说：'战战兢兢，好像面临深渊，好像脚踩薄冰。'从今往后，我知道自己身体会免于毁伤了，诸位！"

【英译】

Master Zeng got seriously ill. He summoned his disciples and said, "Take a look at my feet, and take a look at my hands. *The Book of Songs* says, 'trembling and shaking as if approaching a deep abyss, as if walking on thin ice.' From now on, I am sure of saving my body from any injury, my boys!"

8·4　曾子有疾，孟敬子问之。曾子言曰："鸟之将死，其鸣也哀；人之将死，其言也善。君子所贵乎道者三：动容貌，斯远暴慢矣；正颜色，斯近信矣；出辞气，斯远鄙倍矣。笾豆之事①，则有司存。"

【注释】

①笾（biān）豆之事：指祭祀礼仪。笾豆：祭祀时装祭品的器皿。笾用竹制，豆用木制。

【今译】

曾子病危，孟敬子去探望他。曾子说："鸟将要死的时候，鸣叫里充满悲哀；人将要死的时候，说话充满善意。君子重视道有三点：容貌庄重，别人就不会轻慢相待；神色严肃，就接近了诚信；讲究言词语气，别人就不会粗野悖理。至于礼仪的细节，则有主管的官吏执掌。"

【英译】

Master Zeng was seriously ill, and Meng Jingzi visited him. Master Zeng said to him, "When a bird is about to die, its cries are mournful. When a man is about to die, his words are well-intended. There are three principles of conduct a gentleman values most in the Way: staying clear of slighting by putting on a serious countenance, being trusted by wearing a proper expression on his face, and avoiding being boorish and unreasonable by speaking in proper tones. As to the details of rites like offering sacrifices, just leave them to the minor officials who are in charge."

8·5　曾子曰："以能问于不能，以多问于寡；有若无，实若虚；犯而不校①。昔者吾友尝从事于斯矣。"

【注释】

①犯：被人侵犯或欺侮。校（jiào）：同"较"，计较。

【今译】

曾子说："有才能而向没有才能的人请教，知识多而向知识少的人请教；有本事却好像没有，很充实却好像很空虚；被人冒犯也不计较。从前我的朋友曾经这样做过。"

Master Zeng said, "To be capable yet ask for advice from the less capable; to be knowledgeable yet consult the less knowledgeable; to have a lot yet to appear to be wanting; to be full yet to appear to be empty; to be offended yet not to mind. Such were the ways one of my friends used to conduct himself."

8·6 曾子曰：“可以托六尺之孤，可以寄百里之命，临大节而不可夺也。君子人与？君子人也。”

【今译】

曾子说：“可以把年幼的君主托付给他，可以把国家大事交付给他，遇到生死存亡的紧要关头而不变节。这样的人是君子吗？这样的人是君子啊！”

【英译】

Master Zeng said, "If a man can be entrusted with the care of an orphan ruler, or the administration of a state of one hundred square *li*, if he is unyielding in moments of crisis, is he a gentleman? He is, indeed, a gentleman."

8·7 曾子曰：“士不可以不弘毅，任重而道远。仁以为己任，不亦重乎？死而后已，不亦远乎？”

【今译】

曾子说：“士不可不抱负远大，意志坚定，因为责任重大而道途遥远。把仁作为自己的责任，不重大吗？直到死才可停止，不遥远吗？”

Master Zeng said, "A gentleman must be broad-minded and perseverant, for his responsibility is weighty and the trip long. Taking the practice of benevolence as his responsibility—is it not weighty? Only with death does his trip come to an end—is it not long?"

8·8 子曰："兴于《诗》，立于礼，成于乐。"

【今译】

夫子说："从《诗》起身，以《礼》立身，以《乐》成身。"

【英译】

The Master said, "Start being aroused by learning *The Book of Songs*, become established by learning *The Book of Rites*, and finally become accomplished by learning *The Book of Music*."

8·9 子曰："民可使，由之；不可使，知之。"

【今译】

夫子说："如果民众可以役使，就引导他们；如果民众不可役使，就教育他们。"

【英译】

The Master said, "If the people can be employed, lead them; if they cannot be employed, educate them."

【辨正】

古代没有标点符号，但有语助词。"与朋友交而不信乎"，没有问号，却有"乎"字表疑问。"孝悌也者其为人之本与"没有逗号，却有"也者"表提顿。"民可使由之？不，可使知之。"这种断句法不靠疑问语助词，只靠问号，"不可"也断开，是现代人不顾文法的强行断句。

句子里有"可（使）"与"不可（使）"的对照，有"由之"与"知之"的对照，以及"不可使"前省略的"民"。"民可使，由之不可，使知之。"这种断句，将这一切抛置一旁，视而不见。

"民可，使由之；不可，使知之。"这种断句，从语法上讲，杨伯峻《论语译注》里说："若是古人果是此意，必用'则'字，甚至'使'下再用'之'字以重指'民'，作'民可，则使（之）由之，不可，则使（之）知之'，方不致晦涩而误解。"再说，"使"字与"可"分而与"由之""知之"相连，还有一个问题："由"、"知"都是使动用法，已经暗含一个"使"字了。

"民可使由之，不可使知之"的断句。"使"字与"由之""知之"的使动重叠，"之"字指"民"也是问题。"民可使由民"如何解？"民可使由，不可使知"即"可使民由，不可使民知"，语义已完整，"之"字附赘，如骈拇枝指。

"民可使，由之；不可使，知之。""民"为与统治者相对的"百姓"。"使"为"役使""驱使"，即"使民以时"，"上好礼，则民易使也"句里的"使"。"由"，从，行，道（导），使动，即"使民沿（民）道行"。"知（智）"，"愚"的反面，也是使动。

8·10 子曰："好勇疾贫，乱也。人则不仁，疾之已甚，乱也。"

【今译】

夫子说："好勇逞强而憎恶贫困，是祸乱的根源。对没有仁德的人，憎恶得太过分，也是祸乱的根源。"

【英译】

The Master said, "Being fond of courage while detesting poverty will lead to insubordination. Excessive detestation of men who are not benevolent will also lead to insubordination."

8·11 子曰："如有周公之才之美，使骄且吝，其余不足观也已。"

【今译】

夫子说："即使有周公那样的才能和美德，只要他骄傲自大而且吝啬小气，余下的也就不值一看了。"

【英译】

The Master said, "Even with a man as gifted as the Duke of Zhou, were he arrogant and niggardly, then the rest of his qualities would not be worthy of admiration."

8·12 子曰："三年学，不至于谷①，不易得也。"

【注释】

①至：想到。谷：谷子，小米。古代官吏以谷子来计算俸

禄，所以"谷"常代指做官及其俸禄。

【今译】

夫子说："学习三年，心思不在做官拿俸禄上，这就很难得了。"

【英译】

The Master said, "It is rare that one has been at school for three years and yet has no intention of earning an official's salary."

8·13 子曰："笃信好学，守死善道。危邦不入，乱邦不居。天下有道则见^①，无道则隐。邦有道，贫且贱焉，耻也；邦无道，富且贵焉，耻也。"

【注释】

①天下有道：国家政治清明。见（xiàn）：同"现"。

【今译】

夫子说："忠实守信，爱好学习，坚守信念，热爱真理。危险的邦国不进入，动乱的邦国不居住。天下有道就出来做官；天下无道就隐居不出。国家有道而自己贫贱，是耻辱；国家无道而自己富贵，（也）是耻辱。"

【英译】

The Master said, "Be faithful and fond of learning; be steadfast and enjoy exploring the truth. Enter not a state that is in peril; dwell not in a state that is in turmoil. Come and take office when good government prevails in a state, and remain reclusive when ill government prevails. It is shameful to be poor and humble when good government prevails. It is equally shameful to be rich and noble when ill government prevails."

8·14 子曰：“不在其位，不谋其政。”

【今译】

夫子说：“不在某个职位上，就不要考虑那一职位上的事情。”

【英译】

The Master said, "He who does not hold a certain position shall not involve himself with its affairs."

8·15 子曰：“师挚之始①，《关雎》之乱②，洋洋乎盈耳哉！”

【注释】

①师挚之始：师挚是鲁国的太师。“始”是乐曲的开端，即序曲。

②《关雎》之乱：“乱”是乐曲的终了。“乱”是合奏乐。此时奏《关雎》乐章，所以说“《关雎》之乱”。

【今译】

夫子说：“从太师挚演奏的序曲开始，到最后演奏《关雎》的结尾，丰富而优美的音乐在我耳边回荡。”

The Master said, "From the moment Zhi, the Grand Musician, began the performance with the prelude, till it came to an end with 'Guanju', the exquisite melody lingered around my ears!"

8·16　子曰："狂而不直，侗^①而不愿^②，悾悾^③而不信，吾不知之矣。"

【注释】
①侗（tóng）：幼稚无知。
②愿：谨慎，老实。
③悾（kōng）悾：诚恳。

【今译】
夫子说："狂放而不正直，无知而不谨慎，表面上诚恳而不守信用，我真不知道人为什么会是这个样子。"

【英译】

The Master said, "Men who are unrestrained but not upright, men who are ignorant yet inattentive, men who are incompetent yet not sincere—These are people I don't appreciate."

8·17　子曰："学如不及，犹恐失之。"

【今译】
夫子说："学习就要像追赶不上那样，追上了，还担心会失去。"

【英译】

The Master said, "Learn as if you were chasing something, fearing that you might never get hold of it, or fearing that, after getting holding of it, you might lose it."

8·18　子曰："巍巍①乎，舜禹之有天下也而不与②焉！"

【注释】

①巍巍：崇高、高大的样子。

②与（yù）：参与。何晏《论语集解》："舜、禹以受禅有天下，复任人治之，而己无所与。"

【今译】

夫子说："多么崇高啊！舜和禹得天下而不据为己有。"

【英译】

The Master said, "How lofty were Shun and Yu in staying aloof when they were in possession of the Empire."

8·19　子曰："大哉！尧之为君也。巍巍乎！唯天为大，唯尧则之。荡荡乎！民无能名焉。巍巍乎！其有成功也，焕乎！其有文章。"

【今译】

夫子说："真伟大啊！尧这样的君主。多么崇高啊！只有天最高大，只有尧才能效法天。（他的恩德）多么广大啊！百姓无法用语言来表达对他的称赞。他的功绩多么崇高！他的礼仪制度多么光辉灿烂啊！"

The Master said, "What a great ruler Yao was! How lofty! It is Heaven alone that is greatest and it was Yao alone who could model himself on it. His mind was so boundless that the people failed to find adequate expression to extol him. Lofty was he in his successes, and brilliant was he in his civilized accomplishments!"

8·20　舜有臣五人而天下治。武王曰："予有乱臣十人。"孔子曰："才难，不其然乎？唐虞之际，于斯为盛。有妇人焉，九人而已。三分天下有其二，以服事殷。周之德，其可谓至德也已矣。"

【今译】

舜有五位贤臣，就能治理好天下。周武王说："我有十位治国之臣。"孔子说："人才难得，难道不是这样吗？唐尧、虞舜时期，在这点上最为突出。十个大臣当中有一个是妇女，实际上只有九个人而已。周文王得了天下的三分之二，仍然事奉殷朝，周朝的道德，可以说是最高尚的了。"

【英译】

Shun had five ministers and the Empire was well governed. King Wu of Zhou said, "I have ten capable ministers." Confucius commented, "Isn't it true that talented people are really difficult to find? It is especially true during the period of Tang and Yu. Among the ten ministers of King Wu of Zhou, one was a woman, so actually he had only nine men. The Zhou continued to serve the Yin when they came to possess two thirds of the whole Empire. Its virtue can be said to have reached the zenith."

8·21　子曰："禹，吾无间^①然矣。菲饮食而致^②孝乎鬼神，恶衣服而致美乎黻冕^③，卑^④宫室而尽力乎沟洫^⑤。禹，吾无间然矣。"

【注释】
①间（jiàn）：本义空隙。此处用作动词，挑剔、批评、非议。
②致：致力、努力。
③黻冕（fǔ miǎn）：祭祀时穿的礼服叫黻；祭祀时戴的帽子叫冕。
④卑：低矮。这里用作动词，使宫室低矮简陋。
⑤沟洫（xù）：沟渠。

【今译】
夫子说："对于禹，我没有什么可以挑剔的了；他的饮食菲薄却尽力孝敬鬼神；他的衣服很简朴，而祭祀时努力穿得华美，他住的宫室很低矮，而致力于兴修水利。对于禹，我没有什么挑剔的了。"

【英译】
The Master said, "With Yu I can find no fault. He ate simple food but offered grand sacrifices to the ancestral spirits. He wore coarse clothes but dressed magnificently on sacrificial occasions. He lived in a humble house but devoted his all to fighting the floods. With Yu I can find no fault."

子罕第九

9·1　子罕言利，与命与仁。

【今译】

夫子很少谈到功利，他赞同天命，赞许仁德。

【英译】

Seldom did the Master talk about profit. He believed in destiny and benevolence.

【辨正】

史绳祖《学斋佔毕》："《论语》谓'子罕言利与命与仁'，古注及诸家皆以为三者子所希言，余独疑之。利者固圣人深耻而不言也。虽孟子犹言'何必曰利'，况孔圣乎！故《鲁论》中止言'放于利而行多怨'及'小人喻于利'之外，深斥之而无言焉。至如命与仁，则自乾坤之元，孔子《文言》已释为体仁矣。又曰'乾道变化，各正性命'，何尝不言？且考诸《鲁论》二十篇，问答言仁凡五十三条，张南轩已集为'洙泗言仁'，断之曰言矣。又命字亦言之非一，如：'道之将行，命也；将废，命也。公伯寮其如命何？'又曰'亡之，命矣夫'，又曰'五十知天命'，又曰'死生有命'，又曰'不幸短命'，又曰'不知命，无以为君子'，是岂不言哉？盖子罕言者独利而已，当以此句作一义；曰命曰仁，皆平日所深与，此句别作一义。与者，许也。《论语》中'与'字自作两义，如'吾与点也'，'吾无行而不与二三子者'，又'与其进'，'与其洁也'，'吾非斯人之徒与而谁与'，'义之与比'，'丘不与易也'，'吾不与也'等字，皆其比也。当以理推之。"

白平《杨伯峻〈论语译注〉商榷》："认为原文中的两个'与'都是连词，意思是'利、命、仁'三者，孔子都很少主动谈到，翻译出来就成了'孔子很少谈利和命和仁'，这一理解在言语习惯上让人觉得味道很怪，'与'字这样连用的情况不经见。如果真是那样的话，还不如说成'子罕言利、命、仁'，就像'子不语怪、力、乱、神'、'子以四教：文、行、忠、信'、'子之所慎：齐、战、疾'一样，不会引起歧义。说孔子很少谈仁，这是无论如何也不能自圆其说的。"

9·2　达巷党人曰："大哉孔子！博学而无所成名。"子闻之，谓门弟子曰："吾何执？执御乎？执射乎？吾执御矣。"

【今译】

达巷这个地方人说："孔子真伟大啊！他学问渊博，没有哪一方面能定其名声。"夫子听说了，对他的学生说："我要专于哪方面呢？驾车呢？还是射箭呢？我还是专于驾车吧。"

【英译】

A man from a village in Daxiang said, "Great indeed is Confucius! He is learned, and no particular title can define him. The Master, on hearing of this, said to his disciples, "What should I make my speciality? Chariot-driving? Or archery? I think I prefer chariot-driving."

9 · 3 子曰："麻冕，礼也；今也纯，俭，吾从众。拜下，礼也；今拜乎上，泰也。虽违众，吾从下。"

【今译】

夫子说："用麻布制礼帽，是礼的规定。现在大家都用黑丝绸制作，这样比过去节省了，我赞同大家（的做法）。（臣见国君，先在）堂下跪拜，这是礼的规定。现在大家都在堂上跪拜，太倨傲了。虽然与大家看法不一样，我还是主张堂下拜。"

【英译】

The Master said, "A hemp cap is what is prescribed by the rites, but nowadays people make caps with black silk, which is more economical. I approve of the multitude. To kowtow before ascending the steps is required by the rites. But nowadays people kowtow only after having ascended the steps, which is haughty. Although going against the multitude, I approve of the practice of kowtowing before ascending."

9 · 4 子绝四——毋意，毋必，毋固，毋我。

【今译】

夫子杜绝了四种毛病：不主观猜疑，不绝对肯定，不固执拘泥，不自我中心。

【英译】

The Master was free of four defects: He never made groundless speculation, did not claim absolutely certainty, was not inflexible, and was not self-centered.

9·5 子畏于匡，曰："文王既没，文不在兹乎？天之将丧斯文也，后死者不得与于斯文也；天之未丧斯文也，匡人其如予何？"

【今译】

夫子在匡被围困，他说："周文王死了以后，（世上的）文化不（都）在（我）这里吗？老天如果要灭掉这种文化，那么，后死者就再也见不到了；上天如果不想灭掉这种文化，那么，匡人又能把我怎么样呢？"

【英译】

When besieged in Kuang, the Master said, "After King Wen died, can the culture（Wen）be found elsewhere except here in me? If Heaven intends to destroy it, latecomers will have no chance of accessing it. If Heaven does not intend to destroy it, then what can the men of Kuang do to me?"

9·6 太宰问于子贡曰："夫子圣者与？何其多能也？"子贡曰："固天纵之将圣，又多能也。"

子闻之，曰："太宰知我乎？吾少也贱，故多能鄙事。君子多乎哉？不多也。"

【今译】

太宰问子贡说："夫子是位圣人吧？他怎么会这么多技能啊？"子贡说："这本是上天让他成为圣人，又使他多才多艺。"夫子听到后说："太宰了解我吗？我年少时地位低贱，所以会许多卑贱的技艺。君子觉得这些技艺多吗？不（觉得）多。"

A high officer（Tai Zai）asked Zigong, "Is the Master a sage? Why is he skilled in so many ways?" Zigong said, "It is Heaven that intended him to be a sage, and made him capable of so many skills."

The Master, on hearing of this, said, "Does the officer really know much about me? I was humble when young, so I became skilled in many menial skills. Will a gentleman think it's too much for him? No, he won't."

【辨正】

"君子多乎哉? 不多也。"孔子并不是说"君子不会有这么多能力""君子不必多能",而是说"君子不以这些（能）为多"。也就是说,这里的"多"字是形容词意动用法,"以……为多"。

9·7 牢曰:"子云,'吾不试,故艺'。"

【今译】

子牢说:"夫子说过,'我（年轻时）没有去做官,所以会很多技艺'。"

【英译】

Lao said, "The Master said, 'I did not hold any official post when young. That's why I was able to learn so many different arts.'"

9·8 子曰：“吾有知乎哉？无知也。有鄙夫问于我，空空如也。我叩其两端而竭焉。”

【今译】

夫子说：“我有知识吗？（我）没有知识。有一个乡下人问我，样子很诚恳。我从问题的两端叩问，知识就用尽了。”

【英译】

The Master said, "Am I a learned man? No, I am not. A farmer once asked me a question in a sincere manner. I tackled the problem from beginning to end and I soon had a feeling of exhausting my learning."

【辨正】

杨逢彬《论语新注新译》：“先秦两汉典籍中‘空空’‘悾悾’常见，都是‘诚恳’的意思。因此，我们不能把《论语》的‘空空如也’理解为‘什么都没有’‘一点也不知道’。至于现成成语‘空空如也’表示什么都没有，那是后世语言的变化所致，正如‘桃之夭夭’变化成‘逃之夭夭’一样，只是后者连文字也变了。”

9·9 子曰：“凤鸟①不至，河不出图②，吾已矣夫！”

【注释】

①凤鸟：古代传说中的一种神鸟。传说凤鸟在舜和周文王时代都出现过，它的出现象征着“圣王”将要出世。

②河不出图：传说在上古伏羲氏时代，黄河中有龙马背负八卦图而出。它的出现也象征着“圣王”将要出世。

【今译】

夫子说：“凤鸟不来了，黄河中也不出现八卦图了。（世上无圣君）我这辈子完了！”

【英译】

The Master said, "The Phoenix does not show up, nor does the Yellow River present the Diagram. Alas, I am done for."

【辨正】

《论衡》注引《易坤凿度》曰：“仲尼偶筮其命，得旅，泣曰：‘天也，命也！凤鸟不来，河无图至，呜呼，天命之也！叹讫，而后息志。”

9·10　子见齐衰①者、冕衣裳者②与瞽③者，见之，虽少，必作④；过之，必趋⑤。

【注释】

①齐衰（zī cuī）：丧服，古时用麻布制成。
②冕：官帽；衣：上衣；裳：下服，这里统指官服。冕衣裳者指贵族。
③瞽（gǔ）：盲。
④作：起，表示敬意。
⑤趋：快步走，表示敬意。

【今译】

夫子遇见穿丧服的人、当官的人和盲人，即使他们年轻，也一定会站起来；经过他们身边，一定会快步走过。

When the Master saw a person who was in mourning clothes or ceremonial robe, or who was blind, he would rise to his feet, even though they were younger than he was. When passing them, he would quicken his steps.

9·11　颜渊喟然叹曰："仰之弥高，钻之弥坚。瞻之在前，忽焉在后。夫子循循然善诱人，博我以文，约我以礼，欲罢不能。既竭吾才，如有所立卓尔。虽欲从之，末由也已。"

【今译】

颜渊感叹地说："（对于老师的学问与道德），我抬头仰望，越望越觉得高；我努力钻研，越钻研越觉得坚固。看着好像在前面，忽然又像在后面。老师循序渐进善于诱导，用典籍来丰富我的知识，又用礼节来约束我的言行，让我想停止学习都不可能。我已用尽我的全力，好像仍然巍峨地立在我前面。虽然我想要追近，却找不到路径。"

【英译】

Yan Yuan said with a sigh, "The more I look to the Master's doctrine, the loftier it seems to be. The more I delve into it, the more solid it seems. It looms before me and suddenly it seems to have shifted behind. The Master skillfully guides me step by step, broadening my mind with culture and restraining me with the rites, which I cannot help following. Having exerted all my talent, I find it still towering before me. I find no way to approach it although I am eager to do so."

9·12　子疾病，子路使门人为臣。病间，曰："久矣哉，由之行诈也！无臣而为有臣。吾谁欺？欺天乎？且予与其死于臣之手也，无宁死于二三子之手乎！且予纵不得大葬，予死于道路乎？"

【今译】

夫子患了重病，子路让门徒去作夫子的家臣。夫子的病愈后，说："仲由干这种虚假的事情已经很久了。没有家臣却偏偏要装作有家臣，我骗谁呢？我骗上天吗？我与其死在家臣手里，不如死在你们几个人手里！我即使不能以大夫之礼来安葬，难道会死在路边吗？"

【英译】

The Master got seriously ill. Zilu told his fellow disciples to act as retainers. When he had recovered, the Master said, "Zilu has long been practicing deception. By pretending that I had retainers while I should not have, who would he be deceiving? Heaven? Besides, I would rather have you, my disciples, and not retainers at my side when I die. And will I be left to die by the roadside even if I am not entitled to a grand funeral?"

9·13　子贡曰："有美玉于斯，韫椟①而藏诸？求善贾②而沽③诸？"子曰："沽之哉！沽之哉！我待贾者也。"

【注释】

①韫椟（yùn dú）：韫，藏。椟，木匣。
②善贾（gǔ）：识货的商人。行商曰商，坐商曰贾。
③沽：卖。

【今译】

子贡说："这里有一块美玉，是把它放在木匣里藏起来呢？还是找一个识货的商人卖掉呢？"夫子说："卖掉啊，卖掉啊！我是等待出售（的人）啊。"

【英译】

Zigong said, "If you had a piece of beautiful jade here, would you put it away safely in a box or would you try to sell it to a good buyer who knows its real value?"

The Master said, "Sell it, of course. Sell it! I myself am one who is expecting to be sold out."

【辨正】

刘宝楠《论语正义》："古人重玉，凡用玉必经贾人，况鬻之乎？"卖玉者求识货之善贾，君子出仕则等待明君。程树德《论语集释》："范氏曰'士之待礼，犹玉之待贾也。若伊尹之耕于野，伯夷、太公之居于海滨，世无成汤、文王，则终焉而已，必不枉道以从人，衒玉而求售也。'"杨伯峻《论语译注》："与其说孔子是等价钱的人，不如说他是等识货者的人。"

康有为《论语注》里"沽"作"贾"："子贡曰：'有美玉于斯，韫匵而藏诸？求善贾而贾诸？'子曰：'贾之哉，贾之哉！我待贾者也。'"并注曰："汉石经'沽'作'贾'，今不从'沽'，从石经作'贾'"。从"贾诸""贾之"里的动词"贾"来看，"待贾"之贾可能就是一个动词"贾（沽）"，就如林语堂《谈〈论语〉句解》："用白话解是：出卖啊！出卖啊！我在此地等出卖啊！"

9·14　子欲居九夷。或曰："陋，如之何?"子曰："君子居之，何陋之有?"

【今译】

夫子想搬到九夷去居住。有人说："那里非常僻陋，不开化，怎么办?"夫子说："有君子去住，怎么还会僻陋呢?"

【英译】

The Master wanted to settle among the Nine Tribes of the East. Someone said, "But those places are pretty wild. How could you do it?"

The Master said, "How could it still be wild when a gentleman goes to dwell there?"

9·15　子曰："吾自卫反鲁，然后乐正，《雅》、《颂》各得其所。"

【今译】

夫子说："我从卫国返回到鲁国以后，乐才得以拨正，雅乐和颂乐各归于适当位置。"

【英译】

The Master said, "It was after my return from the State of Wei to the State of Lu that the Music was put right, with the *Ya* and the *Song* assigned their proper places."

9·16 子曰："出则事公卿，入则事父兄，丧事不敢不勉，不为酒困，何有于我哉?"

【今译】

夫子说："在外事奉公卿，在家服侍父兄，办理丧事不敢不尽力，不被酒所困，这些事对我来说有什么困难呢?"

【英译】

The Master said, "To serve high officials in public life, tend to the elders at home, spare no effort in funeral arrangements and not be overcome with wine—Is it difficlut at all for me to do all those things?"

9·17 子在川上，曰："逝者如斯夫! 不舍昼夜。"

【今译】

夫子站在河边感慨地说："时光就像这河水一样流逝，昼夜不停啊。"

【英译】

While standing by a river, the Master said, "Thus time flows by, never ceasing day or night."

9·18 子曰："吾未见好德如好色者也。"

【今译】

夫子说："我没有见过像好色那样好德的人。"

The Master said, "I have never met anyone who loves virtue the way he does beauty."

9·19 子曰："譬如为山①，未成一篑②，止，吾止也。譬如平地③，虽④覆一篑，进，吾往也。"

【注释】

①为山：造山，堆土成山。

②篑（kuì）：土筐。

③平地：平坦的地面。

④虽：通"惟（唯）"，副词，只，独。清俞樾《古书疑义举例·四十七》："此虽字当读为唯（惟），言平地之上唯覆一篑，极言其少。"

【今译】

夫子说："譬如用土堆山，哪怕只差一筐土时停了下来，那也是我没有完成。譬如在平地上刚倒下一筐土，只要继续下去，那我必将成功。"

【英译】

The Master said, "It is like making a mound. If I stop before the last basket of earth, I will not get it finished. On the other hand, even if I just tip the first basket on the bare ground, as long as I keep going, I am moving toward fulfillment.

【辨正】

"吾往也"当为"吾进也"。这一章在形式上分为前后两部分，对照明显。按照前面"止，吾止也"动词重复的句式，后面"进，吾往也"也当重复"进"字。毛子水注译的《论语今注今译》里怀疑："经文'往'字疑是'进'字的形误？"

按说，从"为山"的动宾结构可以看出，与之相对的"平地"中"平"字当为动词，即"平整；使变平"，而不是形容词"平坦"。然而，杨逢彬《论语新注新译》说："所谓与'为山'对文，是用骈文兴起以后的观念范围古人。清人姚永概指责王念孙往往据类书误改古书时说：'古人属辞，意偶而辞不必偶，往往有一字而偶二三字者。王氏每以句法参差不齐为疑，据类书以改古本。不知类书多唐以后人作，其时排偶之文，务尚工整。故其援引，随乎更乙，使之比和。况古人引书，但取大义，文句之多寡，字体之同异，绝不计焉。'（《书〈经义述闻〉〈读书杂志〉后》）"

毛子水注译的《论语今注今译》说："'譬如平地'四字，在这章里一点意义也没有，当是后人所妄加的。"把进德修业比作"为山"，积篑土而终成山，可谓恰当，而比作"平（整土）地"，有何可类比之处？这里对比的不是"堆山"与"平地"，而是为山刚开始与将结束时，"虽（唯）覆一篑"与"未成一篑"的情形。

"止"与"进"相对，这应该没有什么异议。《论语·子罕》9·21中说："子谓颜渊，曰：'惜乎！吾见其进也，未见其止也。'"也是进止相对而言。

"进"字在此不是水平方向上"前进"，也不是"进行""继续"，应当是指堆土为山时，一天比一天增高，一天比一天更具山形，恰好类似"进德"之"进"。

《论语集释》说："荀子宥坐篇：'孔子曰"如垤而进，吾与之。如丘而止，吾已矣。"'即此章异文。"这说法若成立，这一章就有了另外的解法。它不仅仅是说"为山""进德"者的

"止"与"进"，更重要的是说"吾"对"止"与"进"的态度。

9·20　子曰："语①之而不惰者，其回也与!"

【注释】

①语（yù）：告诉。

【今译】

夫子说："听我讲话而能毫不懈怠的，就数颜回吧!"

【英译】

The Master said, "If anyone can listen to me with unflagging attention, it is Hui, I suppose."

9·21　子谓颜渊，曰："惜乎! 吾见其进也，未见其止也。"

【今译】

夫子对颜渊说："可惜呀! 我只见他不断前进，从未见他停止过。"

【英译】

Speaking of Yan Yuan, the Master said, "What a pity! I saw him making progress, yet I never saw him ceased."

9·22　子曰："苗而不秀者有矣夫! 秀而不实者有矣夫!"

【今译】

夫子说："庄稼出了苗而不能吐穗扬花的情况有! 吐穗扬

花而不结果实的情况也有！"

【英译】

The Master said, "There are plants that grow without blossoming, and plants that blossom without bearing any fruit."

9·23　子曰："后生可畏，焉知来者之不如今也？四十、五十而无闻焉，斯亦不足畏也已。"

【今译】

夫子说："年轻人是值得敬畏的，怎么就知道后一代不如前一代呢？如果到了四五十岁时还默默无闻，那他就没有什么值得敬畏的了。"

【英译】

The Master said, "Youngsters should be held in awe. How do you know the next generation will not surpass the present? If one remains undistinguished at the age of forty or fifty, then he does not deserve to be held in awe."

9·24　子曰："法语之言，能无从乎？改之为贵。巽与之言，能无说乎？绎之为贵。说而不绎，从而不改，吾末如之何也已矣。"

【今译】

夫子说："符合礼法的正言规劝，能不听从吗？但改正错误才可贵。恭顺赞许的话，听了能不高兴吗？但认真分析才可贵。高兴却不去分析，听从却不改正错误，（对这样的人）我拿他没有办法。"

【英译】

The Master said, "How can anyone refuse to follow the admonitions? Yet what is more valuable is to reform oneself. How can anyone not be pleased by flattering remarks? Yet, what is more valuable is to analyze them. I do not know what I can do with those who are pleased with what others say but do not analyze, or who follow the admonitions but do not reform themselves.

9·25　子曰："主忠信，毋友不如己者，过则勿惮改。"①

【注释】

①见《学而第一》1·8。

【今译】

夫子说："坚持忠信。不与不如自己的人交朋友；有了过错，就不要怕改正。"

【英译】

The Master said, "Remain true and trustworthy. Do not befriend those who are less virtuous. Do not be afraid to correct his faults if he finds any."

9·26 子曰："三军可夺帅也，匹夫不可夺志也。"

【今译】

夫子说："一国军队，可以失去主帅。一个普通人，不可失去志向。"

【英译】

The Master said, "An army can manage without its commander; a man cannot manage without his will."

【辨正】

"夺"不是"抢夺"。自家的三军有帅，为何要抢人家的？一个人的志向，该怎么"抢夺"？

"夺"也不是"更换""去旧换新"。"三军可以换新帅，匹夫不可换新志"，同样是志，为何旧的就好，好到不可更换？

"夺"是"失去""从有到无"。《吕氏春秋·诚廉》："石可破也，而不可夺坚；丹可磨也，而不可夺赤。"是说"石可打碎，其坚硬依旧；丹可研磨，其红色不变。""不可夺志"是"志不可失""志不可无"。

白平《杨伯峻〈论语译注〉商榷》："此两'夺'字均当依其本义而训为'失去'。《史记·穰侯列传》：'及其贵极富溢，一夫开说，身折势夺而以忧死。'《素问·通评虚实论》：'邪气盛则实，精气夺则虚。'谢惠连《雪赋》：'皓鹤夺鲜，白鹇失素。'《后汉书·李膺传》：'本谓膺贤，遣子师之，岂可以漏夺名籍，苟安而已？'凡古书中脱失文字，校勘者谓之为'夺文'。这都是'夺'用为'失去'义的例证。……若解'夺'为'失去'义，则本章主旨就是勉励匹夫立志，此正是育人之要务所在。三军失去主帅不一定就会失败，而任何一个人失去志气就将一事无成，这个道理是很自然的。"

9·27　子曰："衣^①敝缊袍^②，与衣狐貉^③者立，而不耻者，其由也与？'不忮不求，何用不臧？^④'"子路终身诵之。子曰："是道也，何足以臧？"

【注释】

①衣：穿，当动词用。

②敝：坏。缊：旧的丝棉絮。敝缊（yùn）袍：指破旧的丝棉袍。

③狐貉：用狐和貉的皮做的裘皮衣服。

④不忮（zhì）不求，何用不臧：这两句见《诗经·邶风·雄雉》。忮：嫉妒。臧：善，好。

【今译】

夫子说："穿着破旧的丝棉袍子，与穿着狐貉皮袍的人站在一起而不觉得羞惭的，大概只有仲由吧。'不嫉妒，不贪求，做什么能不好呢？'"子路听后，反复背诵这句诗。夫子又说："只做到这样，怎么能说够好了呢？"

【英译】

The Master said, "If there is anyone wearing a worn- out gown standing beside a man dressed in fur and not feel ashamed, it must be Zilu, I suppose. 'If a man is neither envious nor covetous, he will be successful in whatever he is doing.'" Thereafter, Zilu constantly repeated these verses. The Master said, "How is this way sufficient if you want to become successful?"

9·28　子曰："岁寒，然后知松柏之后凋也。"

【今译】

夫子说："到了寒冷的季节，才知道松柏是最后凋谢的。"

【英译】

The Master said, "Only when the cold season comes is the point brought home that the pine and the cypress are the last to lose their leaves."

9·29　子曰："知者不惑，仁者不忧，勇者不惧。"

【今译】

夫子说："有智慧的人不迷惑，有仁德的人不忧愁，有勇气的人不畏惧。"

【英译】

The Master said, "The man of wisdom is never in two minds; the man of benevolence never worries; the man of courage is never afraid."

9·30　子曰："可与共学，未可与适道；可与适道，未可与立；可与立，未可与权。"

【今译】

夫子说："可以一起学习的人，未必能一起追求道；能够一起追求道的人，未必能一起守道；能够一起守道的人，未必能一起应变。"

The Master said, "A companion in study may not be a companion in the pursuit of the Way. A companion in the pursuit of the Way may not share your principles. And he who shares your principles may not share your moral discretion."

9·31 "唐棣之华，偏其反而。岂不尔思？室是远而。"子曰："未之思也，夫何远之有？"

【今译】

古代有一首诗这样写道："唐棣的花朵啊，翩翩地摇摆。我岂能不想念你吗？只是由于家住的地方太远了。"夫子说："他还是没有真的想念，如果真的想念，有什么遥远呢？"

【英译】

"O the blossoms of shadberry,

Swing and twist elegantly.

Not that I do not miss you,

But that your home is so far away."

The Master commented, "He did not really miss her. If he did, there is no such thing as being far away."

乡党第十

10 · 1　孔子于乡党，恂恂①如也，似不能言者。
其在宗庙朝廷，便便②言，唯谨尔。

【注释】

①恂（xún）恂：温和恭顺。

②便（pián）便：善辩，善于辞令。

【今译】

孔子在乡里，显得很温和恭敬，像是不会说话的样子。但
他在宗庙里、朝廷上，却很善于言辞，只是比较谨慎。

【英译】

In his hometown, Confucius appeared moderate and courteous, as if at a loss for words. In the ancestral temple or at court,
he spoke articulately but was selective of words.

10 · 2　朝，与下大夫言，侃侃如也；与上大夫言，訚訚①
如也。君在，踧踖②如也，与与③如也。

【注释】

①訚（yín）訚：正直，和颜悦色而又不苟同。

②踧踖（cù jí）：恭敬而局促不安的样子。

③与与：小心谨慎、威仪合度的样子。

【今译】

上朝的时候，跟下大夫说话，温和而快乐；跟上大夫说话，正直而公正；国君在时，恭敬而略显拘谨，但又仪态合度。

【英译】

At court, when conversing with junior ministers, he spoke freely and affably; when conversing with senior ministers, he spoke respectfully. In the presence of his Lord, his bearing was composed yet appropriate.

10·3 君召使摈①，色勃如也②，足躩③如也。揖所与立，左右手，衣前后，襜④如也。趋进，翼如也。宾退，必复命曰："宾不顾矣。"

【注释】

①摈（bìn）：同"傧"，动词，负责招待宾客。
②色勃如也：脸色立即庄重起来。
③足躩（jué）：脚步快的样子。躩：快步走。
④襜（chān）：整齐的样子。

【今译】

国君召夫子去接待宾客，夫子脸色立即振奋起来，脚步也快起来，他向和他站在一起的人作揖，手向左或向右作揖，衣服前后摆动，却整齐不乱。快步走的时候，像鸟儿展开双翅一样。宾客走后，必定向君主回报说："客人（已去）不再回顾了。"

When summoned by his lord to receive foreign guests, he looked solemn and walked briskly. He bowed to his colleagues, turning to the right and the left, his robes swinging back and forth without being disarranged. He approached the guest in quick steps, as though he was gliding on wings. When the guest had left, he would surely report to his lord, "The guest is out of sight."

10·4　入公门，鞠躬如也，如不容。

立不中门，行不履阈①。

过位，色勃如也，足躩如也，其言似不足者。

摄齐②升堂，鞠躬如也，屏气似不息者。

出，降一等③，逞④颜色，怡怡如也。

没阶⑤，趋进，翼如也。

复其位，踧踖如也。

【注释】

①履阈（yù）：脚踩门坎。阈：门槛，

②摄齐（zī）：提起衣服的下摆。摄：提起。齐：衣服的下摆。

③降一等：从台阶上走下一级。

④逞：舒展开，松口气。

⑤没阶：走完了台阶。

【今译】

走进朝廷的大门，弓着身子，像是门里容不下。站，不站在门中央；走，不踩门坎。经过国君的座位时，神色振奋，脚步迅速，说话像气力不足。提起衣服下摆登堂，弓着身子，屏住气息像不呼吸一样。退出，走下一级台阶，脸色才舒解，神色怡然。下完台阶，快步向前，像鸟儿展翅。回到自己的位子上，（又）像是恭敬而不安的样子。

【英译】

On entering the palace gate, he bent his body slightly forward, as if the gate was too narrow. He did not stand in the doorway, or tread on the threshold. When he passed the throne, he seemed to be summoned up, quickened his pace, and spoken below his breath. When he ascended the court, he lifted the hem of his robe with both hands, bent his head and held his breath. When he came out, he began to look relaxed only after taking a flight down. When he had reached the bottom of the steps, he went forward with quickened steps as though he was gliding on wings. When he was back at his seat, he resumed his respectful and uneasy look.

10·5　执圭①，鞠躬如也，如不胜。上如揖，下如授。勃如战色，足蹜蹜②如有循③。

享礼④，有容色。

私觌⑤，愉愉如也。

【注释】

①圭：一种上圆下方的玉器。举行典礼时，不同身份的人执不同的圭。出使邻国，大夫执圭作为代表君主的凭信。

②蹜（sù）蹜：形容脚步细碎紧密，小步走路的样子。

③循：沿着。如有循：好像沿着一条直线往前走一样。

④享：献上。享礼：指向对方贡献礼物的仪式。使者受到接见后，接着举行献礼仪式。

⑤觌（dí）：会见。

【今译】

拿着圭，恭敬谨慎，像是拿不动似的。上举时像是在作揖，下放时像是递与对方。脸色振奋得像是战栗，步子小而快，好像沿着一条直线走。在举行赠送礼物的仪式时，显得和颜悦色。私下会见，则显得轻松愉快。

【英译】

When he held the jade tablet, he bent his body slightly forward, as if it was too heavy for him to carry. When he raised it, he seemed to be bowing with his hands clasped. When he lowered it, he seemed to be handing it to someone before him. He looked as though to be in fear and trembling, and his feet were constrained as though following a marked line. When making a presentation, he looked amiable and courteous. When meeting in a private capacity with the hosts, he appeared relaxed and cheerful.

10·6　君子不以绀緅饰①，红紫不以为亵服②。

当暑，袗絺绤③，必表而出之④。

缁衣⑤，羔裘⑥；素衣，麑⑦裘；黄衣，狐裘。

亵裘长，短右袂⑧。

必有寝衣⑨，长一身有半。

狐貉之厚以居⑩。

去丧，无所不佩。

非帷裳⑪，必杀之⑫。

羔裘玄冠⑬不以吊⑭。

吉月⑮，必朝服而朝。

【注释】

①不以绀（gàn）緅（zōu）饰：不以深青透红或黑中透红的颜色布给平常穿的衣服镶边作饰物。绀：深青透红，斋戒时服装的颜色。緅：黑中透红，丧服的颜色。

②红紫不以为亵（xiè）服：古人认为，红紫不是正色，便服不宜用红紫色。亵服：平时在家里穿的衣服。

③袗（zhěn）绤（chī）绤（xì）：穿粗的或细的葛布单衣。袗：单衣。绤：细葛布。绤：粗葛布。

④必表而出之：把麻布单衣穿在外面，里面还要衬有内衣。

⑤缁衣：黑色的衣服。

⑥羔裘：羔皮衣。古代的羔裘都是黑羊皮，毛皮向外。

⑦麑（ní）：白色小鹿。

⑧短右袂（mèi）：右袖短一点，便于做事。袂：袖子。

⑨寝衣：睡衣。

⑩狐貉之厚以居：狐貉之厚，厚毛的狐貉皮。居：坐。

⑪帷裳：上朝和祭祀时穿的礼服，用整幅布制作，不加裁剪，而要折叠缝上。

⑫必杀（shài）之：一定要裁去多余的布。杀：裁削。

⑬羔裘玄冠：黑色皮礼帽。

⑭不以吊：不用于丧事。

⑮吉月：每月初一。

君子不用深青透红或黑中透红的布做镶边，不用红色或紫色的布做平常在家穿的便服。夏天穿粗的或细的麻布单衣，但一定要套在内衣外面。黑色的罩衣，配黑色的羔羊皮袍。白色的罩衣，配白色的鹿皮袍。黄色的罩衣，配黄色的狐皮袍。平常在家穿的皮袍做得长一些，右边的袖子短一些。睡觉一定要有睡衣，长要有上身的一倍半。狐貉的厚毛皮用来制作坐垫。丧服期满，脱下丧服后，可以佩带各种的饰品。如果不是礼服，一定要杀上布边。不穿黑色羔羊皮袍戴黑色帽子去吊丧。每月初一，一定要穿着朝服去上朝。

【英译】

The gentleman does not wear a dress with reddish black or black红ed borders, nor red or violet casual clothes.

In the heat of summer, he wears an unlined gown made of hemp or linen, making sure it covers the undergarment.

He wears a black gown over a black lambskin coat, a white gown over a fawnskin coat and a yellow gown over yellow fox fur.

His informal fur coat is long but with a short right sleeve.

When sleeping, he wears pajamas, which should come down to his knees.

He uses fox or raccoon pelts for cushions because the fur is thick.

Once the period of mourning was over, he places no restrictions on the kinds of ornaments he wears.

For non-ceremonial occasions, his gowns must be border-sewn.

Lambskin coats and black caps are not to be worn at funerals.

On the first day of the month, he will surely wear his court robe and present himself at court.

10 · 7 齐①，必有明衣②，布。
齐必变食③，居必迁坐④。

【注释】

①齐：同"斋"。

②明衣：古人在斋戒期间沐浴后所穿的干净内衣。

③变食：改变平常的饮食。指不饮酒，不吃葱、蒜等有刺激味的东西。

④居必迁坐：指居住的地方从内室迁到外室，从"燕寝"迁到"正寝"。

【今译】

斋戒沐浴的时候，一定要有干净的内衣，用布做的。斋戒的时候，一定要改变平常的饮食，居住也一定搬移地方。

【英译】

In periods of fasting, he invariably wears a clean undergarment, which is made of hemp cloth.

In periods of fasting, he invariably changes to a more austere diet and moves his sleeping place to outer room.

10·8　食不厌精，脍①不厌细。

食饐②而餲③，鱼馁④而肉败，不食。色恶，不食。臭恶，不食。失饪，不食。不时⑤，不食。割不正⑥，不食。不得其酱，不食。

肉虽多，不使胜食气⑦。

唯酒无量，不及乱⑧。

沽酒市脯不食。不撤姜食，不多食。

【注释】

①脍（kuài）：切细的肉。

②饐（yì）：腐败发臭。

③餲（ài）：变味。

④馁（něi）：鱼腐烂。

⑤不时：不合时令。

⑥割不正：肉切得不方正。

⑦气（xì）：同"饩"，即粮食。

⑧不及乱：不到酒醉时。乱：指酒醉。

【今译】

饭食不嫌做得精，鱼和肉不嫌切得细。饭放时间长，变味了，鱼、肉腐烂了，不吃。食物的颜色不正常，不吃。气味难闻，不吃。烹调不当，不吃。不合时令的东西，不吃。不以正当方式切割的，不吃。佐料放得不适当，不吃。席上的肉虽多，但吃的量不超过主食。只有酒没有限制，但不喝醉。从市上买来的肉干和酒，不吃。每餐必须有姜，但不多吃。

【英译】

Rice could never be over-husked and meat could never be

too finely cut.

He did not eat food that went sour, nor did he eat rotten fish or meat. He did not eat food whose color had changed or which had a bad smell. He did not eat anything not properly prepared or not in season. He did not eat meat that had not been slaughtered properly, or served without the proper sauce.

Plenty of meat as there was, he did not take it to exceed the due proportion for the grain.

Only in drinking did he not set himself a rigid limit, but he did not allow himself to get drunk.

He did not consume wine or dried meat bought from a shop.

He rejected no ginger, but did not take too much.

10·9　祭于公，不宿肉[1]。祭肉不出三日。出三日，不食之矣。

【注释】

①不宿肉：不使肉过夜。古代大夫、士都有助君祭祀之礼，须自带祭牲。天子诸侯的祭礼，于当天清晨杀牲，然后举行祭典。第二天又祭，叫做"绎祭"。绎祭之后，助祭之臣可带助祭的肉回去，或分得国君的祭肉。带回的祭肉，须及时向下分赐，以均神惠。不得过宿，以保证三天之内食用。

【今译】

参加公家祭祀分到的肉，不留到第二天。祭祀用过的肉（存放）不超过三天。超过三天，就不吃了。

He did not keep overnight the meat bestowed on him after a sacrifice held by his Lord. In other cases, he did not keep the sacrificial meat over three days. Once it was kept beyond three days, he no longer ate it.

10·10　食不语，寝不言。

【今译】

吃饭的时候不说话，睡觉的时候也不说话。

【英译】

He did not converse at meals; nor did he talk while in bed.

10·11　虽疏食、菜羹、瓜祭，必齐如也。

【今译】

即使用粗饭、菜汤、或用瓜祭祀，也要像斋戒时一样严肃恭敬。

【英译】

Even if the sacrifice he offered at each meal with only coarse grains, vegetable soups or melons, he would do it sincerely as if in fasting.

10 · 12　席不正，不坐。

【今译】

席子放得不端正，不坐。

【英译】

If a mat was not properly laid, he would not sit on it.

10 · 13　乡人饮酒，杖者出，斯出矣。

【今译】

行乡饮酒的礼仪结束后，一定要等老年人先出去，然后自己才出去。

【英译】

When drinking at a village gathering, he would not leave until those with walking sticks had done so.

10 · 14　乡人傩①，朝服而立于阼阶②。

【注释】

①傩（nuó）：古代迎神驱鬼的宗教仪式。

②阼（zuò）阶：主人立在大堂东面的台阶，在这里欢迎客人。阼：东面的台阶。

【今译】

乡里人举行迎神驱鬼的宗教仪式时，夫子总是穿着朝服站在东边的台阶上。

【英译】

When an exorcism was performed in his village, he would attend in his court robe standing on the eastern steps（where the host usually stood to welcome his guests）.

10·15　问人于他邦，再拜而送之。

【今译】

托人向在外国的朋友问好送礼，要拜两次送别受托者。

【英译】

When asking someone to extend his regards to a friend in another state, he would bow deeply twice before sending him off.

10·16　康子馈药，拜而受之。曰："丘未达，不敢尝。"

【今译】

季康子给夫子赠送药品，夫子拜谢之后接受了，说："我对药性不了解，不敢尝。"

【英译】

When Ji Kangzi sent a gift of medicine, Confucius bowed deeply before accepting it, saying, "Not knowing its properties, I dare not try it."

10·17　厩焚。子退朝，曰："伤人乎?"不问马。

【今译】

马棚失火烧掉了。夫子退朝回来，说："伤人了吗?"不问马的情况怎么样。

【英译】

The stables caught fire. Confucius, on returning from court, asked, "Was anyone hurt?" He did not ask about the horses.

10·18　君赐食，必正席先尝之。君赐腥，必熟而荐之。君赐生，必畜之。

侍食于君，君祭，先饭。

【今译】

国君赐给熟食，夫子一定摆正座席先尝一尝。国君赐给生肉，一定煮熟了，先给祖宗上供。国君赐给牲畜，一定要饲养起来。同国君一道吃饭，在国君举行饭前祭礼的时候，一定要先吃饭。

【英译】

When his Lord gave a gift of cooked food, he would set his mat straight and taste the food immediately. When his Lord gave him a gift of uncooked food, he would cook it and offer it to the ancestors. When his Lord gave him a gift of a live animal, he would rear it. When accompanying his Lord at a meal, he would taste the food first while his Lord performed the sacrificial offering.

10·19　疾，君视之，东首，加朝服，拖绅。

【今译】

得了病，国君去探视，他在床上头向东，身上盖上朝服，拖着绅带。

【英译】

When he was ill and his Lord came to see him, Confucius made sure to lie with his head to the east with his court robe draped over him（to show his respect）, his grand sash trailing over the side of the bed.

10·20　君命召，不俟驾行矣。

【今译】

国君召见，他不等车马驾好，就先步行走去了。

【英译】

When summoned by his Lord, he would set off on foot without waiting for his carriage to be ready.

10·21　入太庙，每事问①。

【注释】

①见《八佾第三》3·15。

【今译】

进入太庙，每件事都要问一问。

【英译】

When he entered the Grand Temple, Confucius enquired about everything.

10 · 22　朋友死，无所归^①，曰："于我殡。"

【注释】

①归：往，归宿。无所归，没有人料理后事。

【今译】

朋友死了，没有人敛埋，夫子说："丧葬由我来办吧。"

【英译】

When a friend died and there were no kin to take care of his funeral service, Confucius would say, "Leave it to me."

10 · 23　朋友之馈，虽车马，非祭肉，不拜。

【今译】

朋友馈赠物品，即使是车马，不是祭肉，（夫子在接受时）也是不拜的。

【英译】

He would not bow when accepting gifts from a friend, even if they were carriages and horses, the only exception being sacrificial meat.

10 · 24　寝不尸，居不客。

【今译】

睡觉不像死尸一样挺着，平日家居也不像作客或接待客人时那样庄重严肃。

【英译】

When he slept, he did not lie flat on his back like a corpse. When alone at home, he did not sit as if he were receiving a guest.

10 · 25　见齐衰①者，虽狎②，必变。见冕者与瞽者③，虽亵④，必以貌。

凶服⑤者式⑥之，式负版⑦者。

有盛馔⑧，必变色而作⑨。迅雷风烈必变。

【注释】

①齐衰（zī cuī）：孝服。

②狎（xiá）：亲近的意思。

③瞽者：盲人，指乐师。

④亵（xiè）：常见、熟悉。

⑤凶服：丧服。

⑥式：同"轼"，古代车辆前部的横木。这里作动词用。身子向前微俯，伏在横木上，表示同情或尊敬。这在当时是一种礼节。

⑦负版：斩衰和齐衰丧服上披在背上的粗麻片。负版者是重孝之人，所以，遇到时要轼而致敬。

⑧馔（zhuàn）：饮食。盛馔，盛大的宴席。

⑨作：坐直身。白平《杨伯峻〈论语译注〉商榷》："古人坐着的时候臀部压着脚跟，臀部离开脚跟而将腰伸直叫'作'，并不是指'站立起来'。"

【今译】

看见穿丧服的人，即使是关系很亲密，也一定变得庄重。看见戴冠冕的人和盲人，即使很熟悉，也一定有礼貌。在车上遇见了穿丧服的人，就是孝服上背部有粗麻片的人，俯伏在车前横木上（以示同情）。（作客时，）如果有丰盛的筵席，一定改变仪容，坐直身致谢。遇见迅雷大风，一定要改变神色（以示对上天的敬畏）。

【英译】

When meeting someone in mourning dress, even though it was his intimate, he would turn and look serious. When meeting someone wearing a ceremonial cap or someone blind, even though they were well-known to him, he would show them respect.

On passing a person dressed as a mourner, or rather, a person wearing a solemn mourning dress with a piece of cloth on his shoulder, he would lean forward with his hands on the crossbar of his carriage to show respect.

When a sumptuous feast was brought on, he invariably put on a solemn expression and sat up.

When there was a sudden clap of thunder or a violent wind, he invariably assumed a solemn attitude.

【辨正】

张椿《四书辨证》："《丧服记》：'负广出于适寸。'郑云：'负，在背上者。适，辟领。负出于辟领外旁一寸。''衰长六寸，博四寸。''广衰当心，前有衰，后有负版，左右有辟领，孝子哀戚，无所不在。'孔子式负版者，以其服最重故耳。"

王闿运《论语训》："负版，衰之领也。《记》曰：'负版出于适，适出于衰。三年丧，衰乃有之，卒哭，受齐衰，则除矣。'上言变齐衰，嫌式凶服、式齐衰以下，故特明负版乃为凶服。"

若把"负版者"解作"背负国家图集的人"，则十分怪异，因为"背负国家图集的人"很特殊而具体，难以与穿孝服者、冕者、瞽者这些常见者相并列。白平《杨伯峻〈论语英译〉商榷》："这里讲的都是经常出现的情况，"背负国家图籍的人"不可能坐着马车在街上经常遇到。如果这样的人需要'轼'，那么同类的国家工作人员就都应该'轼'，不会只将这种人单提出来表述。国家图籍为什么会让人背着在街上走，根据什么就能坐在自己的马车上判断出他身上背的是国家图籍，这些都是不好回答的问题。"

10・26　升车，必正立，执绥①。
车中，不内顾②，不疾言③，不亲指④。

【注释】

①绥：上车时拉着上车的索带。

②内顾：回头看。

③疾言：高声说话。疾：大，宏亮。

④不亲指：不用自己的手指划。

【今译】

上车时，一定直立，拉着扶手带。在车上，不回头，不高声说话，不用自己的手指指点点。

【英译】

When mounting a carriage, he would stand squarely and hold on to the handrail. When in the carriage, he would not turn back or talk volubly, nor would he make instructional gestures.

10·27　色斯举矣①，翔而后集②。曰："山梁雌雉，时哉时哉③！"子路共④之，三嗅而作⑤。

【注释】

①色斯：惊骇的样子。举：鸟飞起来。

②翔而后集：飞翔一阵，然后落到树上。鸟群停在树上叫"集"。

③时哉时哉：得其时呀！得其时呀！这是说野鸡时运好，能自由飞翔，自由落下。

④共：同"拱"。

⑤三嗅而作：嗅应为"臭"字之误。臭（jù）：鸟张开两翅。作：飞起来。

【今译】

一群野鸡倏地飞起，在空中飞翔一段时间之后，又都落在树上。夫子说："山梁上的这些雌雉啊，得其时呀！得其时呀！"子路向他们拱拱手，野鸡振翅三次飞走了。

A covey of pheasants burst on the wing swiftly, flew freely for a while and then lit on the branches. Confucius said, "Look at those hen-pheasants on the hill ridge, what good times they are in! What good times they are in!" Zilu saluted the birds with both hands joined before his chest. Thrice the birds flapped their wings and flew away.

先进第十一

11·1　子曰："先进^①于礼乐，野人^②也；后进^③于礼乐，君子^④也。如用之，则吾从先进。"

【注释】

①先进：指先学习礼乐而后再做官的人。

②野人：庶民，乡野平民。

③后进：先做官后学习礼乐的人。

④君子：这里指统治者。

【今译】

夫子说："先学习礼乐的，是（原来没有爵禄的）平民；后学习礼乐的，是君子。如果要使用人才，我主张选用先学习礼乐的人。"

【英译】

The Master said, "Those who first learn the rites and music before taking office are men of common origin; those who learn the rites and music after taking office are men of aristocratic origin. If I were to use them, I'd choose the former."

11·2 子曰："从我于陈、蔡者，皆不及门也。"

【今译】

夫子说："曾跟随我在陈国、蔡国的学生，现在都不在我门下了。"

【英译】

The Master said, "None of those who followed me in Chen and Cai is still with me now."

11·3 德行：颜渊、闵子骞、冉伯牛、仲弓。言语：宰我、子贡。政事：冉有、季路。文学：子游、子夏。

【今译】

德行好的有：颜渊、闵子骞、冉伯牛、仲弓。善于辞令的有：宰我、子贡。擅长政事的有：冉有、季路。通晓文献知识的有：子游、子夏。

【英译】

Morality: Yan Yuan, Min Ziqian, Ran Boniu and Zhonggong. Eloquence: Zaiwo and Zigong. Administrative talent: Ran You and Ji Lu. Letters: Ziyou and Zixia.

11·4 子曰："回也非助我者也，于吾言无所不说。"

【今译】

夫子说："颜回不是对我有帮助的人，他对我说的话无不心悦诚服。"

The Master said, "Hui is not a help to me, for he is pleased with everything I say."

11·5 子曰："孝哉闵子骞！人不间^①于其父母昆^②弟之言。"

【注释】

①间：间隔、闲隙。用作动词，生闲隙。
②昆：哥哥，兄长。

【今译】

夫子说："闵子骞真是孝顺呀！不因他的父母兄弟的话而生闲隙。"

【英译】

The Master said, "What a good son Min Ziqian is! He will not be alienated from his parents and brothers by what they said."

11·6 南容三复白圭^①，孔子以其兄之子妻之。

【注释】

①白圭：白圭指《诗经·大雅·抑之》的诗句："白圭之玷，尚可磨也，斯言之玷，不可为也。"意思是白玉上的污点还可以磨掉，我们言论中有毛病，就无法挽回了。这是告诫人说话要谨慎。

【今译】

南容反复诵读"白圭"的诗句。孔子把兄长的女儿嫁给他为妻。

【英译】

Nan Rong repeated over and over again the lines about the white jade.（A blemish on the white jade can be polished away; a blemish in words cannot be removed at all.）Confucius married his niece to him.

11·7　季康子问："弟子孰为好学?"孔子对曰："有颜回者好学，不幸短命死矣，今也则亡。"

【今译】

季康子问孔子："你的学生中谁最好学?"孔子回答："有一个叫颜回的，很好学。不幸短命死了。现在没有这样的人了。"

【英译】

Ji Kangzi asked Confucius, "Who among your disciples truly loves to learn?" Confucius answered, "There was a Yan Hui; he loved to learn. Unfortunately, he died young and now there is no such man."

11·8　颜渊死，颜路请子之车以为之椁①。子曰："才不才，亦各言其子也。鲤也死，有棺而无椁。吾不徒行以为之椁。以吾从大夫之后②，不可徒行也。"

【注释】

①椁（guǒ）：古人所用棺材，内为棺，外为椁。根据礼

制，大夫以下的人死后三天入棺，埋葬前灵柩停放三个月。这三个月棺材要装在一辆车上，这车叫"辁"。辁外四面都用木料堆积起来，然后用泥封，这就是殡殓时的"椁"。

②从大夫之后：跟随在大夫后面，意即当过大夫。孔子在鲁国曾任司寇，是大夫一级的官员。

【今译】

颜渊死了，（他的父亲）颜路请求夫子把车借给他作殡殓之椁。夫子说："（不说颜渊和鲤）有才无才，也都是做儿子的。孔鲤殡殓时，也只有内棺而没有外椁。我没有把车给他做殡殓之椁，是因为我跟在大夫之后上朝，按礼不可以步行。"

【英译】

When Yan Yuan died, （his father） Yan Lu asked the Master to lend his carriage to be the outer coffin for a while. The Master said, "Everyone speaks up for his own son whether he is talented or not. When my son Li died, he had a coffin but no outer coffin. I did not use my carriage as an outer coffin at the cost of going out without a carriage, as it would be improper for me, a former senior official, to go on foot."

【辨正】

从"请子之车以为之椁"看不出"卖车买椁"来，实际应是借孔子车作殡棺之椁，而不是葬时之椁，借期不超三个月。

针对"卖车买椁"的解法，程树德《论语集释》里引宦懋庸《论语稽》予以反驳："按卖车买椁之说有八不可解。《丧大记》：'士棺六寸，棺椁之间容瓹。'瓹，酒器也。则椁大于棺无几，其值要亦不多。颜氏贫不能办，容或有之，孔子何不能为办？一也。孔子制于中都，四寸之棺，五寸之椁，其葬鲤也固当以士礼，然与其有棺无椁，何不从庶人之礼，为具四寸棺五寸椁乎？二也。孔子未闻甚贫，颜路但请助一椁可也，安见遂无一帛一粟而独以车请？三也。孔子有羔、麑、狐之裘，皆贵服，且亦当有他器物，何于回、鲤之椁皆以不徒行为辞，若车外更无长物可卖？四也。《王制》：'命车不粥于市。'孔子为大夫，其车当亦命车，颜路何敢请卖？五也。即谓路非真欲请车，特以探厚葬之可否，然必以车为指名何也？六也。孔子在卫，脱骖以赠馆人之丧，必更买骖而反鲁，路何不以骖为请？七也。且经本文曰请车，曰为椁，绝无买卖意义，八也。今考《礼经》，乃知以车为殡棺之椁。《檀弓》：'天子之殡也，菆涂龙輴以椁，加斧于椁上，毕涂屋。'又曰：'天子龙輴而椁帱，诸侯輴而设帱。'《丧大记》：'君殡用輴欑，至于上毕涂屋。大夫殡以帱欑，至于西序，涂不暨于棺。士殡见衽涂上帷之。'《士丧礼》：'士殡掘肂见衽。'按輴，车也。天子画龙，故曰龙輴。菆欑训丛，丛木也。为殡也以椁者，非葬时之椁，乃涂所丛之木如椁也。曰加斧于椁上，则此亦名椁矣。斧者，画覆棺之衣为斧文，即帱也。肂者，埋棺之坎也。衽者，古人棺不钉，于棺盖之缝加衽而以皮束之。君三衽三束，大夫士皆二也。《王制》：'大夫士庶人三日而殡，三月而葬。'颜子，士也。三日之后，三月未葬之前，当殡于西序。其殡也，当掘肂见衽，帷其上而涂之，不当用车。颜路请车为椁，盖欲殡时以孔子之车菆涂为椁，非葬时之椁也。"

11·9 颜渊死。子曰："噫！天丧予！天丧予！"

【今译】

颜渊死了，夫子说："唉！老天要我的命呀！老天要我的命呀!"

When Yan Yuan died, the Master said, "Alas! Heaven is be-reaving me! Heaven is bereaving me!"

11·10　颜渊死，子哭之恸。从者曰："子恸矣！"曰："有恸乎？非夫人之为恸而谁为？"

【今译】

颜渊死了，夫子哭得很悲痛。跟随夫子的人说："夫子太悲痛了！"夫子说："太悲痛了吗？我不为这个人悲痛，还为谁呢？"

【英译】

When Yan Yuan died, the Master wept bitterly. His disciples said, "Master, you are over-grieved." The Master said, "Over-grieved? If I do not grieve over this man's death, who else should I grieve for?"

11·11　颜渊死，门人欲厚葬之。子曰："不可。"

门人厚葬之。子曰："回也视予犹父也，予不得视犹子也。非我也，夫二三子也。"

【今译】

颜渊死了，众弟子想厚葬他，夫子说："不能这样做。"（结果）众弟子（还是）厚葬了他。夫子说："颜回待我如父亲，我却不能把他当儿子一样对待。这不是我的过错，是那几个学生干的。"

【英译】

When Yan Yuan died, the disciples wanted to hold a grand funeral for him. The Master said, "It would not be proper."

All the same, the disciples went ahead and buried him in grand style. The Master said, "Hui treated me as a father, yet I could not treat him as a son. This is not my fault, but that of your fellow disciples."

11·12　季路问事鬼神。子曰："未能事人，焉能事鬼?"曰："敢问死。"曰："未知生，焉知死?"

【今译】

季路问怎样去事奉鬼神。夫子说："不能事奉人，怎么能事奉鬼?"季路说："请问死是怎么回事?"（夫子回答）说："还不知道活着的道理，怎么知道死呢?"

【英译】

Jilu asked about serving the ghosts and spirits. The Master said, "How can you serve the spirits when you are not able to serve the living?"

Jilu went on, "May I ask about death?" The Master said, "How can you understand death when you do not even understand life?"

11·13　闵子侍侧，訚訚如也；子路，行行①如也；冉有、子贡，侃侃如也。子乐。"若由也，不得其死然。"

【注释】

①行（hàng）行：刚强的样子。

【今译】

闵子骞侍立夫子身边，一副和悦而正直的样子；子路（侍立夫子身边），一副刚强的样子；冉有、子贡（侍立夫子身边），一副温和快乐的样子。夫子很高兴。夫子说："像仲由这样，只怕得不到善终！"

【英译】

When in attendance on the Master, Min Ziqian looked pleasant and upright; Zilu looked unbending; Ran You and Zigong looked affable. The Master was happy. "A man like Zilu will not die a natural death."

11·14　鲁人为长府。闵子骞曰："仍旧贯，如之何？何必改作？"子曰："夫人不言，言必有中。"

【今译】

鲁国翻修长府的国库。闵子骞道："沿用旧例怎么样？何必改建呢？"夫子道："平时不大开口的人，一开口就说到要害上。"

【英译】

The authority of Lu wanted to rebuild the treasury. Min Ziqian said, "Why not simply restore it? Why must it be totally rebuilt?"

The Master said, "A man of few words, when he speaks, will hit the nail on the head."

11·15 子曰："由之瑟奚为于丘之门①?"门人不敬子路。子曰："由也升堂矣，未入于室也②。"

【注释】

①奚为于丘之门：为什么在我这里弹呢？奚：为什么。为：弹。据《说苑·修文篇》，孔子对于子路弹瑟表示不满，是因为子路性情刚猛，中和不足，故弹出的音调过于激越，"有杀伐之声"。

②升堂入室：堂是正厅，室是内室，用以形容学习程度的深浅。

【今译】

夫子说："仲由弹奏的这种瑟，为什么要在我门下弹呢？"众弟子因此都不尊敬子路。夫子便说："仲由嘛，他在学习上已经达到升堂的程度了，只是还没有入室罢了。"

【英译】

The Master said, "Why does Zilu play this kind of music here?" The other disciples ceased to treat Zilu with respect. The Master said, "Zilu may have entered the hall but has not yet reached the inner chamber."

11·16　子贡问：“师与商也孰贤?”子曰：“师也过，商也不及。”

曰：“然则师愈与?”子曰：“过犹不及。”

【今译】

子贡问夫子：“师和商二人谁更好一些呢?”夫子回答说：“师啊过头了，商有些不足。”子贡说：“但是，师更好，对吗?”夫子说：“过头与不足同样不好。”

【英译】

Zigong asked, "Who is better, Shi or Shang?"

The Master said, "Shi tends to go too far, while Shang falls short."

"Does that mean that Shi is in fact better?" Zigong queried.

The Master said, "Going too far is as bad as falling short."

11·17　季氏富于周公，而求也为之聚敛而附益之。子曰：“非吾徒也。小子鸣鼓而攻之，可也。”

【今译】

季氏比周朝的公侯还富有，而冉求都他搜刮来增加他的钱财。夫子说：“他不是我的学生了，你们可以大张旗鼓地去攻击他了!”

【英译】

The Ji family was wealthier than some Dukes of Zhou, yet Qiu helped them add further to their wealth by all sorts of villainous means. The Master said, "He is no disciple of mine. You pupils may attack him openly to the beating of drums."

11·18　柴^①也愚^②，参也鲁，师也辟^③，由也喭^④。

【注释】

①柴：高柴，字子羔。

②愚：愚直之愚，指愚而耿直，不是傻的意思。

③辟（pì）：偏，偏激，邪。

④喭（yàn）：鲁莽，粗鲁，刚猛。

【今译】

高柴愚直，曾参迟钝，颛孙师偏激，仲由鲁莽。

【英译】

The Master said, "Chai is dumb; Shen is slow; Shi is radical; and（Zhong）You is rash."

11·19　子曰："回也其庶乎，屡空。赐不受命，而货殖焉，亿则屡中。"

【今译】

夫子说："颜回啊，或许是命啊，他（安于天命而）常常贫乏。端木赐不听天命而行商，谋度常常得中（而致富）。"

【英译】

The Master said, "Hui is constantly in poverty, which might be his destiny, while Ci, refusing to accept his lot, constantly succeeds in making money by doing business, which might, too, be his destiny."

11·20　子张问善人之道。子曰："不践迹，亦不入于室。"

【今译】

子张问做善人的方法。夫子说："如果不踏着前人的脚印走，其为善也不能做到家。

【英译】

Zizhang asked about the way of becoming a good man. The Master said, "If you do not follow the footprints of others, you will not be able to enter the inner chamber（be perfectly good）."

11·21　子曰："论笃是与，君子者乎？色庄者乎？"

【今译】

夫子说："言论笃实就赞许，这样的人是君子呢？还是仅仅是表情上庄重的人呢？"

【英译】

The Master said, "Is the man, who applauds whoever speaks sincerely, really a gentleman, or merely putting on a dignified appearance?"

11·22 子路问："闻斯行诸?"子曰："有父兄在,如之何其闻斯行之?"

冉有问："闻斯行诸?"子曰："闻斯行之。"

公西华曰："由也问闻斯行诸,子曰,'有父兄在';求也问闻斯行诸,子曰,'闻斯行之'。赤也惑,敢问。"子曰："求也退,故进之;由也兼人①,故退之。"

【注释】
①兼人:指其做事行为兼倍于人,冒进。

【今译】
子路问:"听到就做吗?"夫子说:"有父兄在,怎么能听到就做呢?"冉有问:"听到就做吗?"夫子说:"听到就做。"公西华说:"仲由问'听到就做吗?'你回答说'有父兄健在',冉求问'听到就做吗?'你回答'听到就做'。我被弄糊涂了,请问(怎么回事)。"夫子说:"冉求(做事总)退缩,所以我向前推他;仲由(做事)冒进,所以我向后拉他。"

【英译】
Zilu asked, "Should I immediately put into practice what I have learned?" The Master said, "How can you do that as your father and elder brother are still alive?" Ran You asked, "Should I immediately put into practice what I have learned?" The Master said, "Yes, you should."

Gongxi Hua said, "When Zhong You asked whether he should immediately put into practice what he had learned, you pointed out that he should not do that as his father and elder brothers are still alive. When Qiu asked the same question, you answered that he should. I am puzzled. May I be enlightened?"

The Master said, "Qiu usually holds himself back, so I urged him on.（Zhong）You has the drive of two men, so I tried to hold him back."

11·23 子畏于匡，颜渊后。子曰："吾以女为死矣。"曰："子在，回何敢死?"

【今译】

夫子在匡地受到当地人围困，颜渊最后才逃出来。夫子说："我以为你已经战死了呢。"颜渊说："夫子还活着，我怎么敢死呢?"

【英译】

When the Master was besieged in Kuang, Yan Yuan was the last to break the siege. The Master said, "I thought you had died in the breakout."

To which Yan Yuan replied, "How would I dare to die when you, my Master, are still alive."

11·24 季子然问："仲由、冉求可谓大臣与?"子曰："吾以子为异之问，曾由与求之问。所谓大臣者，以道事君，不可则止。今由与求也，可谓具臣矣。"

曰："然则从之者与?"子曰："弑父与君，亦不从也。"

【今译】

季子然问："仲由和冉求可以算是大臣吗？夫子说："我以为你是问别人，原来是问由和求呀。所谓大臣，（应该）以道的要求来事奉君主；如果不行，他宁肯辞职。现在由和求这两个人，可以算是有才能的臣子。"季子然问："那么他们会顺从主人吗？"夫子说："杀父亲、杀君主的事，他们也不会顺从。"

【英译】

Ji Ziran asked, "Could Zhong You and Ran Qiu be counted as great ministers?"

The Master said, "I thought you would ask about someone else, never expecting you would mention（Zhong）You and Qiu. The term 'great minister' refers to those who serve their Lord according to the Way and who, when this is no longer possible, relinquish office. Now men like（Zhong）You and Qiu can be described as capable ministers."

"In that case, would they always do what they are told to do?"

"No, not to the extent of killing their father or ruler."

11·25　子路使子羔为费宰。子曰："贼夫人之子。"
子路曰："有民人焉，有社稷焉，何必读书，然后为学？"
子曰："是故恶夫佞者。"

【今译】

子路让子羔去作费邑的长官。夫子说："这简直是害人子弟。"子路说："那个地方有老百姓，有社稷，治理百姓和祭祀神灵都是学习，何必一定要读书，然后才能为学呢？"夫子说："所以我讨厌那种花言巧语狡辩的人。"

Zilu recommended Zigao to be the prefect of Bi. The Master said, "You are ruining another man's son."

Zilu said, "In Bi, there are the people from whom he can learn how to govern; there are altars where he can learn how to perform sacrificial ceremonies. Why must he read books before he can be considered as educated?"

The Master said, "It is for this reason that I dislike men who are eloquent in defending."

11·26　子路、曾皙①、冉有、公西华侍坐。

子曰："以吾一日长乎尔，毋吾以也②。居③则曰：'不吾知也！'如或知尔，则何以哉④？"

子路率尔⑤而对曰："千乘之国，摄⑥乎大国之间，加之以师旅，因之以饥馑；由也为之，比及⑦三年，可使有勇，且知方⑧也。"

夫子哂⑨之。

"求，尔何如？"

对曰："方六七十⑩，如⑪五六十，求也为之，比及三年，可使足民。如其礼乐，以俟君子。"

"赤，尔何如？"

对曰："非曰能之，愿学焉。宗庙之事⑫，如会同⑬，端章甫⑭，愿为小相⑮焉。"

"点，尔何如？"

鼓瑟希⑯，铿尔，舍瑟而作，对曰："异乎三子者之撰。"

子曰："何伤乎？亦各言其志也。"

曰："莫⑰春者，春服既成，冠者五六人，童子六七人，浴乎沂，风乎舞雩⑱，咏而归。"

夫子喟然叹曰："吾与点也！"

三子者出，曾皙后。曾皙曰："夫三子者之言何如？"

子曰："亦各言其志也已矣。"

曰："夫子何哂由也？"

曰："为国以礼。其言不让，是故哂之。

唯求则非邦也与？安见方六七十如五六十而非邦也者？

唯赤则非邦也与？宗庙会同，非诸侯而何？赤也为之小，孰能为之大？"

【注释】

①曾皙（xī）：名点，字子皙，曾参的父亲，也是孔子的学生。

②以吾一日长乎尔，毋吾以也：不要因为我比你们年长一些而不敢说话。

③居：平日。

④则何以哉：何以，即何以为用。

⑤率尔：轻率，急切。

⑥摄：夹在其中受局促，受逼迫。

⑦比（bì）及：等到。

⑧方：礼法。

⑨哂（shěn）：微笑，讥笑。

⑩方六七十：纵横各六七十里。

⑪如：或者。

⑫宗庙之事：指祭祀之事。

⑬会同：诸侯会见。

⑭端章甫：端，古代礼服的名称。章甫，古代礼帽的名称。

⑮相：在祭祀、会同时，行赞礼的人，也叫傧相。

⑯希：同"稀"，稀疏（指弹瑟速度放慢）。

⑰莫：同"暮"。

⑱舞雩（yú）：鲁国祭天求雨的台子，在今山东曲阜南。

【今译】

子路、曾皙、冉有、公西华（四人）陪夫子坐着。

夫子说："不要因为我比你们年龄大一些而不敢说。你们平时总说：'没有人了解我呀！'假如有人了解你，你将做什么呢？"

子路不假思索地回答："一个方圆百里之诸侯国，夹在大国中间，受到别的国家侵犯，加上国内又闹饥荒，让我去治理，只要三年，就可以使百姓勇敢善战，而且懂得礼仪。"

夫子听了，微微一笑。

（夫子又问：）"冉求，你怎么样呢？"

（冉求）答道："方圆六七十里或五六十里的国家，让我去治理，三年以后，就可以使百姓富足。至于礼乐教化，就要等君子来了。"

（夫子又问）："公西赤，你怎么样？"

（公西赤）答道："不敢说我能做到，但是我愿意学习。在宗庙祭祀或者诸侯会盟中，我愿意穿着礼服，戴着礼帽，做一名小司仪。"

（夫子又问：）"曾点，你怎么样呢？"

弹瑟的节奏逐渐慢下来，接着"铿"的一声停止了，曾皙放下瑟，站起来，回答说："我与他们三位不一样。"

夫子说："那有什么关系呢？也就是各人讲自己的志向而已。"

（曾皙）说："暮春三月，已经穿上了春天的衣服，我和五六位成年人，六七个少年，去沂河里洗澡，在舞雩台上吹风，一路唱着歌走回来。"

夫子长叹一声说："我赞同曾皙啊。"

其他三人都出去了，曾皙留在后面。他问夫子说："他们三人的话怎么样？"

夫子说："也就是各自谈谈自己的志向罢了。"

（曾皙）说："夫子为什么要笑仲由呢？"

（夫子）说："治理国家要讲礼，可是他说话一点也不谦让，所以我笑他。冉求讲的就不是治理国家吗？何以见得六七十里或五六十里见方的地方就不是国家呢？公西赤讲的就不是治理国家吗？宗庙祭祀和诸侯会盟，这不是诸侯的事是什么？像赤这样的人如果只能做一个小相，那谁又能做大相呢？"

【英译】

When Zilu, Zeng Xi, Ran You and Gongxi Hua were seated in attendance, the Master said, "Do not feel constrained simply because I am somewhat older than you are. You often say, 'No one recognizes my worth!' If someone did recognize your worth, what would you do?"

Zilu promptly answered, "If I were to administer a state of a hundred square *li*, situated between several powerful states, troubled by armed invasions and repeated famines, I could, within three years, imbue all the people with courage and courtesy."

The Master smiled at him.

"Qiu, what about you?"

"If I were to administer an area measuring sixty or seventy square *li*, or even fifty or sixty square *li*, I could, within three years, make the people prosperous. As for the rites and music, I would leave that to abler gentlemen."

"Chi, how about you?"

"I dare not say that I am already capable, but I would be willing to learn. On ceremonial occasions in the ancestral temple or at diplomatic gatherings, I should like to serve as a minor official in charge of protocol, properly dressed in ceremonial robes and cap."

"Dian, how about you?"

After strumming a few dying notes and the final chord, he stood up from his lute. "My idea is different from theirs."

The Master said, "No harm in that. After all, each of you is entitled to talk about your own aspirations."

Zeng Xi said, "In late spring when everyone has put on spring clothes, I would, in the company of five or six adults and six or seven children, go bathing in the River Yi and enjoy the breeze on the Rain Altar, and then sing our way home."

The Master sighed and said, "I am all in favour of Dian."

When the three left, Zeng Xi stayed behind. He asked the Master, "What do you think of what the other three said?"

The Master said, "Each spoke of his own aspiration, that's all."

"Why did you smile at（Zhong）You?"

The Master said, "It is by the rites that a state is administered, but in the way he spoke,（Zhong）You showed no modesty. That is why I smiled at him. Was Qiu not talking about administering a state? Why can't a territory of sixty to seventy, or fifty to sixty square *li* be called a state? Was Chi not talking about administering a state? What are ancestral temples and diplomatic gatherings, if they are not state affairs? If Chi can play a minor part, then who else can play a major role?"

颜渊第十二

12·1　颜渊问仁。子曰："克己复礼^①为仁。一日克己复礼，天下归仁焉。为仁由己，而由人乎哉?"

颜渊曰："请问其目。"子曰："非礼勿视，非礼勿听，非礼勿言，非礼勿动。"

颜渊曰："回虽不敏，请事斯语矣。"

【注释】

①复礼：使自己的言行符合于礼的要求。

【今译】

颜渊问怎样做才是仁。夫子说："约束自己，践行礼，这就是仁。一旦这样做了，天下的一切都将归依仁德。实行仁德，完全在于自己，难道还在于别人吗?"颜渊说："请问实行仁的条目。"夫子说："不合于礼的不要看，不合于礼的不要听，不合于礼的不要说，不合于礼的不要做。"颜渊说："我虽然愚笨，但请让我按照您这话去做吧。"

【英译】

Yan Yuan asked about benevolence. The Master said, "To restrain oneself to observe the rites constitutes benevolence. Once everyone restrains himself and observes the rites, benevolence will prevail in the whole Empire. The practice of benevolence depends on oneself alone, and not on others."

Yan Yuan asked, "May I know about the detailed requirements?"

The Master said, "Do not look unless it is in accordance with the rites, do not listen unless it is in accordance with the rites, do not speak unless it is in accordance with the rites, and do not do anything that is not in accordance with the rites."

Yan Yuan said, "Though I am not intelligent, let me try to live up to your words."

12 · 2　仲弓问仁。子曰："出门如见大宾，使民如承大祭。己所不欲，勿施于人。在邦无怨，在家无怨。"

仲弓曰："雍虽不敏，请事斯语矣。"

【今译】

仲弓问怎样做才是仁。夫子说："出门如同去接待贵宾，役使百姓如同承当重大的祭祀。自己不愿要的，不要强加于别人；在朝廷上做事无怨无悔；在卿大夫家做事无怨无悔。"仲弓说："我虽然愚笨，但请让我按照您这话去做吧。"

【英译】

Zhonggong asked about benevolence. The Master said, "Every time you go out, do it as if you were receiving an important guest. Every time you employ the people, do it as if you were officiating at an important sacrifice. Do not impose on others what you yourself do not desire. Harbour no discontent when serving at the imperial court or in a noble family.

Zhonggong said, "Though I am not intelligent, let me try to

live up to your words."

12·3　司马牛问仁。子曰："仁者，其言也讱^①。"

曰："其言也讱，斯谓之仁已乎？"子曰："为之难，言之得无讱乎？"

【注释】

①讱（rèn）：话难说出口。这里引申为说话谨慎。

【今译】

司马牛问怎样做才是仁。夫子说："仁人，说话（缓慢）谨慎。"司马牛说："说话谨慎，就叫做仁了吗？"夫子说："做起来困难，说话能不谨慎吗？"

【英译】

Sima Niu asked about benevolence. The Master said, "A benevolent man speaks cautiously as if with difficulty."

"Can a man be regarded as benevolent if he speaks cautiously as if with difficulty?" asked Sima Niu.

The Master said, "How can a man speak lightly without caution when it is difficult to put his words into action?

12·4　司马牛问君子。子曰："君子不忧不惧。"

曰："不忧不惧，斯谓之君子已乎？"子曰："内省不疚，夫何忧何惧？"

【今译】

司马牛问怎样做一个君子。夫子说："君子不忧愁，不恐惧。"司马牛说："不忧愁，不恐惧，这样就可以叫做君子了吗？"夫子说："自己问心无愧，那还有什么忧愁和恐惧呢？"

【英译】

Sima Niu asked about being a gentleman. The Master said, "A gentleman is free from worries and fears."

"Can a man be called a gentleman if he is free from worries and fears?" asked Sima Niu.

The Master said, "If one has a clear conscience, what has he to worry about and fear?"

12·5　司马牛忧曰："人皆有兄弟，我独亡。"子夏曰："商闻之矣：死生有命，富贵在天。君子敬而无失，与人恭而有礼，四海之内，皆兄弟也。君子何患乎无兄弟也？"

【今译】

司马牛忧愁地说："别人都有兄弟，唯独我没有。"子夏说："我听说过：'死生有命，富贵在天。'君子只要做事认真，不放纵自己，对人恭敬有礼，那么，天下人就都是自己的兄弟。君子何愁没有兄弟呢？"

【英译】

Sima Niu appeared worried, saying, "All men have brothers. I alone have none."

Zixia said, "I have heard it said that life and death are predetermined by destiny; wealth and honour depend on Heaven. A gentleman is dedicated to his duty, without indulging himself, and is respectful and courteous to others. Thus, all men under the sun are brothers. Why should a gentleman worry about having no brothers?"

12·6　子张问明。子曰："浸润之谮①，肤受之愬②，不行焉，可谓明也已矣。浸润之谮，肤受之愬不行焉，可谓远③也已矣。"

【注释】

①浸润之谮（zèn）：像水那样一点一滴地渗进来的谗言，不易觉察。谮：谗言。

②肤受之愬：像皮肤感觉到疼痛那样的诬告，即直接的诽谤。

③远：明之至，明智的最高境界。

【今译】

子张问怎样做才算是明智。夫子说："像水浸润般的谗言，像尘垢落在皮肤那样的诽谤，在你那里行不通，那你可以算是明察秋毫了。像水浸润般的谗言，像尘垢落在皮肤那样的诽谤，在你那里行不通，那你可以算是有远见了。"

【英译】

Zizhang asked about perceptiveness and insight. The Master said, "When a man is immune to slanders which gradually soak his mind like water, or to calumnies which gradually accumulate like dust on his skin, he can be called clear-sighted. He can at the same time be said to be far-sighted."

12·7　子贡问政。子曰：“足食，足兵，民，信之。”

子贡曰：“必不得已而去，于斯三者何先？”曰：“去兵。”

子贡曰：“必不得已而去，于斯二者何先？”曰：“去食。自古皆有死，民无信不立。”

【今译】

子贡问怎样治理国家。夫子说，“使粮食充足，使军备充足，使百姓守信。”子贡说：“如果迫不得已去掉一项，那么在三项中先去掉哪一项呢？”夫子说：“去掉军备。”子贡说：“如果迫不得已再去掉一项，那么这两项中去掉哪一项呢？”夫子说：“去掉粮食。自古以来人总是要死的，百姓如果没有信用就不能立足。”

【英译】

Zigong asked about governing a state. The Master said, "Make food sufficient, make arms sufficient, and make people trustworthy."

Zigong said, "If one of these three essentials had to be dispensed with, which one should it be?"

The Master said, "Arms."

Zigong asked again, "If one of the two had to be dispensed with, which one should it be?"

"Food." The Master said, "After all, everyone has to die eventually. The people will not be able to maintain their footing without being trustworthy."

【辨正】

“食”“兵”“信”三件事，源自“足食，足兵，民信之矣"一句，而"自古皆有死，民无信不立"用来解释为何"信"不可去，可以看出"信"字尽管在"民信之"里用作动词，在"民无信"里用作名词，其义却是相同的。

陈天祥《四书辨疑》："一章中两信本是一意，《注》文解'民信之矣'则云'民信于我'，此以信为国家之信也。解'民无信不立'则云'民无食必死，然死者人之所不免，无信则虽生而无以自立'此却说信为民之信，立亦民之自立也。又曰'宁死而不失信于民，使民亦宁死而不失信于我'，前一句信在国，后一句信在民。后又分人情民德二说。云'以人情而言，则兵食足而后吾之信可以孚于民'，此说信亦在国也。继云'以民德而言，则信本人之所固有，非兵食所得而先'，此说又信在民矣。不惟信字交互无定，而兵食与信先后之说自亦不一，圣人本旨，果安在哉？"

"民信之"，很容易让人理解成主—谓—宾结构，即"人民相信政府"，然后移来解释"民无信不立"，就成了"民无信则国不立"或者"国无民信则不立"。"自古皆有死"是说"人之死"，不是"国之亡"；"民无信不立"是说"人不讲信用就无法立身"，都与"国"无涉。

"足食""足兵"之"足"，并非形容词"充足/富裕"，而是动词"使……充足"。足食足兵不单是民自己的事，更是为政者的"政"事。而"民信之矣"一句，程树德《论语集释》里说：高丽本"民信"上有"使"字。皇本"民信"上有"令"字。"使民信之""令民信之"不也是为政者的"政"事吗？"足食"是使民有足够的粮食；"足兵"是使民有足够的武器，使足够的民能拿起武器为兵；"民信之"是使民讲信用。这不但是为政，而且还是为政三要事中最重要的：兵可去，食可去，信不可去。

"民信之矣"一句，毛子水《论语今注今译》里断为：

"民，信之"，并解释说："民信之矣"的"矣"字，当是衍文。孔子举出为政三要事：足食；足兵；民，信之。（"信之"是"使民信任政府"的意思。）——不是"使民信任政府"，而是"使民讲信用"。

12·8 棘子成曰："君子质而已矣，何以文为？"子贡曰："惜乎，夫子之说君子也！驷不及舌①。文犹质也，质犹文也。虎豹之鞟②犹犬羊之鞟。"

【注释】

①驷不及舌：指话一说出口，就收不回来了。驷，拉一辆车的四匹马。

②鞟（kuò）：去掉毛的皮，即革。《刘宝楠正义》："然鞟为革，凡去毛不去毛，皆得称之，不必专主去毛一训。"

【今译】

棘子成说："君子只要内在的品质好就行了，要那些外在的文饰做什么呢？"子贡说："太遗憾了，夫子您这样谈论君子。一言既出，驷马难追。（如果）质就像文，文就像质，（没有区别），那么，虎、豹的外表就像犬、羊的外表一样了。"

【英译】

Ji Zicheng said, "The important thing to a gentleman is his intrinsic essence. What need is there for extrinsic refinement?

Zigong commented, "What a pity that you should talk about a gentleman in such a way. A word once spoken cannot be caught up even by a team of four horses. If the essence is no different from the refinement, then a tiger or a leopard is no different in appearance from a dog or a sheep."

12·9　哀公问于有若曰："年饥，用不足，如之何？"

有若对曰："盍彻乎？"

曰："二，吾犹不足，如之何其彻也？"

对曰："百姓足，君孰与不足？百姓不足，君孰与足？"

【今译】

鲁哀公问有若说："遭了饥荒，国家用度困难，怎么办？"有若回答说："为什么不实行彻法，只抽十分之一的田税呢？"哀公说："现在抽十分之二，我还不够，如何能实行什一税呢？"有若说："如果百姓的用度足，您怎么会不足呢？如果百姓的用度不足，您又怎么会足呢？"

【英译】

Duke Ai asked You Ruo, "What should be done when there is a poor harvest and the state has a strained budget?"

You Ruo answered, "What about taxing the people one part in ten?

The Duke said, "I do not have enough to spend even if I tax them two parts in ten. How could I possibly tax them one part in ten?"

To which You Ruo replied, "When the people have plenty, how can you alone be left in want? If the people are in want, how can you alone live in plenty?"

12·10 子张问崇德辨惑。子曰："主忠信，徙义，崇德也。爱之欲其生，恶之欲其死。既欲其生，又欲其死，是惑也。'诚不以富，亦祇以异。'"

【今译】

子张问怎样提高道德修养、辨别迷惑。夫子说："以忠信为主，唯义是从，就是提高道德修养。爱一个人，希望他活下去，厌恶起来就想让他死去，既要他活，又要他死，这就是迷惑。（正如《诗经》所说的：）'的确不是因为富有，只是因为不一样。'"

【英译】

Zizhang asked about how one could cultivate virtue and solve perplexities. The Master said, "Make it your guiding principle to be faithful and trustworthy, and pursue justice, then you will be cultivating virtue. When you love a man, you want him to live a long life and when you hate him you want him to die. When you want him both to live and to die, that is perplexity. "It is indeed not because of the wealth, but of different pursuit."

【辨正】

"诚不以富，亦祇以异"一句引语与上文格格不入，因而程颐怀疑是错简，即别章的文句，因书页次序错乱而误置此处。详见《季氏第十六》第12章。

12·11　齐景公问政于孔子。孔子对曰："君君①，臣臣，父父，子子。"公曰："善哉！信如君不君，臣不臣，父不父，子不子，虽有粟，吾得而食诸？"

【注释】

①君君：君主要以君主的礼仪规范行事，要像君主的样子。即"君尽君道"。

【今译】

齐景公问孔子如何治理国家。孔子说："做君主的要像君主的样子，做臣子的要像臣子的样子，做父亲的要像父亲的样子，做儿子的要像儿子的样子。"齐景公说："讲得好呀！如果君不像君，臣不像臣，父不像父，子不像子，即使有粮食，我能吃得上吗？"

【英译】

Duke Jing of Qi asked Confucius about how to govern a state. Confucius answered, "Let the Lord be a Lord, the minister a minister, the father a father, the son a son."

The Duke remarked, "Well said. If the Lord did not act like a Lord, the minister not like a minister, the father not like a father, the son not like a son, then even if there were plenty of grain, would I get my share?"

【辨正】

与下文"君不君，臣不臣，父不父，子不子"对照，可以看出"君君、臣臣、父父、子子"每一句的前一字为主语，后一字为谓语，意思是君尽君道，臣尽臣道，父尽父道，子尽子道。

《左传·昭公二十六年》："齐侯与晏子坐于路寝。公叹曰：'美哉室！其谁有此乎？'晏子曰：'敢问何谓也？'公曰：'吾以为在德。'对曰：'如君之言，其陈氏乎？陈氏虽无大德，而有施于民。豆、区、釜、钟之数，其取之公也薄，其施之民也厚。公厚敛焉，陈氏厚施焉，民归之矣。《诗》曰："虽无德与女，式歌且舞。"陈氏之施，民歌舞之矣。后世若少惰，陈氏而不亡，则国其国也已。'公曰：'善哉！是可若何？'对曰：'唯礼可以已之。在礼，家施不及国，民不迁，农不移，工贾不变，士不滥，官不滔，大夫不收公利。'公曰：'善哉！我不能矣。吾今而后知礼之可以为国也。'对曰：'礼之可以为国也久矣，与天地并。君令臣共，父慈子孝，兄爱弟敬，夫和妻柔，姑慈妇听，礼也。君令而不违，臣共而不贰，父慈而教，子孝而箴；兄爱而友，弟敬而顺；夫和而义，妻柔而正；姑慈而从，妇听而婉：礼之善物也。'公曰：'善哉！寡人今而后闻此礼之上也。'对曰：'先王所禀于天地，以为其民也，是以先王上之。'"

12·12　子曰："片言①可以折狱②者，其由也与？"子路无宿诺。

【注释】
①片言：古代打官司，原告与被告叫"两造"，听讼须听两造之辞，一面之辞叫"片言"或"单辞"。片：偏。
②折狱：制狱，断案。狱：案件。

【今译】
夫子说："他的一面之辞就能让人断案的，只有仲由吧。"

子路没有隔夜的承诺。

【英译】

The Master said, "If there's anyone whose one-sided words can be safely taken as truth to settle a lawsuit, it is, perhaps, (Zhong) You." Zilu will not postpone the fulfillment of his promise till the next day.

【辨正】

杨伯峻《论语译注》：孔子说："根据一方面的语言就可以判决案件的，大概只有仲由吧！"子路从不拖延诺言。

黄怀信《论语新校释》：先生说："一言半语（就）可以断官司的，大概是仲由吧！"

毛子水《论语今注今译》："根据一面的话判断讼案，似只有仲由的话才可以！"子路答应别人的事，一定马上替人做到。

这三种译法正代表了三种理解。前两种，杨、黄的解法，共同点是子路听讼断案，不同点是对"片言"的解释。第三种理解不同于前两种，子路是讼者，即听讼于子路。

毛子水的白话翻译："根据一面的话判断讼案，似只有仲由的话才可以！"就把子路放在了被听的位置。子路性急人直不撒谎，他的话，虽是一面之词，却可以听而断案。这是孔子对子路很高的评价。皇《疏》引孙绰云："谓子路心高而言信，未尝文过以自卫。听讼者便宜以子路单辞为正，不待对验而后分明也，非谓子路闻人片言便能断狱也。"

12·13 子曰："听讼,吾犹人也。必也使无讼乎!"

【今译】

夫子说："审理诉讼,我同别人没有区别。如果一定（要说区别）,那就是不使诉讼出现!"

【英译】

The Master said, "In settling a lawsuit, I am no different from others. If there is a difference, it is, perhaps, that I try to make sure no lawsuit will occur."

12·14 子张问政。子曰："居之无倦,行之以忠。"

【今译】

子张问如何治理政事。夫子说："居于官位不懈怠,做事尽职尽责。"

【英译】

Zizhang asked about government. The Master said, "Never slacken your effort at your post, and carry out your duties with dedication."

12·15 子曰："博学于文,约之以礼,亦可以弗畔矣夫!"①

【注释】

①见《雍也第六》6·27。

The Master said, "A gentleman, who is widely versed in literature and historical records and regulates himself with rites, can be relied upon not to go astray."

12·16　子曰："君子成人之美，不成人之恶。小人反是。"

【今译】

夫子说："君子成全别人的好事，而不助成别人作恶。小人与此相反。"

【英译】

The Master said, "A gentleman helps others fulfill their good wishes but not their evil ones. The petty man does the opposite."

12·17　季康子问政于孔子。孔子对曰："政者，正也。子帅以正，孰敢不正？"

【今译】

季康子问孔子如何治理国家。孔子回答说："政就是正。您若以正做表率，那么谁敢不正呢？"

【英译】

Ji Kangzi asked Confucius about government. Confucius answered, "Government（*zheng*）is being upright（*zheng*）. If you set an example by being upright, who would dare to be otherwise?"

12·18　季康子患盗，问于孔子。孔子对曰："苟子之不欲，虽赏之不窃。"

【今译】

季康子苦于盗窃太多，问孔子怎么办。孔子回答说："假如你自己不贪图财利，即使奖赏偷窃，也没有人做。"

【英译】

Troubled by theft in the state, Ji Kangzi came to consult Confucius, who said, "If you yourself were a man of few desires, no one would steal even if they are rewarded for doing that."

12·19　季康子问政于孔子曰："如杀无道，以就有道，何如?"孔子对曰："子为政，焉用杀? 子欲善而民善矣。君子之德风，小人之德草。草上之风，必偃。"

【今译】

季康子问孔子执政之道，说："如果杀掉无道的人来成全有道的人，怎么样?"孔子说："您治理政事，哪里用得着杀戮呢? 您追求良善，老百姓就会跟着良善。在位者的品德好比风，在下的人的品德好比草。风吹到草上，草就必定倒伏。"

【英译】

Ji Kangzi asked Confucius about government, saying, "What would you think of killing those who do not follow the Way in order to support those who do?

Confucius answered, "In governing the state, what need is there for you to kill? Pursue goodness yourself and the common people will naturally become good. The morality of a gentleman is like wind while that of the common people is like grass. The grass is sure to bend when the wind blows."

【辨正】

赞同黄怀信《论语新校释》里的断句：君子之德，风也，人小之德，草也。草，上之风，必偃。

12·20 子张问："士何如斯可谓之达矣？"子曰："何哉，尔所谓达者？"子张对曰："在邦必闻，在家必闻。"子曰："是闻也，非达也。夫达也者，质直而好义，察言而观色，虑以下人。在邦必达，在家必达。夫闻也者，色取仁而行违，居之不疑。在邦必闻，在家必闻。"

【今译】

子张问："士怎样才可以叫做通达？"夫子说："你说的通达是什么意思？"子张答道："在朝廷里一定知名，在卿大夫家也一定知名。"夫子说："这是知名，不是通达。所谓通达，要品质正直，崇尚道义，察颜观色，时常想着谦恭待人。这样的人，在朝廷里一定通达，在卿大夫家也一定通达。而知名者，表面上装出仁的样子，而行动上却违背仁，自己还以仁人自居不惭愧。在朝廷里一定知名，在卿大夫家一定会知名。"

【英译】

Zizhang asked, "What must a scholar do to become prestigious?"

The Master said, "What do you mean by 'prestigious'?"

Zizhang answered, "To be well-known whether he serves in a state or in a noble family."

The Master said, "That is being well-known, not being prestigious. To become prestigious, one must be upright by nature and value justice highly, sensitive to other's words and observant of the expression on their faces, and always ready to give precedence to others. Such a man is bound to become prestigious whether he serves in a state or in a noble family. To become well-known, one may assume the appearance of being benevolent, but he does the opposite in action, and prides himself on that appearance without misgiving. Such a man is sure to be well-known, whether he serves in a state or in a noble family."

12·21 樊迟从游于舞雩之下，曰："敢问崇德，修慝①，辨惑。"子曰："善哉问！先事后得，非崇德与？攻其恶，无攻人之恶，非修慝与？一朝之忿，忘其身，以及其亲，非惑与？"

【注释】

①慝（tè）：恶念。修：治而去之。修慝：这里是指改正邪恶的念头。

【今译】

樊迟陪着（先生）在舞雩台下散步，说："请问（怎样）提高道德、怎样根治恶念、怎样辨别迷惑？"夫子说："问得好！先做事，后获得，不是提高道德吗？反省自己的不良言行，而不去指责他人的过错，不是去除恶念吗？由于一时的气愤，就忘记了自身的安危，以至于牵连自己的亲人，这不就是迷惑吗?"

【英译】

While accompanying the Master on a walk at the foot of the Rain Altar, Fan Chi said, "May I ask how one can cultivate virtue, clear up one's resentment and recognize foolishness?"

The Master said, "What an excellent question! Isn't a person cultivating virtue when he places service before reward? Isn't he clearing up resentment when he criticizes his own faults rather than those of others? Isn't it foolishness when, in a sudden fit of anger, one forgets the safety of his family as well as his own?"

12·22 樊迟问仁。子曰："爱人。"问知。子曰："知人。"

樊迟未达。子曰："举直错诸枉①，能使枉者直。"

樊迟退，见子夏曰："乡②也吾见于夫子而问知，子曰'举直错诸枉，能使枉者直'，何谓也?"

子夏曰："富哉言乎! 舜有天下，选于众，举皋陶③，不仁者远④矣。汤有天下，选于众，举伊尹，不仁者远矣。"

【注释】

①举直错诸枉：选拔直者，罢黜枉者。错：同"措"，放置。枉：不正直，邪恶。

②乡（xiàng）：同"向"，过去。

③皋陶（gāo yáo）：传说中舜时掌握刑法的大臣。

④远（yuàn）：动词，远离，远去。

樊迟问什么是仁。夫子说:"爱人。"

樊迟问什么是智,夫子说:"了解人。"

樊迟还不明白。夫子说:"选拔正直的人,置于不正直的人之上,这样就能使不正直的人归向正直。"

樊迟退出来,见到子夏说:"刚才我见到老师,问他什么是智,他说'选拔正直的人,置于不正直的人之上,这样就能使不正直的人归向正直。'这是什么意思?"

子夏说:"这话说得多么深刻呀!舜有天下,在众人中挑选人才,把皋陶选拔出来,不仁的人就远离了。汤有了天下,在众人中挑选人才,把伊尹选拔出来,不仁的人就远离了。"

【英译】

Fan Chi asked about benevolence. The Master said, "Love your fellow men."

He asked about wisdom. The Master said, "Know your fellow men." Seeing that Fan Chi failed to grasp his meaning, the Master added, "Promote the upright over the crooked. This can make the crooked upright."

Fan Chi withdrew and went to see Zixia, saying, "Just now, I went to see the Master and asked about wisdom. The Master said, 'Promote the upright over the crooked. This can make the crooked upright.' What did he mean?"

Zixia said, "Rich, indeed, is the meaning of his words. When Shun took over the Empire, he promoted Gao Yao from the multitude and those who were not benevolent fled. When Tang took over the Empire, he promoted Yi Yin from the multitude and those who were not benevolent fled."

12·23 子贡问友。子曰："忠告而善道之，不可则止，毋自辱焉。"

【今译】

子贡问怎样交友。夫子说："忠诚地劝告他，好好地引导他，不听从就作罢，不要自取其辱。"

【英译】

Zigong asked how to associate with friends. The Master said, "Advise them in earnest and guide them properly, but let it be if they are reluctant to follow. Do not invite disgrace."

12·24 曾子曰："君子以文会友，以友辅仁。"

【今译】

曾子说："君子以文章学问来结交朋友，以朋友来帮助培养仁德。"

【英译】

Master Zeng said, "A gentleman makes friends through his learning, and looks to friends for support in cultivating benevolence."

子路第十三

13·1　子路问政。子曰："先之劳之。"请益。曰："无倦。"

【今译】

子路问怎样处理政事。夫子说："把政事放在首位，为之竭心尽力。"子路请求多讲一点。夫子说："不要懈怠。"

【英译】

Zilu asked about government. The Master said, "Give it the first priority, and take pains with it." Zilu asked for more. The Master said, "Never slacken your efforts."

【辨正】

俞樾《群经平议》："'先之劳之'四字作一句读，犹《阳货》'使之闻之'，不得因有两'之'字而分为二事也。《诗·绵蛮》'为之载之'，《孟子·滕文公下》'与之食之'，句法皆与此同。"对于这种说法，杨逢彬《论语新注新译》辨得清晰透彻："俞说不确。俞樾所举三例中，'为之载之'和'与之食之'是'【介词+宾语】+【动词+宾语】'结构，介词结构只能修饰谓语，不能独立；'使之闻之'是'【使令动词+宾语】+【行为动词+宾语】'形成的兼语结构，兼语结构也是一个整体，不能分开，因此这三例都'不得因有两"之"字而分为二事也’。而‘先之劳之’是两个【动词+宾语】结构，这两个谓宾结构却是可以并列而二的；所以，‘先之劳之’和俞樾所举三例看似相同，其实有异。”因此，“先之劳之”不可解为“先之劳”。

“之”字指代，应该从上文里找。它承接上文，就是指“政”。孔子回答“先政劳政”，且“勤政不倦”。“先”字是“把……当作首要的事”，“放在第一位”。“劳”是“为……操心”。

清代简朝亮《论语集注补正述疏》：“《孟子》云：‘劳于王事。’，信哉！……今《经》接‘问政’而曰“先之、劳之’，明乎其身先此政也，勤劳此政也。其所为‘之’者，各接上文有所指焉。孔《注》云：‘先导之以德，使民信之，然后劳之。《易》曰：‘说以使民，民忘其劳。’盖孔引《易·况·象传》文也。今考《经》云：‘君子信而后劳其民。’又《经》言‘民利’者，遂云‘择可劳而劳之’。此孔说所由也，然在本文则病添文矣。如孔说，苟不添言‘民’，惟接‘问政’而曰‘先之’，然后‘劳之’，则其所谓‘之’者，乌知其所指乎？且下文‘无倦’当双承矣，岂可曰劳民无倦乎？经学为文学，非辩文法则不明也。”辨得同样清晰而透彻。

13·2　仲弓为季氏宰，问政。子曰：“先有司，赦小过，举贤才。”

曰：“焉知贤才而举之？”曰：“举尔所知；尔所不知，人其舍诸？”

【今译】

仲弓做了季氏的家宰，问怎样处理政事。夫子说：“行在办事人员前头，不计较小过错，举用贤才。”仲弓又问：“怎样知道贤才而举用呢？”夫子说：“举用你知道的，你不知道的，别人难道会舍弃吗？"

【英译】

While serving as a steward to the Ji family, Zhonggong asked about government. The Master said, "Set an example for your subordinates, be lenient on minor faults and promote men of virtue and talent."

"How do I recognize the men of virtue and talent so as to promote them?" asked Zhonggong.

"Promote those you have recognized. As for those you did not recognize, will others neglect them?"

13·3　子路曰："卫君待子为政，子将奚先？"

子曰："必也正名乎！"

子路曰："有是哉，子之迂也！奚其正？"

子曰："野哉，由也！君子于其所不知，盖阙如也。名不正，则言不顺；言不顺，则事不成；事不成，则礼乐不兴；礼乐不兴，则刑罚不中；刑罚不中，则民无所措手足。故君子名之必可言也，言之必可行也。君子于其言，无所苟而已矣。"

【今译】

子路（对夫子）说："卫国国君若是留您去治理国家，您将先做什么？"夫子说："一定要做的话，那就是正名分吧。"子路说："您竟如此不切实际！有什么要正的？"夫子说："仲由啊，你见识太浅陋了。君子对于他所不知道的事情，采取存疑的态度。名分不正，说起话来就不顺当合理；说话不顺当合理，事情就办不成；事情办不成，礼乐就不能兴盛；礼乐不能兴盛，刑罚就不会公平允当；刑罚不公平允当，百姓就不知如何是好。所以，君子给一名分，一定要说得通，说出来一定要行得通。君子对于自己的话，严肃不马虎才行。"

【英译】

Zilu asked the Master, saying, "If the Lord of Wei were expecting you to administer his state, what would you do first?"

The Master said, "If something has to be done first, it is the rectification of names."

"Fancy you being so pedantic!" said Zilu. "What need is there to rectify the names?"

"How boorish you are, （Zhong）You!" said the Master. "A gentleman would appear uncertain when it comes to what he does not know. If your name is not licit, your words will not carry weight. If your words do not carry weight, your administrative goal will not be accomplished. If your goal is not accomplished, the rites and music will not come to prevail. If the rites and music do not prevail, penalties will not be properly executed. If penalties are not properly executed, the people will be at a loss as to what to do. Therefore, when a gentleman gives a name, it must be justifiable; when he sets a goal, it must be executable. A gentleman will be anything but casual with his words."

【辨正】

卫灵公夫人南子不守妇道，世子蒯聩欲杀之，不果而出奔宋、晋。灵公欲立公子郢，郢辞。灵公死，南子欲立郢，郢又辞曰："有亡人之子辄在"。乃立蒯聩之子辄，即卫出公。蒯聩从晋国归，晋国赵鞅帅师纳蒯聩于戚，卫人群然拒之。父子相持13年（哀公2—14年）。蒯聩与其姊伯姬谋，逼迫握有大权的孔悝（kuī）（伯姬之子）结盟，推翻出公。出公出奔鲁。蒯聩即位，即卫庄公。

全祖望《鲒埼亭集·正名论》："孔子以世子称蒯聩，则其尝为灵公所立无疑矣。观《左传》累称之为'太子'，固有明文矣。不特此也，其出亡之后，灵公虽怒，而未尝废之也。灵公欲立子郢而郢辞，则灵公有废之意而未果，又有明文矣。惟蒯聩未尝为灵公所废，特以得罪而出亡，则闻丧而奔赴，则卫人所不可拒也。蒯聩之归有名，而卫人之拒无名也，况诸侯之子得罪于父而归者，亦不一矣。晋之乱也，夷吾奔屈，重耳奔蒲，及奚齐、卓子之死，夷吾兄弟相继而归，不闻以得罪而晋人拒之也。然则蒯聩何尤焉？故孔子之正名也，但正其世子之名而已。既为世子，则卫人所不可拒也。"

刘宝楠《论语正义》："愚谓《春秋》之义，世子继体以为君，为辄计者，内迫于南子，不能迎立蒯聩，则惟如叔齐及公子郢之所为，逊避弗居斯已耳。乃辄俨然自立，当时必援无适子立適孙之义，以王父命为辞，是辄不以世子予蒯聩。观于公子郢之言'有亡人之子辄在'，忠贞如子郢，在辄未立时，已不敢以世子称蒯聩，则辄既立后，假以王父之命，其谁敢有称蒯聩为世子者？所以蒯聩入戚，卫命石曼姑同齐国夏帅师围戚，明是待蒯聩为寇仇，其不以世子称蒯聩审矣。《太史公自序》云：'南子恶蒯聩，子父易名。'谓不以蒯聩为世子，而辄继立也。名之颠倒，未有甚于此者。夫子亟欲正之，而辄之不当立，不当与蒯聩争国，顾名思义，自可得之言外矣。"

夫子以哀公6年返卫，出公"待子为政"，此时名义未决，正须辨定。名不正则言不顺，言不顺则事不成。人伦正则天理得，政通人和，否则，名不正，则国必乱。——其后卫国发生的事，都不幸为夫子所言中。

《王阳明传习录》里的答问，可以看作孔子将如何帮助卫出公正名："孔子既肯与辄为政，必已是他能倾心委国而听。圣人盛德至诚，必已感化卫辄，使知无父之不可以为人，必将痛哭奔走，往迎其父。父子之爱，本于天性。辄能悔痛真切如此，蒯聩岂不感动底豫？蒯聩既还，辄乃致国请戮。聩已见化于子，又有夫子至诚调和其间，当亦决不肯受，仍以命辄，群臣百姓又必欲得辄为君。辄乃自暴其罪恶，请于天子，告于方伯诸侯，而必欲致国于父。聩与群臣百姓亦皆表辄悔悟仁孝之美，请于天子，告于方伯诸侯，必欲得辄而为之君。于是集命于辄，使之复君卫国。辄不得已，乃如后世上皇故事，率群臣百姓尊聩为太公，备物致养。而始退复其位焉。则君君、臣臣、父父、子子，名正言顺，一举而为政于天下矣。孔子正名，或是如此。"

"盖阙"即"阙盖"，也作"区盖"、"丘盖"。程树德《论语集释》："谓疑而不明。《荀子·大略》：'言之信者，在乎区盖之间，疑则不言，未问则不立。'杨倞注：'区、藏物处，盖、所以覆物者。凡言之可信者，如物在区皿之间，言有分限，不流溢也。'《汉书·儒林传》：'疑者丘盖不言。'苏林曰：'丘盖不言，不知之意。'如淳曰：'齐俗以不知为丘。'区、阙声之转。《论语》之盖阙，即荀子之区盖，为未见阙疑之意，故曰'盖阙如也'，与'踧踖如也'同词。读'阙如'连文者非。"

13·4 樊迟请学稼。子曰："吾不如老农。"请学为圃①。曰："吾不如老圃。"

樊迟出。子曰："小人哉，樊须也！上好礼，则民莫敢不敬；上好义，则民莫敢不服；上好信，则民莫敢不用情。夫如是，则四方之民襁负其子而至矣，焉用稼？"

【注释】
①圃（pǔ）：菜地，引申为种菜的人。

樊迟请教如何种庄稼。夫子说："我不如老农民。"樊迟又请教如何种菜。夫子说："我不如老菜农。"樊迟退出以后，夫子说："樊迟真是小人。在上位者只要重视礼，老百姓就没有人敢不严肃认真；在上位者只要重视义，老百姓就没有人敢不服从；在上位的人只要重视信，老百姓就没有人敢不说实话。要是做到这样，四面八方的老百姓就会背着自己的小孩来投奔，哪里用得着种庄稼？"

【英译】

Fan Chi asked about growing crops. The Master said, "I am not as good as an old farmer." He then asked about growing vegetables. "I am not as good as an old gardener."

After Fan Chi left, the Master said, "Fan Chi is indeed a petty man. If those at the top observe the rites, none of the common people will dare not be conscientious. If they love to be upright, none of the common people will dare not to comply. If they promote trustworthiness, none of the common people will dare to be deceitful. If so, the common people will come to him from all corners of the country, with their babies strapped on the backs. What need is there for those at the top to learn farming?"

13·5　子曰："诵《诗》三百，授之以政，不达；使于四方，不能专对；虽多，亦奚以为？"

【今译】

夫子说："《诗经》三百篇能背诵，交给他政事，却不能处理；派他出使外国，不能独立地应对；背得虽多，又做什么用呢?"

The Master said, "If a man who is able to recite the three hundred poems in *The Book of Songs* is not competent at government when given a post, or cannot exercise his own initiative when sent to foreign states, what use is it for him to recite so many poems?"

13·6　子曰:"其身正,不令而行;其身不正,虽令不从。"

【今译】

夫子说:"自身品行端正,即使不发布命令,老百姓也会去做;自身品行不正,即使发布命令,老百姓也不会服从。"

【英译】

The Master said, "If a man is correct in his own person, then there will be obedience without orders being given; but if he is not correct in his own person, there will be no obedience even though orders are given."

13·7　子曰:"鲁卫之政,兄弟也。"

【今译】

夫子说:"鲁和卫两国的政事,就像兄弟(的政事)一样。"

【英译】

The Master said, "In terms of government, the states of Lu and Wei are like brothers."

13·8　子谓卫公子荆，"善居室。始有，曰：'苟合矣。'少有，曰：'苟完矣。'富有，曰：'苟美矣。'"

【今译】

夫子谈到卫国的公子荆时说："他善于持家。刚开始有一点，他说：'几乎够了。'稍为多一点时，他说：'几乎完备了。'更多一点时，他说：'几乎完美了'。"

【英译】

Speaking of Childe Jing of Wei, the Master said, "He knows well about the economy of the family. When there was just a little in the house, he would say, 'That's pretty good indeed.' When there was a little more, he would say, 'That's enough indeed.' And when there was plenty, he would say, 'That's perfect indeed.'"

13·9　子适卫，冉有仆。子曰："庶矣哉！"
冉有曰："既庶矣，又何加焉?"曰："富之。"
曰："既富矣，又何加焉?"曰："教之。"

【今译】

夫子到卫国，冉有为他驾车。夫子说："人口真多呀！"冉有说："人口已经多了，还要做什么呢?"夫子说："使他们富起来。"冉有说："富了以后，还要做什么呢?"夫子说："对他们进行教化。"

【英译】

When the Master went to the state of Wei, Ran You drove for him. The Master said, "What a teeming population!"

"When the population is already teeming, what can be done further?" demanded Ran You.

"Enrich them." replied the Master.

"When they have become rich, what can be done further?"

"Educate them." said the Master.

13·10 子曰："苟有用我者，期月①而已可也，三年有成。"

【注释】

①期月：一个月。期：稘，周年，也写作"朞"，误读成"其月"，校书者改"其"为"期"，遂衍出一"月"字。

【今译】

夫子说："如果有人用我治理国家，一年停止就可以，三年就会有大成。"

【英译】

The Master said, "If anyone employs me to govern the state, in one year's time a difference can be made, and in three years' time, great results can be achieved."

13·11　子曰："'善人为邦百年，亦可以胜残去杀矣。'诚哉是言也！"

【今译】

夫子说："'善人治理国家一百年，也可以消除残暴与杀戮了。'这话真对啊！"

【英译】

The Master said, "If a state is governed by a good man for a hundred years, cruelty and killings can well be eliminated. How true the saying is!"

13·12　子曰："如有王①者，必世②而后仁。"

【注释】

①王（wàng）：以仁义取天下。
②世：三十年为一世。

【今译】

夫子说："即使有王者兴起，也需要一世的时间才能实现仁政。"

【英译】

The Master said, "Even with a good king, it would still require an entire generation for benevolence to prevail."

13·13　子曰："苟正其身矣，于从政乎何有？不能正其身，如正人何？"

【今译】

夫子说："如果端正了自身，管理政事还有什么难呢？如果不能端正自身，如何能端正别人呢？"

【英译】

The Master said, "If one makes himself upright, what difficulty will he have in governance? If he cannot make himself upright, how can he make others upright?"

13·14　冉子退朝。子曰："何晏也？"对曰："有政。"子曰："其事也？如有政，虽不吾以，吾其与闻之。"

【今译】

冉求退朝回来，夫子说："为什么回来得这么晚呀？"冉求说："有政事。"夫子说："只是一般的事务吧？如果有政事，虽然不用我了，我也会知道的。"

【英译】

Ranzi returned from court. The Master said, "Why so late?"

"There were affairs of state to attend to."

The Master said, "They could only have been routine matters. Were they affairs of state, I would have heard about them, even though I am no longer in office."

13·15　定公问："一言而〔可以〕兴邦，有诸？"

孔子对曰："言不可以若是。其几也。人之言曰：'为君难，为臣不易。'如知为君之难也，不几乎一言而兴邦乎？"

曰："一言而丧邦，有诸？"

孔子对曰："言不可以若是。其几也。人之言曰：'予无乐乎为君，唯其言而莫予违也。'如其善而莫之违也，不亦善乎？如不善而莫之违也，不几乎一言而丧邦乎？"

【今译】

鲁定公问："一句话就使国家兴盛，有这样的话吗？"孔子答道："话语不能如此绝对，但很接近。有人说：'做君难，做臣不易。'如果理解了做君很难，这不近乎于一句话使国家兴盛吗？"鲁定公又问："一句话使国家衰亡，有这样的话吗？"孔子回答说："话语不能如此绝对，但很接近。有人说：'我不乐于做君主，只乐于我说的话没有人敢违抗。'如果说得对而没有人违抗，不也好事吗？如果说得不对而没有人违抗，那不就近乎于一句话使国家衰亡吗？"

【英译】

Duke Ding asked, "Is there such a thing as a single saying makes a state prosper?"

Confucius answered, "It cannot be said so absolutely, but it is almost so. There is a saying which goes: 'It is not easy to be a Lord, nor is it easy to be a Minister.' If the Lord realizes how difficult his role is, then is that not almost a case of a single saying making a state prosper?"

Duke Ding asked, "Is there such a thing as a single saying ruins a state?"

Confucius answered, "It cannot be said so absolutely, but it is almost so. There is a saying which goes: 'I do not at all enjoy being a Lord, except for that no one dare disobey me.' If what he says is right, isn't it good that no one disobeys him? But if what he says is wrong and no one dares to disobey him, isn't it almost a case of a single saying ruining a state?"

【辨正】

王若虚《论语辨惑》："定公问'一言而可以致丧'者，子曰'言不可以若是，其几也。'几，近也。即下文'不几乎'之'几'耳。三字自为一句，一言得失，何遽至于兴丧，然亦有近之者。此意甚明，无可疑。"

13·16　叶公问政。子曰："近者说，远者来。"

【今译】

叶公问怎样处理政事。夫子说："（使）近处的人高兴，远处的人来归附。"

【英译】

The Governor of She asked about government. The Master said, "Make the local people happy, and win over those who are far away."

13·17 子夏为莒父宰，问政。子曰："无欲速，无见小利。欲速，则不达；见小利，则大事不成。"

【今译】

子夏做莒父的总管，问夫子怎样处理政事。夫子说："不要求快，不要贪求小利。求快反而达不到目的，贪求小利就做不成大事。"

【英译】

When Zixia was steward of Jufu and asked about government, the Master said, "Do not make haste. Do not covet petty gains. More haste, less speed. Coveting petty gains will mean failure in great accomplishments."

13·18 叶公语孔子曰："吾党有直躬者，其父攘羊，而子证之。"孔子曰："吾党之直者异于是：父为子隐，子为父隐。直在其中矣。"

【今译】

叶公告诉孔子说："我的家乡有个正直的人，他的父亲偷了人家的羊，他告发了父亲。"孔子说："我家乡的正直的人和你讲的正直人不一样：父亲为儿子隐瞒，儿子为父亲隐瞒。正直就在其中了。"

【英译】

The Governor of She said to Confucius, "In my village there is a man of integrity. He denounced his father for stealing a sheep."

Confucius answered, "In my village, men of integrity do things differently. A father covers up for his son, and a son covers up for his father. In such behavior is integrity to be found as a matter of course."

【辨正】

《汉书·宣帝纪》："夏五月，诏曰：'父子之亲，夫妇之道，天性也。虽有患祸，犹蒙死而存之，诚爱结于心，仁厚之至也，岂能违之哉！自今，子首匿父母、妻匿夫、孙匿大父母，皆勿坐。其父母匿子、夫匿妻、大父母匿孙，罪殊死，皆上请廷尉以闻。'"

白平《杨伯峻〈论语译注〉商榷》："攘羊之类的事情不体面，'隐'的原因就是'知耻'，就是对家族声誉的维护，所谓'家丑不可外扬'。从'隐'的动因来看，它还是包含着一定的积极意义的。子女对父母的过失要'隐'，虽然有碍公理，但却是事理人情的自然趋向，在任何社会环境下，要求人们做到大义小义都'灭亲'，事事处处都'存天理而灭人欲'，这显然有点不切实际。尤其是在'小过'的范畴内，更有通过'法治'解决问题和通过'情治'解决问题的区别。

"儒家主张为父母'隐'过，但并不主张对父母之过视而不见，子女对父母之过有'谏'的责任。如果子女平时能对父母之过不失其谏，便可以降低父母之过的频率和程度，不至于小过酿成大过。父亲攘羊，平时必有贪利的不当表现，当儿子的应当谏阻。攘羊的事实已经形成，当儿子的还可以再谏，哪怕谏到'父母怒，不说，而挞之流血'的地步，如果能达到妥善处理的结果，也总比告发出来要好。

"告发父亲攘羊，这种正直无疑是一种偏激而简单的正直。'父为子隐，子为父隐'的做法貌似不直，但如果纳入儒家的思想体系中，确实有'直在其中'的道理可言。"

13·19　樊迟问仁。子曰："居处恭，执事敬，与人忠。虽之夷狄，不可弃也。"

【今译】

樊迟问怎样是仁。夫子说："居家恭敬规矩，办事严肃认真，待人忠实诚恳。即使到了夷狄，（这些）也不可背弃。"

【英译】

Fan Chi asked about benevolence. The Master said, "Be courteous in everyday life, conscientious at work and faithful to others. These are qualities that cannot be forsaken, even if you go and live among the barbarians."

13·20　子贡问曰："何如斯可谓之士①矣？"

子曰："行己有耻，使于四方，不辱君命，可谓士矣。"

曰："敢问其次。"曰："宗族称孝焉，乡党称弟焉。"

曰："敢问其次。"曰："言必信，行必果②，硁硁③然小人哉！——抑亦可以为次矣。"

曰："今之从政者何如？"子曰："噫！斗筲之人④，何足算也？"

【注释】

①士：士在周代贵族中位于最低层。此后，士成为古代社会知识分子的通称。

②果：果断，坚决。

③硁（kēng）硁：象声词，敲击石头的声音。这里指固执

的样子。

④斗筲（shāo）之人：比喻器量狭小的人。筲：竹器，容一斗二升。

【今译】

子贡问道："怎样才可以叫做士？"

夫子说："自己在做事时有知耻之心，出使外国各方，能够完成君主交付的使命，可以叫做士。"

子贡说："请问次一等的呢？"

夫子说："宗族中的人称赞他孝顺父母，乡党称赞他敬兄爱弟。"

子贡又问："请问再次一等的呢？"

夫子说："说到一定做到，做事一定坚持到底，不问是非地固执己见，那是小人啊。但也可以说是再次一等的士了。"

子贡说："现在的执政者，您看怎么样？"

夫子说："唉！这些器量狭小的人，哪里能数得上呢？"

【英译】

Zigong asked, "What should a scholar do before he deserves the title?"

The Master said, "He should have a sense of shame in his conduct and, when sent abroad, accomplishes his mission, then he can be called a scholar."

"May I ask about the grade below?"

"Someone who is praised by his clan for being a good son and by his fellow villagers for being a respectful young man."

"And the next?"

"A man who insists on keeping his word and seeing his actions through to the end can, perhaps, qualify to come next, even though he is stubbornly petty."

"What about those engaged in government today?" Zigong asked finally.

"Oh, they are so narrow-minded and of such limited capacity that they are unworthy to be taken into account," said the Master.

13·21　子曰："不得中行①而与之，必也狂狷②乎！狂者进取，狷者有所不为也。"

【注释】

①中行：行为合乎中庸。

②狷（juàn）：拘谨，有所不为。

【今译】

夫子说："找不到奉行中庸之道的人交往，必得交往，就与狂者、狷者吧。狂者敢作敢为，狷者有些事是不肯干的。"

【英译】

The Master said, "Failing to find moderate men for associates, one should, if there is no alternative, turn to the radical and the over-scrupulous. The former are enterprising, while the latter are highly principled as to what they cannot do."

13·22　子曰："南人有言曰：'人而无恒，不可以作巫医。'善夫！"

"不恒其德，或承之羞。"子曰："不占而已矣。"

【今译】

　　夫子说："南方人有句话说：'人如果做事没有恒心，不能当巫医。'这句话说得真好啊！""人不能持之以恒，常会遭受耻辱。"夫子说："（这句话是说，没有恒心的人）用不着去占卦了。"

【英译】

The Master said, "There is a saying among the southerners: 'A person who lacks constancy will not make a healer.' How true that is!" "A man who cannot persevere will often suffer disgrace." The Master commented, "The import of the saying is simply that for someone like that, there is no point in consulting the oracle."

13·23　子曰："君子和而不同，小人同而不和。"

【今译】

　　夫子说："君子讲求和谐而与人不同，小人讲求完全一致而不追求和谐。"

【英译】

The Master said, "A gentleman seeks harmony without seeking identical views whereas the petty man seeks identical views but not true harmony."

13·24　子贡问曰："乡人皆好之，何如?"子曰："未可也。"

"乡人皆恶之，何如?"子曰："未可也；不如乡人之善者好之，其不善者恶之。"

【今译】

子贡问："全乡人都喜欢他，怎么样?"夫子说："不行。"子贡又问："全乡人都讨厌他，怎么样?"夫子说："不行。不如全乡的好人都喜欢他，全乡的坏人都厌恶他。"

【英译】

Zigong asked, "What do you think of a person who is liked by everyone in the village?"

The Master said, "That won't do."

"What do you think of a person who is disliked by everyone in the village?"

"That won't do, either! It would be better to be liked by all the good people and disliked by all the bad people in his village."

13·25　子曰："君子易事而难说也。说之不以道，不说也；及其使人也，器之。小人难事而易说也。说之虽不以道，说也；及其使人也，求备焉。"

【今译】

夫子说："君子容易事奉，却难以取悦。不按正道取悦他，他不会高兴；等他用人的时候，会如使用器皿一样，用其所长；小人难以事奉，却容易取悦。不按正道取悦他，他也会高兴；等他用人的时候，却希望人各方面都完美。"

The Master said, "A gentleman is easy to serve but hard to please. He will not be pleased unless you try in the right way, but when it comes to employing his men, he will do what accords with their capacity. The petty man is hard to serve but easy to please. He will be pleased even if one goes against the right way, and when he employs his men, he expects them to be perfect."

13·26　子曰:"君子泰而不骄,小人骄而不泰。"

【今译】

夫子说:"君子安静坦然而不傲慢无礼,小人傲慢无礼而不安静坦然。"

【英译】

The Master said, "The gentleman is composed but not arrogant, while the petty man is just the opposite."

13·27　子曰:"刚、毅、木、讷近仁。"

【今译】

夫子说:"刚强、果敢、朴实、谨慎,这四种品德接近于仁。"

【英译】

The Master said, "Being firm, resolute, simple and slow in speech makes one almost a benevolent man."

13·28 子路问曰："何如斯可谓之士矣?"子曰："切切偲偲①，怡怡②如也，可谓士矣。朋友切切偲偲，兄弟怡怡。"

【注释】

①偲（sī）偲：勉励、督促、诚恳的样子。

②怡（yí）怡：和气、亲切、顺从的样子。

【今译】

子路问："怎样才可以称为士呢?"夫子说："互助督促勉励，相处和和气气，可以算是士了。朋友之间互相督促勉励，兄弟之间相处和和气气。"

【英译】

Zilu asked, "What should a man do before he deserves to be called a Scholar?"

The Master said, "One who is exacting and cordial toward others can be called a Scholar—exacting toward his friends and cordial toward his brothers."

13·29 子曰："善人教民七年，亦可以即戎矣。"

【今译】

夫子说："善人教练百姓七年，也可以叫他们当兵打仗了。"

【英译】

The Master said, "The common people will be ready to take up arms after being taught for seven years even by a good man."

13·30　子曰："以不教民战，是谓弃之。"

【今译】

夫子说："用未经训练的百姓去打仗，这就是抛弃他们。"

【英译】

The Master said, "To send people to war without giving them proper training is to discard them."

宪问第十四

14·1　宪问耻。子曰："邦有道，谷；邦无道，谷，耻也。"

"克、伐、怨、欲不行焉，可以为仁矣?"子曰："可以为难矣，仁则吾不知也。"

【今译】

原宪问夫子什么是耻辱。夫子说："国家政治清明，就做官拿俸禄；国家政治黑暗，还做官拿俸禄，这就是耻辱。"原宪又问："好胜、自夸、怨恨、贪欲都戒掉了，这样可以算做到仁了吧?"夫子说："可以说难能可贵了，但至于是不是做到了仁，我不知道。"

【英译】

Xian asked about shame. The Master said, "It is alright to hold office when good government prevails in a state, yet it is shame to hold office when ill government prevails."

"Can a man be considered 'benevolent' if he has abstained from loving superiority, boasting, grudging and being covetous?"

The Master said, "It may be estimable, but whether it is benevolent, I do not know."

14·2 子曰："士而怀居，不足以为士矣。"

【今译】

夫子说："做士如果留恋家庭的安逸生活，就不配做士了。"

【英译】

The Master said, "A scholar is not a qualified one if he indulges in domestic comfort."

14·3 子曰："邦有道，危言危行；邦无道，危行言孙。"

【今译】

夫子说："国家政治清明，应该言正、行正；国家政治昏乱，行为还要正直，但说话要谦逊谨慎。"

【英译】

The Master said, "When good government prevails in a state, act in an upright way and speak boldly; when ill government prevails in a state, act in an upright way but speak with caution."

14·4 子曰："有德者必有言，有言者不必有德。仁者必有勇，勇者不必有仁。"

【今译】

夫子说："有道德的人，一定有言论，有言论的人不一定有道德。仁人一定勇敢，勇敢的人不一定都有仁德。"

The Master said, "A virtuous man is sure to have his famous sayings, but a man who has his famous sayings is not necessarily virtuous. A benevolent man is sure to courageous, but a courageous man is not necessarily benevolent."

14·5 南宫适问于孔子曰："羿善射，奡①荡舟②，俱不得其死然。禹稷③躬稼而有天下。"夫子不答。

南宫适出，子曰："君子哉若④人！尚德哉若人！"

【注释】

①奡（ào）：传说中寒浞的儿子，后来为夏少康所杀。

②荡舟：摇船，以舟师冲杀。传说中奡力大，善于水战。

③禹：夏朝开国之君，善于治水，注重发展农业。稷：传说是周朝的祖先，又为谷神，教民种植庄稼。

④若：这个。

【今译】

南宫适问孔子："羿善于射箭，奡善于水战，最后都不得好死。禹和稷都亲自种植庄稼，却得到了天下。"夫子没有回答，南宫适出去后，夫子说："这个人真是个君子啊！这个人真崇尚道德啊！"

【英译】

Nangong Kuo asked Confucius, "Yi was an excellent archer and Ao was skilled in water battles, yet neither of them met a natural death. Both Yu and Ji, on the other hand, won their empires while farming the land. (Why did these things happen？）" The Master made no reply.

After Nangong Kuo had left, the Master commented, "How gentlemanly that man is! How reverent towards virtue that man is!"

14·6 子曰："君子而不仁者有矣夫，未有小人而仁者也。"

【今译】

夫子说："君子中没有仁德的人是有的，小人中有仁德的人却没有。"

【英译】

The Master said, "There are gentlemen who are not benevolent, but there are no petty men who are benevolent."

14·7 子曰："爱之，能勿劳乎? 忠焉，能勿诲乎?"

【今译】

夫子说："爱他，能不（为他）担心吗? 忠于他，能不（为他）打算吗?"

【英译】

The Master said, "Could you love someone without worrying about him? Could you be devoted to someone without considering for him?"

"劳"与"诲"对举，置于"勿"后，应为动词，而不是"勤""苦"之类的形容词。"劳"这一动作是"施爱者"发出的，若把"劳"解作"使之劳"，"劳"就成"受爱者"的行为了。程树德《论语集释》："刘氏《正义》'劳当训忧'。《淮南·精神训》'竭力而劳万民'，《泛论训》'以劳天下之民'，高诱《注》并云：'劳，忧也。'正此处确诂。"

程树德《论语集释》里说："《孟子》曰'教人以善谓之忠'，即此处忠字注脚。"为讲通这一句而去寻"忠"字更宽泛的定义，其实不必。可参阅《论语·学而》"为人谋而不忠乎"句里的"忠"字，而"诲"字也正是"谋"。李零《丧家狗：我读〈论语〉》："战国文字，谋字的写法，最常见，是从心从母，相当悔（如中山王鼎和郭店楚简）。《说文·言部》，谋字的古文写法，也是从口从母，相当诲。"吴大澂古籀补："古谋字从言从每，与许书诲字相类，疑古文谋诲为一字。《说命》'朝夕纳诲'当读为'纳谋'。"

14·8　子曰："为命①，裨谌②草创之，世叔讨论之，行人子羽修饰之，东里子产润色之。"

【注释】

①命：指国家的政令。
②裨谌（pí chén）：人名，郑国的大夫。

【今译】

夫子说："（郑国）制定外交的文书，都是由（大夫）裨谌草拟初稿，由世叔审阅，外交官子羽加以修饰，东里子产润色。"

The Master said, "In producing a diplomatic document, Pi Chen would first write the draft, Shi Shu would examine and review its content, Zi Yu, the master of protocol, would revise it and Zi Chan of Dong Li would give the finishing touches.

14·9 或问子产。子曰："惠人也。"
问子西。曰："彼哉！彼哉！"
问管仲。曰："（仁）人也。夺伯氏骈邑三百，饭疏食，没齿无怨言。"

【今译】

有人问子产是个怎样的人。夫子说："是个施恩的人。"又问子西。夫子说："他呀！他呀！"又问管仲。夫子说："他是个有仁德的人，他剥夺伯氏的骈邑三百家，伯氏终生食粗饭，直到老死没有怨言。"

【英译】

When asked about Zichan, the Master said, "He was a man beneficial to the people." When asked about Zixi, the Master said, "Oh, that man! Oh, that man!" When asked about Guan Zhong, the Master said, "He was a benevolent man. He took three hundred households from the fief of the Bo family in the city of Pian and Bo lived on coarse grain for the rest of his life, yet the latter never uttered a single word of complaint."

14·10 子曰:"贫而无怨难,富而无骄易。"

【今译】

夫子说:"贫穷而能够没有怨恨,很难;富裕而不傲慢,容易。"

【英译】

The Master said, "It is difficult to be poor without making complaints, whereas it is easy to be rich without arrogance."

14·11 子曰:"孟公绰为赵魏老则优,不可以为滕、薛大夫。"

【今译】

夫子说:"孟公绰做晋国赵氏、魏氏地位最高的家臣,绰绰有余,但不能做滕、薛(这类小国)的大夫。"

【英译】

The Master said, "Meng Gongchuo would be more than adequate serving as a steward of the Zhao or Wei family, but he would not be suitable to serve as a minister even in a small state like Teng or Xue."

【辨正】

为何孟公绰不宜任小国的大夫呢?朱熹《论语集注》:"大家势重,而无诸侯之事;家老望尊,而无官守之责。"

14·12　子路问成人。子曰:"若臧武仲之知,公绰之不欲,卞庄子之勇,冉求之艺,文之以礼乐,亦可以为成人矣。"曰:"今之成人者何必然?见利思义,见危授命,久要不忘平生之言,亦可以为成人矣。"

【今译】

子路问怎样做才是一个德行完备的人。夫子说:"像臧武仲那样智慧,孟公绰那样克制,卞庄子那样勇敢,冉求那样多才多艺,再用礼乐加以修饰,也就可以算德行完备的人了。"夫子又说:"现在的完人何必一定要这样呢?只要见到财利想到道义,遇到危难能献出生命,长久交往不忘旧日的诺言,也可以算德行完备的人了。"

【英译】

Zilu asked about how to be an accomplished man.

The Master said, "A man can be considered accomplished if he is as wise as Zang Wuzhong, as free from desires as Meng Gongchuo, as courageous as Zhuangzi of Bian and as versatile as Ran Qiu, and is further refined by the rites and music." "Yet," added the Master, "an accompoished man today does not have to possess all those merits. He will be accomplished all the same so long as he considers justice before a gain, is ready to give his life at a critical moment, and does not forget his promises he made long ago."

14·13 子问公叔文子于公明贾曰：“信乎，夫子不言，不笑，不取乎？”

公明贾对曰：“以告者过也。夫子时然后言，人不厌其言；乐然后笑，人不厌其笑；义然后取，人不厌其取。”

子曰：“其然？岂其然乎？”

【今译】

夫子向公明贾问到公叔文子，说：“先生他不说、不笑、不取钱财，是真的吗？”公明贾回答道：“是传话的人说错了。先生该说时才说，别人觉得他话少；快乐时才笑，别人觉得他笑少；认为合礼时才取，别人觉得他取得少。”夫子说：“是那样么？难道真是那样吗？”

【英译】

The Master asked Gongming Jia about Gongshu Wenzi, "Is it true that your master never spoke, never laughed and never took anything from others?"

Gongming Jia answered, "Whoever told you that got it entirely wrong. My master spoke only when it was necessary for him to do so. So, people never grew tired of his speaking. He laughed only when he was happy. So, people never grew tired of his laughing. He took only what was his due. So, people never grew tired of his taking."

The Master said, "Is that so? Is it really so?"

14·14　子曰："臧武仲以防求为后于鲁，虽曰不要①君，吾不信也。"

【注释】

①要（yāo）：胁迫，要挟。

【今译】

夫子说："臧武仲请求鲁君立其子弟为鲁国卿大夫他才离开防邑，即使说他没要挟鲁君，我也不相信。"

【英译】

The Master said, "Zang Wuzhong pleaded with the Duke of Lu to appoint his successors to be ministers of Lu so that he could leave his fief of Fang. Should it be said that he was not coerving his lord, I would not believe it."

14·15　子曰："晋文公谲①而不正，齐桓公正而不谲。"

【注释】

①谲（jué）：欺诈，玩弄权术。

【今译】

夫子说："晋文公诡诈而不正派，齐桓公正派而不诡诈。"

【英译】

The Master said, "Duke Wen of Jin was crafty and not upright. Duke Huan of Qi, on the other hand, was upright and not crafty."

14·16　子路曰："桓公杀公子纠，召忽死之，管仲不死。"曰："未仁乎?"子曰："桓公九合诸侯，不以兵车，管仲之力也。如其仁，如其仁。"

【今译】

子路说："齐桓公杀了公子纠，召忽自杀殉节，但管仲却没有自杀。管仲不能算是仁人吧?"夫子说："桓公多次召集各诸侯国盟会，不用武力，都是管仲的力量啊。这就是他的仁德，这就是他的仁德。"

【英译】

Zilu said, "When Duck Huan had Childe Jiu killed, Zhao Hu died for Jiu but Guan Zhong failed to do so." He added, "In that case, did he fall short of benevolence?" The Master said, "It was due to Guan Zhong that Duke Huan was able, without resorting to armed forces, to assemble the feudal lords many times. Such was his benevolence. Such was his benevolence."

14·17　子贡曰："管仲非仁者与? 桓公杀公子纠，不能死，又相之。"子曰："管仲相桓公，霸诸侯，一匡天下，民到于今受其赐。微管仲，吾其被发左衽①矣。岂若匹夫匹妇之为谅②也，自经③于沟渎而莫之知也。"

【注释】

①其被发左衽（rèn）：其：大概。被：通"披"。衽：衣襟。"被发左衽"是当时的夷狄之俗。

②谅：遵守信用。这里指小节小信。

③自经：自缢，上吊自杀。

【今译】

子贡问："管仲不是仁人吗？桓公杀了公子纠，他不能为公子纠殉死，反而做了齐桓公的宰相。"夫子说："管仲辅佐桓公，称霸诸侯，匡正了天下，老百姓到了今天还享受着他带来的好处。如果没有管仲，我大概要披散着头发，衣襟向左开了。（他）哪能像普通百姓那样恪守小节，自杀在沟渠里，而没有人知道啊。"

【英译】

Zigong said, "Wasn't Guan Zhong a man of benevolence? He did not die for his lord Jiu who was killed by Duke Huan, and lived to be the Duke's prime minister."

The Master said, "Guan Zhong, acting as the prime minister, assisted Duke Huan in gaining dominance over the feudal lords and bringing order to all the states in the Empire. To this day, the common people still enjoy the benefits of his contribution. Had it not been for Guan Zhong, I might well be wearing my hair down and folding my robes to the left. Surely he had not the petty faithfulness of the common people who, without being well-known, commit suicide in a ditch."

【辨正】

刘向《说苑》："子路问于孔子曰：'昔者管仲欲立公子纠而不能，召忽死之，管仲不死，是无仁也。'孔子曰：'召忽者，人臣之材。不死则三军之虏也，死之则名闻于天下矣，何为不死哉？管子者，天子之佐、诸侯之相也。死之则不免于沟渎之中，不死则功复用于天下，夫何为死之哉？'"

14·18 公叔文子之臣大夫僎①与文子同升诸公②。子闻之，曰："可以为'文'矣。"

【注释】

①僎（zhuàn）：公叔文子的家臣。

②升诸公：这是说僎由家臣升为大夫，与公叔文子同位。公：公室。

【今译】

公叔文子的家臣僎与文子一道晋升为卫国的大夫。夫子知道了这件事以后说："（他死后）可以给他'文'的谥号了。"

【英译】

Zhuan, the steward of Gongshu Wenzi, was promoted to high office in the state, serving side by side with Gongshu Wenzi. On hearing of this, the Master commented, "Gongshu Wenzi deserved to be accorded the posthumous title 'Wen'."

14·19 子言卫灵公之无道也，康子曰："夫如是，奚而不丧？"孔子曰："仲叔圉治宾客，祝鮀治宗庙，王孙贾治军旅。夫如是，奚其丧？"

【今译】

夫子讲到卫灵公的无道，季康子说："既然如此，为什么他却没有败亡呢？"孔子说："因为他有仲叔圉接待宾客，祝鮀管理宗庙祭祀，王孙贾统率军队，像这样，怎么会败亡呢？"

The Master was speaking of the immorality of Duke Ling of Wei, Ji Kangzi asked, "If that was the case, why did he not lose his state?"

Confucius said, "With Zhongshu Yu in charge of diplomatic affairs, Zhu Tuo managing the ancestral temple and Wangsun Jia commanding the army, how could he lose his state?"

【辨正】

王肃《孔子家语·贤君》："哀公问于孔子曰：'当今之君，孰为最贤？'孔子对曰：'丘未之见也，抑有卫灵公乎？'公曰：'吾闻其闺门之内无别，而子次之贤，何也？'孔子曰：'臣语其朝廷行事，不论其私家之际也。'公曰：'其事何如？'孔子对曰：'灵公之弟曰公子渠牟，其智足以治千乘，其信足以守之，灵公爱而任之。又有士曰林国者，见贤必进之，而退与分其禄，是以灵公无游放之士。灵公贤而尊之。又有士曰庆足者，卫国有大事，则必起而治之；国无事，则退而容贤。灵公悦而敬之。又有大夫史鳅，以道去卫，而灵公郊舍三日，琴瑟不御，必待史鳅之入，而后敢入。臣以此取之，虽次之贤，不亦可乎。'"

14·20　子曰："其言之不怍①，则为之也难。"

【注释】

①怍（zuò）：惭愧。

【今译】

夫子说："一个人说起话来大言不惭，那么他实际做起来就很困难。"

The Master said, "He who talks big without feeling ashamed will find it difficult to put his words into practice."

14·21 陈成子弑简公。孔子沐浴而朝，告于哀公曰："陈恒弑其君，请讨之。"公曰："告夫三子。"

孔子曰："以吾从大夫之后，不敢不告也。君曰'告夫三子'者。"

之三子告，不可。孔子曰："以吾从大夫之后，不敢不告也。"

【今译】

陈成子杀了齐简公。孔子沐浴后去上朝，向鲁哀公报告说："陈恒把他的君主杀了，请出兵讨伐他。"哀公说："你去报告那三位大夫吧。"孔子说："因为我居大夫之位，所以不敢不来报告，君主却说'你去告诉那三位大夫吧'!"孔子去向那三位大夫报告，但他们都不同意派兵讨伐。孔子说："因为我居大夫之位，所以不敢不来报告!"

【英译】

Chen Chengzi killed Duke Jian of Qi. Confucius took a bath and went to court to report to Duke Ai, saying, "Chen Heng has slain his ruler. May I request that an army be sent to punish him?"

The Duke answered, "Report it to the three lords."

Confucius said, "I dared not conceal the incident simply because I was a minister, yet he told me to 'report it to the three lords'."

Confucius went and reported to the three lords, but they refused to take any action.

"I dared not to conceal the incident simply because I was a minister," said Confucius.

14·22　子路问事君。子曰："勿欺也，而①犯之。"

【注释】
①而：能。

【今译】
子路问怎样事奉君主。夫子说："不能欺骗他，但能犯颜直谏。"

【英译】
Zilu asked about the way to serve a ruler. The Master said, "Do not deceive him. Rather, tell him the truth even if it offends him."

14·23　子曰："君子上达，小人下达。"

【今译】
夫子说："君子追求知晓高层次的道理，小人追求明白低层次的道理。"

【英译】

The Master said, "A gentleman aims to reach upward（for lofty virtue）while the petty man aims to reach downward （for personal benefit）."

14·24　子曰:"古之学者为己,今之学者为人。"

【今译】

夫子说:"古代的人学习是为了提高自己,而现在的人学习是为了给别人看。"

【英译】

The Master said, "In ancient times, men learnt to improve themselves; men today learn to impress others."

14·25　蘧伯玉①使人于孔子。孔子与之坐而问焉,曰:"夫子何为?"对曰:"夫子欲寡其过而未能也。"
　　使者出,子曰:"使乎! 使乎!"

【注释】

①蘧(qú)伯玉:姓蘧,名瑗(yuàn),字伯玉,卫国大夫。孔子到卫国时曾住在他的家里。

【今译】

蘧伯玉派使者去拜访孔子。孔子与使者一同坐下,然后问道:"先生最近在做什么?"使者回答说:"先生想要减少自己的错误,但未能做到。"使者走了以后,夫子说:"好一位使者啊,好一位使者啊!"

Qu Boyu sent a messenger to Confucius. Confucius sat with him and asked, "What does your master do?" He answered, "My master seeks to reduce his errors but has not yet succeeded."

When the messenger had left, the Master commented, "What a messenger! What a messenger!"

14·26　子曰：“不在其位，不谋其政。”
曾子曰：“君子思不出其位。”

【今译】

夫子说：“不在那个职位上，就不要考虑那个职位上的事情。”曾子说：“君子考虑问题，不超越自己的职位。”

【英译】

The Master said, "He who does not hold a certain position shall not involve himself with its affairs."

Master Zeng commented，"A gentleman does not allow his thoughts to exceed his authority."

14·27　子曰：“君子耻其言而过其行。”

【今译】

夫子说：“君子认为言过其行是可耻的。”

【英译】

The Master said, "A gentleman considers it a disgrace to let his words outstrip his deeds."

【辨正】

由于连词"而"字的并列作用，"耻其言而过其行"容易被理解成"耻其言"与"过其行"两件事。朱熹《论语集注》里说："耻者，不敢尽之意。过者，欲有余之辞。"即代表了这种断成两截的解法。

针对朱熹这种解法，《论语集释》里辨析得非常清楚："圣人之言，恐不如此之迂曲也。且言不过行，有何可耻？行取得中，岂容过余？过中之行，君子不为，过犹不及，圣人之明论也。《注》文本因而字故为此说，本分言之，止是耻其言过于行。旧说君子言行相顾，若言过其行，谓有言而行不副，君子所耻。南轩曰："言过其行，则为无实之言，是可耻也。耻言之过行，则其笃行可知矣。"二论意同，必如此说义乃可通，"而"字盖"之"字之误。

钱穆《论语新解》里说："本章或作耻其言之过其行。今按：君子所耻，乃其言而过其行，即言之过其行也。不当分耻其言与过其行作两项解。"杨伯峻《论语译注》里说："而——用法同'之'，说详词诠。皇侃所据本，日本足利本，这一'而'字者作'之'字。"

此处"之"字用在主谓语结构之间，使"其言过其行"成为名词性词组，作"耻"字的宾语。应该清楚地指出"而"字乃"之"字之误，不应当模糊地说此处"而"字用法同"之"。

14·28　子曰："君子道者三，我无能焉：仁者不忧，知者不惑，勇者不惧。"子贡曰："夫子自道也。"

【今译】

夫子说："君子之道有三个方面，我都未能做到：仁德的人不忧愁，聪明的人不迷惑，勇敢的人不畏惧。"子贡说："这正是老师的自我写照啊！"

【英译】

The Master said, "The way a gentleman abides entails three qualities, none of which I have been able to accomplish: The benevolent is free from anxieties; the wise is free from doubts; the bold is free from fear." Zigong said, "What the Master said is in fact a description of himself."

【辨正】

"夫子自道也"的"夫子"不是呼语，不是子贡当着老师面，喊着"老师，您这是自我描述啊。""夫子"一旦离开句子去扮"呼语"角色，"自道"就没了主语。在结构上，"夫子"恐怕一身难兼二任，既当呼语，又当主语。子贡是对其他人说的："（这是）夫子说他自己啊！"子贡的意思是说，夫子"我无能焉"是谦辞，而"仁者不忧，知者不惑，勇者不惧"正可用来描述夫子。

"自道"不止是"自己说"，还是"说自己"。因此, 理雅各译"that is what you yourself say"，没有译全, 还必须加上"of oneself"：That is what our Master said of himself。

14·29　子贡方人。子曰："赐也贤乎哉？夫我则不暇。"

【今译】

子贡评论别人的短处。夫子说："赐啊，你就那么贤良吗？我就没有空闲去评论别人。"

Zigong was talking about the faults of others. The Master said, "Ci, are you so perfect yourself? For my part I have no time for such things."

14·30　子曰："不患人之不己知，患其不能也。"

【今译】

夫子说："不忧虑别人不知道自己，只担心自己没有能力。"

【英译】

The Master said, "Worry not about whether people appreciate you, but whether you are competent."

14·31　子曰："不逆诈，不亿不信，抑亦先觉者，是贤乎！"

【今译】

夫子说："不事先怀疑别人欺诈，也不猜测别人不诚实，却能事先觉察别人的欺诈和不诚实，这是贤人啊。"

【英译】

The Master said, "He who, without suspecting others of fraud or doubting other's credibility, is able to perceive them before they actually occur, is a truly sagacious man."

14·32 微生亩①谓孔子曰："丘何为是栖栖②者与？无乃为佞乎？"孔子曰："非敢为佞也，疾固③也。"

【注释】

①微生亩：姓微生，名亩，鲁国人。

②栖（xī）栖：忙碌不安、不安定的样子。

③疾：恨。固：顽固。

【今译】

微生亩对孔子说："孔丘你为什么这样栖栖遑遑？莫非你在花言巧语？"孔子说："不敢花言巧语，只是痛恨那些顽固不化的人。"

【英译】

Weisheng Mu said to Confucius, "（Kong）Qiu, why are you so restless? Don't you mean to show off your eloquence?"

"I dare not show off my eloquence," responded Confucius, "but I simply detest obstinant diehards."

14·33 子曰："骥不称其力，称其德也。"

【今译】

夫子说："千里马值得称赞的不是它的能力，而是它的品德。"

【英译】

The Master said, "A steed which covers a thousand *li* a day is praised for its virtue, not for its strength."

14 · 34　或曰："以德报怨，何如?"子曰："何以报德?
以直报怨，以德报德。"

【今译】

有人说："用恩德来报答怨恨怎么样?"夫子说："那用什
么来报答恩德呢? 应该是用正直来报答怨恨，用恩德来报答恩
德。"

【英译】

Someone asked, "What do you think of 'Requiting malice
with goodness'?"

The Master said, "What, then, do you requite goodness
with? 'Requite malice with righteousness, but requite goodness
with goodness.'"

14 · 35　子曰："莫我知也夫!"子贡曰："何为其莫知子
也?"子曰："不怨天，不尤人。下学而上达。知我者其天乎!"

【今译】

夫子说："没有人了解我啊!"子贡说："怎么没有人了解
您呢?"夫子说："我不埋怨天，也不责备人，下学礼乐而上达
天命，了解我的只有天吧!"

【英译】

The Master said, "Alas! It seems that no one understands
me."

Zigong said, "How is it that no one understands you?"

The Master said, "I bear no grudges against Heaven or

man. I learn downward the basics and reach upward to what is up above. If I am understood at all, it is, perhaps, by Heaven alone."

14·36 公伯寮愬子路于季孙。子服景伯以告，曰："夫子固有惑志。于公伯寮，吾力犹能肆诸市朝①。"

子曰："道之将行也与，命也；道之将废也与，命也。公伯寮其如命何!"

【注释】

①肆：指处以死刑后陈尸示众。市朝：被处死的罪犯中，自士以下的，陈尸于市集，自大夫以上的，陈尸于朝廷。

【今译】

公伯寮向季孙告发子路。子服景伯把这件事告诉给夫子，并且说："他老人家固然有些糊涂的想法，但对于公伯寮，我的力量还能够把他杀了，陈尸于市。"夫子说："道能够得到推行，是天命决定的；道不能得到推行，也是天命决定的。公伯寮能把天命怎么样呢？"

【英译】

Gongbo Liao spoke ill of Zilu to Jisun. Zifu Jingbo reported this to Confucius, saying, "My lord is certainly being led astray by Gongbo Liao, and I am still powerful enough to have him killed and his corpse exposed in the market."

The Master said, "It is destiny if my doctrine prevails; it is equally destiny if my doctrine falls into disuse. What can Gongbo Liao do in defiance of destiny?"

14·37　子曰："贤者辟世，其次辟地，其次辟色，其次辟言。"

子曰："作者七人矣。"

【今译】

夫子说："贤人躲避动荡的社会，次一等的人躲避讨厌的地方，再次一等的人躲避讨厌的脸色，又次一等的人躲避讨厌的言语。"夫子又说："这样做的已经有七个人了。"

【英译】

The Master said, "It is the wisest men who shun a troubled society; the less-wise shun troubled places; the still-less-wise shun troublesome looks; the yet-less-wise shun troublesome speeches."

The Master said, "There were seven men who accomplished these feats."

14·38　子路宿于石门。晨门曰："奚自？"子路曰："自孔氏。"曰："是知其不可而为之者与？"

【今译】

子路夜里住在石门，看门的人问："从哪里来？"子路说："从孔家来。"看门的人说："是那个知道做不到却偏要去做的人吗？"

【英译】

Zilu stayed for the night at the Stone Gate. The gatekeeper asked him, "Where are you from?"

Zilu answered, "From Confucius."

"Is that the man who persists in working towards a goal when he knows it is almost impossible to achieve?"

14·39　子击磬于卫，有荷蒉^①而过孔氏之门者，曰："有心哉，击磬乎！"既而曰："鄙哉！硁硁乎！莫己知也，斯己而已矣。深则厉^②，浅则揭^③。"

子曰："果^④哉！末之难矣^⑤。"

【注释】

①荷蒉（kuì）：肩背着草筐。

②深则厉：穿着衣服涉水过河。

③浅则揭：提起衣襟涉水过河。"深则厉，浅出揭"是《诗经·卫风·匏有苦叶》的诗句。

④果：诚，真。

⑤末：无。难：困难。

【今译】

夫子在卫国，有一次正在击磬，一位背草筐的人从门前走过，说："有心声啊，这磬击得！"

过了一会又说："（心地多）狭窄啊，磬声硁硁地。人不懂你，只有自己懂了。（就像涉水，）水深就穿着衣服趟，水浅就撩起衣服过。"

夫子说："果真这样，就不难了。"

【英译】

Once while he was in the state of Wei, the Master was playing the stone chimes when a man passed by and said, "The man playing the stone chimes seems to be deeply troubled in his mind." Presently, he added, "How narrow-minded this stubborn sound suggests. It seems that no one understands you, except you yourself. 'When the water is deep, go across by wading; when it is shallow, lift your hem and cross.'"

The Master said, "If it is really so, it will not be difficult at all."

【辨正】

俞樾《群经平议》："《淮南子·道应篇》'令不果往'，高诱注：'果，诚也。'果哉末之难矣，犹曰诚哉无难矣。盖如荷蒉者之言，随世以行己，视孔子所为，难易相去何啻天壤？故孔子闻其言而叹之，一若深喜其易者，而甘为其难之意自在言外。圣人辞意微婉，初非与之反唇也。"

14·40　子张曰："《书》云：'高宗①谅阴②，三年不言。'何谓也？"子曰："何必高宗，古之人皆然。君薨，百官总己以听于冢宰③三年。"

【注释】

①高宗：商王武宗。

②谅阴：古时天子守丧之称。

③冢宰：官名，相当于后世的宰相。

【今译】

子张说："《尚书》上说，'高宗住在墓庐（守丧），三年不谈政事。'这是什么意思？"夫子说："何必是高宗，古人都是这样。国君死了，朝廷百官都约束自己，听命于冢宰三年。"

【英译】

Zizhang asked, "*The Book of Documents* says, 'King Gaozong confined himself to his mourning hut, and for three years he did not attend to state affairs.'What does this mean?"

The Master said, "There is no need to mention King Gaozong as an example. People in ancient times did the same. When the lord died, all the officials would be under the command of the prime minister for three years."

14 · 41 子曰："上好礼，则民易使也。"

【今译】
夫子说："在上位的人喜好礼仪，那么百姓就容易役使。"

【英译】
The Master said, "When those in the upper position observe the rites, the common people will be easy to employ."

14 · 42 子路问君子。子曰："修己以敬。"
曰："如斯而已乎?"曰："修己以安人。"
曰："如斯而已乎?"曰："修己以安百姓。修己以安百姓，尧舜其犹病诸。"

【今译】
子路问什么叫君子。夫子说："修养自己，保持严肃恭敬的态度。"子路说："这样就够了吗?"夫子说："修养自己，使周围的人安乐。"子路说："这样就够了吗?"夫子说："修养自己，使所有百姓都安乐。修养自己使所有百姓都安乐，尧舜应该都担心没有做到呢。"

【英译】

Zilu asked about how to be a gentleman. The Master said, "He cultivates himself to be sincere."

"Is that all?" asked Zilu.

"He cultivates himself and thereby brings peace and happiness to his fellow men."

"Is that all?"

"He cultivates himself and thereby brings peace and happiness to the common people. This might be hard even for Yao or Shun to accomplish."

14·43 　原壤①夷俟②。子曰："幼而不孙弟③，长而无述焉，老而不死，是为贼。"以杖叩其胫。

【注释】

①原壤：鲁国人，孔子的旧友。

②夷俟（sì）：夷，指"箕踞"，即屁股坐地，双腿左右斜伸出去，又开成八字形，因像"簸箕"故称。古人认为，以这种姿势坐在地上是一种轻慢无礼的表现。俟：等待。

③孙弟：同"逊悌"。

【今译】

原壤又开双腿坐着等待夫子。夫子骂他说："年幼的时候，你不讲孝悌，长大了又没有什么可说的成就，老而不死，真是害人虫。"说着，用手杖敲敲他的小腿。

Yuan Rang sat waiting with his legs spread wide apart. The Master said, "You were defiant when young; you accomplished nothing when grown up; and you refuse to die when old. You are what I call a pest." With these words, the Master tapped him on the shin with his walking stick.

14·44 阙党①童子将命②。或问之曰："益者与?"子曰："吾见其居于位③也，见其与先生并行也。非求益者也，欲速成者也。"

【注释】

①阙党：即阙里，孔子家住的地方。
②将（jiāng）命：奉传主人之命。
③居于位：童子与长者同坐。

【今译】

阙里的一个童子，来向夫子传话。有人问夫子："这是求上进的人吗?"夫子说："我看见他坐在主人的位子上，又见他和长辈并肩而行。他不是求上进的人，是个急于求成的人。"

【英译】

Once in Quedang, a boy came to pass a message to the Master. When the boy left, someone asked about him, saying, "Is he one that is eager to make progress?" The Master said, "I have seen him take the seat of an adult and walk alongside his seniors. What interests him is not how to make progress but how to succeed quickly."

卫灵公第十五

15·1　卫灵公问陈^①于孔子。孔子对曰："俎豆^②之事，则尝闻之矣；军旅之事，未之学也。"明日遂行。

【注释】

①陈：同"阵"，布阵之法。

②俎（zǔ）豆：俎豆是古代祭祀时用以盛牲肉的器具。俎豆之事是指礼节仪式方面的事。

【今译】

卫灵公向孔子问军队列阵之法。孔子回答说："祭祀礼仪方面的事情，我听说过；用兵打仗的事，从来没有学过。"第二天，孔子便离开了卫国。

【英译】

Duke Ling of Wei asked Confucius about military tactics. Confucius answered, "I have heard something about the use of sacrificial vessels, but as to military affairs, I have never studied them." The next day he departed.

15·2　在陈绝粮，从者病，莫能兴①。子路愠见曰："君子亦有穷②乎?"子曰："君子固③穷，小人穷斯滥④矣。"

【注释】

①兴：起身。

②穷：绝境，走投无路的境地。

③固：坚定，坚守不渝。程子曰："固穷者，固守其穷。"

④滥：肆意妄为；漫无准则。

【今译】

（夫子一行）在陈国断了粮，随从的人都饿病了，起不来了。子路生气地去见夫子，问道："君子也有走投无路的时候吗?"夫子说："君子走投无路时能坚持；小人走投无路时就无所不为了。"

【英译】

In Chen when provisions ran out, the followers became too weak to get to their feet. Zilu, with resentment written over his face, came up to the Master and said, "Are there times when gentlemen are caught in such extreme straits?" The Master said, "In extreme straits, gentlemen will remain steadfast while petty men will throw out all restraints."

【辨正】

现代汉语里"穷"与"贫"同义，指"生活贫困，缺少钱财"。古汉语也有相近的含义："多有之者富，少有之者贫，至无有者穷。"（《荀子·大略》）但这一章里的"穷"，却不是财富多少，而是"穷达"之"穷"，指走投无路的困境。白话文翻译时不宜保留"穷"字而译作"君子也有穷得毫无办法的时候吗?"以免读者以为是"钱太少"。

孔子把君子与小人放在一起对照,走投无路时君子如何做,小人如何做。君子固而小人滥。可以看出"固"与"滥"相对,是句中用来描述主语的极重要的形容词,不能把"固"解作副词"当然"。

"滥"字《汉语大字典》里解释为"肆意妄为;漫无准则"。与"滥"相对,"固"字就是指君子在穷境中一如既往,坚守不渝。孔子在没有粮食,从者饿得起不来的时候,仍能"讲诵弦歌不衰",这就是"固"。

15·3 子曰:"赐也,女以予为多学而识之者与?"对曰:"然,非与?"曰:"非也,予一以贯之。"

【今译】

夫子(问子贡)说:"赐啊!你以为我是学得多而记住吗?"子贡答道:"是啊,难道不是这样吗?"夫子说:"不是的。我自始至终都贯穿一种思想。"

【英译】

The Master said, "Ci, do you think that I just learned more and memorized them?"

"Yes, I do. Is it not so?"

"No, I united all my learnings with one principle."

【辨正】

参见《里仁第四》第15章:"子曰:'参乎,吾道一以贯之。'曾子曰:'唯。'子出,门人问曰:'何谓也?'曾子曰:

'夫子之道，忠恕而已矣。'"

程树德《论语集释》："孔子以忠恕之道通天下之志，故无所不知，无所不能，非徒恃乎一己之多学而识也。忠恕者，絜矩也。絜矩者，格物也。物格则后知至，故无不知。由身以达乎家国天下，是一以贯之也。一以贯之，则天下之知皆我之知，天下之能皆我之能，何自多之有？"

15·4　子曰："由！知德者鲜矣。"

【今译】

夫子说："由啊！懂得德的人很少啊。"

【英译】

The Master said, "（Zhong）You, rare are those who understand virtue."

15·5　子曰："无为而治者，其舜也与？夫何为哉？恭己正南面而已矣。"

【今译】

夫子说："能够不作为而治理天下的人，大概只有舜吧？他做了些什么呢？只是庄严端正地坐在君位上罢了。"

【英译】

The Master said, "If there was a ruler who governed the state efficiently without exertion, it was, perhaps, Shun alone. What did he do? He just sat reverently on the throne facing south."

15·6　子张问行①。子曰"言忠信，行笃敬，虽蛮貊②之邦，行矣。言不忠信，行不笃敬，虽州里③，行乎哉？立则见其参④于前也，在舆则见其倚于衡⑤也，夫然后行。"子张书诸绅⑥。

【注释】

①行：行身。

②蛮貊（mò）：古人对少数民族的贬称，蛮在南方，貊在北方。

③州里：五家为邻，五邻为里，四里为族，五族为党，五党为州，二千五百家。州里指本乡本土。

④参：直立。

⑤倚：立。衡：车辕前面的横木。

⑥绅：贵族系在腰间的大带。

【今译】

子张问如何行身处世。夫子说："说话要忠信，行事要笃敬，即使到了蛮貊地区，也可以行得通。说话不忠信，行事不笃敬，就是在本乡本土，能行得通吗？站着，就看到忠信笃敬直立于面前，坐车，就看到它立于车辕的横木前，这样就可以行得通。"子张把这些话写在腰间的大带上。

【英译】

Zizhang asked how to conduct oneself. The Master said, "If you are faithful and truthful in what you say, and sincere and respectful in what you do, you can get on well with such conduct even in backward lands. But if you fail to do so, can you get on well even in your own neighborhood? When you stand, these words seem to be standing right before you, and when you are in a carriage, they seem to be standing right before the handle-bar. Then you will surely get on well everywhere you go."

Zizhang had these words written down on his sash.

15·7 子曰:"直哉史鱼! 邦有道,如矢;邦无道,如矢。君子哉蘧伯玉! 邦有道,则仕;邦无道,则可卷而怀之。"

【今译】

夫子说:"史鱼真是正直啊! 国家有道,他的言行像箭一样直;国家无道,他的言行也像箭一样直。蘧伯玉真是一位君子啊! 国家有道就出来做官,国家无道就辞官归隐,把自己的主张藏在心里。

【英译】

The Master said, "How straight Shi Yu was! When good government prevailed in the state he was as straight as an arrow, and when ill government prevailed in the state he remained the same. How gentlemanly Qu Boyu was! When good government prevailed in the state he took office, but when ill government prevailed in the state, he packed himself off and kept his talent close to his chest."

【辨正】

《孔子家语·困誓》:"卫蘧伯玉贤,而灵公不用;弥子瑕不肖,反任之。史鱼骤谏而不从。史鱼病将卒,命其子曰:'吾在卫朝不能进蘧伯玉,退弥子瑕,是吾为臣不能正君也。生而不能正君,则死无以成礼。我死,汝置尸牖下,于我毕矣。'其子从之。灵公吊焉，怪而问焉。其子以其父言告公，公愕然失容，曰：'是寡人之过也。'于是命之殡于客位，进蘧伯玉而用之，退弥子瑕而远之。孔子闻之，曰：'古之列谏之者，死则已矣，未有若史鱼死而尸谏，忠感其君者也，不可谓直乎?'"

15·8　子曰："可与言而不与之言，失人；不可与言而与之言，失言。知者不失人，亦不失言。"

【今译】

夫子说："可以同他谈的话，却不同他谈，这是待人不当；不可以同他谈的话，却同他谈，这就说话不当。有智慧的人既不会待人不当，又不会说话不当。"

【英译】

The Master said, "To fail to speak to a man you ought to is a wrong you did to the person. To speak to a man you ought not to is a wrong you did to the words. A wise man does not speak to the wrong person, nor does he speak the wrong words."

15·9　子曰："志士仁人，无求生以害仁，有杀身以成仁。"

【今译】

夫子说："志士仁人，不愿贪生怕死而损害仁，宁愿牺牲自己的性命来成就仁。"

【英译】

The Master said, "A man of ideals and benevolence will not

seek to stay alive at the expense of benevolence, but will readily give up his life for its sake."

15·10 子贡问为仁。子曰："工欲善其事，必先利其器。居是邦也，事其大夫之贤者，友其士之仁者。"

【今译】

子贡问怎样实行仁德。夫子说："做工的人想把事做好，必须首先使他的工具锋利。住在这个国家，就要事奉大夫中的那些贤者，与士人中的仁者交朋友。"

【英译】

Zigong asked about the practice of benevolence. The Master said, "A craftsman must first sharpen his tools if he wishes to get his work well done. So, when you live in a state, you should try to serve the most virtuous of the ministers and make friends with the most benevolent scholars."

15·11 颜渊问为邦。子曰："行夏之时，乘殷之辂①，服周之冕②，乐则《韶》、《舞》③。放④郑声⑤，远佞人。郑声淫，佞人殆⑥。"

【注释】

①辂（lù）：天子所乘的车。殷代的大车，木质而无饰，俭朴实用。

②周之冕：周代的礼帽。周代礼帽体制完备而华美。

③《韶》《舞》：即《韶》《武》。见《八佾第三》第25章："子谓《韶》，尽美矣，又尽善也。谓《武》，尽美矣，未尽善

也。"

④放：驱逐，禁绝。

⑤郑声：郑国民间音乐形式活泼，孔子认为是靡靡之音。

⑥殆：危险。

【今译】

颜渊问怎样治理国家。夫子说："用夏代的历法，乘殷代的车子，戴周代的礼帽，奏《韶》《舞》乐，禁绝郑国的乐曲，疏远能言善辩的人，郑国的乐曲浮靡不正派，佞人太危险。"

【英译】

Yan Yuan asked about the government of a state. The Master said, "Follow the calendar of the Xia, ride in the carriage of the Yin, and wear the ceremonial cap of the Zhou. As for music, adopt the *Shao* and the *Wu*. Proscribe the tunes of the State of Zheng and stay away from flatterers. The tunes of the State of Zheng are lascivious, and flatterers are dangerous."

15·12 子曰："人无远虑，必有近忧。"

【今译】

夫子说："人若没有长远的考虑，事到近前，必有忧患。"

【英译】

The Master said, "A man who gives no thought for the distant future is bound to be worried when it comes close at hand."

朱熹《论语集注》："苏氏曰：人之所履者，容足之外，皆为无用之地，而不可废也。故虑不在千里之外，则患在几席之下矣。"对此，《四书辨疑》辩驳得清楚："苏氏论地理远近，义有未安。君子以正心修身为本，近思约守，事来则应，未闻所虑必须长在千里外也。存心于千里之外，以备几席之间，咫尺之患，计亦疏矣。远，久远也。但凡作事不为将来久远之虑，必有日近倾败之忧也。"

"远""近"不是说空间距离，而是说时间，"人无远虑，必有近忧"就是要告诉人凡事要早作打算，否则，事到近前，必有忧患。

15·13　子曰："已矣乎！吾未见好德如好色者也。"

【今译】

夫子说："完了，我从来没有见像好色那样好德的人。"

【英译】

The Master said, "Alas! I have never met a man who loves virtue as much as he loves beauty."

15·14　子曰："臧文仲其窃位者与！知柳下惠之贤而不与立也。"

【今译】

夫子说："臧文仲是一个窃居官位的人吧！他知道柳下惠是个贤人，却不举荐他做官。"

The Master said, "Zang Wenzhong must be one who usurped his post! He knew the excellence of Liuxia Hui and yet would not recommend him to an official post."

15·15 子曰:"躬自厚而薄责于人,则远怨矣。"

【今译】

夫子说:"多要求自己而少要求他人,那就可以避免别人的怨恨了。"

【英译】

The Master said, "If you demand of yourself more and demand of others less, you will stay away from resentment."

【辨正】

徐干《中论修本篇》:"孔子之制《春秋》也,详内而略外,急己而宽人。故于鲁也,小恶必书;于众国也,大恶始笔。夫见人而不自见者谓之矇,闻人而不自闻者谓之聩,虑人而不自虑者谓之瞽。故明莫大乎自见,聪莫大乎自闻,睿莫大乎自虑。"

程树德《论语集释》反对释"厚"为"厚责",不无道理:"皇疏引蔡谟云:儒者之说,虽与义无违,而于名未安也。何者?以自厚为责己,文不辞矣。厚者,厚其德也,而人又若己所未能而责物以能,故人心不服。若自厚其德而不求多于人,则怨路塞,责己之美虽存乎中,然自厚之义不施于责也。"

15 · 16 　子曰："不曰'如之何，如之何'者，吾末如之何也已矣。"

【今译】

夫子说："不说'该怎么办？该怎么办？'的人，我对他真不知该怎么办了。"

【英译】

The Master said, "With those who never ask themselves, 'What should I do? What should I do?' I really don't know what I should do."

15 · 17 　子曰："群居终日，言不及义，好行小慧，难矣哉！"

【今译】

夫子说："整天聚在一起，说话不合义理，喜欢卖弄小聪明，这种人难有所成。"

【英译】

The Master said, "Staying with others all day long, talking about nothing concerning virtue, and indulging in showing off petty cleverness—such a person is not likely to get anywhere!"

15 · 18 　子曰："君子义以为质，礼以行之，孙以出之，信以成之。君子哉！"

【今译】

夫子说："君子（做事）以义为根本，依礼行事，用谦逊的语言表达，靠诚信完成它。这是君子啊!"

【英译】

The Master said, "The gentleman has morality as the essence, and performs it by observing the rites, speaks it out with modesty, and accomplishes it by trustworthiness. Such is a gentleman indeed!"

15·19　子曰:"君子病无能焉，不病人之不己知也。"

【今译】

夫子说:"君子只怕自己没有才能，不怕别人不了解自己。"

【英译】

The Master said, "The gentleman is troubled by his own lack of ability, not by the failure of others to appreciate him."

15·20　子曰:"君子疾没世而名不称焉。"

【今译】

夫子说:"君子担心去世以后没有留下为人称颂的名声。"

【英译】

The Master said, "The gentleman detests not leaving an exemplary reputation behind when he is gone."

15 · 21　子曰："君子求诸己，小人求诸人。"

【今译】

夫子说："君子求之于自己，小人求之于别人。"

【英译】

The Master said, "What the gentleman seeks, he seeks within himself; what the petty man seeks, he seeks in others."

15 · 22　子曰："君子矜而不争，群而不党。"

【今译】

夫子说："君子庄重而不争执，与人合群但不拉帮结派。"

【英译】

The Master said, "The gentleman is dignified without being contentious, and sociable without forming cliques."

15 · 23　子曰："君子不以言举人，不以人废言。"

【今译】

夫子说："君子不凭一个人说的话来举荐他，也不因为一个人不好而鄙弃他正确的话。"

【英译】

The Master said, "The gentleman does not recommend a man because of his words, neither does he dismiss the fine words because of its speaker."

15·24 子贡问曰："有一言而可以终身行之者乎?"子曰："其恕乎! 己所不欲, 勿施于人。"

【今译】

子贡问夫子："有没有一个字可以终身奉行的呢?"夫子说："应当是恕吧! 自己不想要的, 不要强加给别人。"

【英译】

Zigong asked, "Is there a single word which can be a guide for good conduct throughout one's life?"

The Master said, "It should be the word 'forgiveness'. Do not do to others what you would not want others to do to you."

15·25 子曰："吾之于人也, 谁毁谁誉? 如有所誉者, 其有所试矣。斯民也, 三代之所以直道而行也。"

【今译】

夫子说："我对于别人, 诋毁过谁? 赞美过谁? 如有赞美的, 必定是经过考验的。夏商周三代的人都是这样, 所以三代能直道而行。"

【英译】

The Master said, "With regard to others, whom did I ever defame, whom did I ever praise? If I praised someone, it was because he had been put to the test. The people of Xia, Shang and Zhou all followed the same principle, and that was why they were able to keep on the straight path."

15·26　子曰："吾犹及史之阙文①也。有马者借人乘之，今亡矣夫！"

【注释】

①阙文：史官记史，遇到有疑问的地方，缺而不记，称"阙文"。阙，同"缺"。

【今译】

夫子说："我还见过史书存疑以待后人的地方，（如同）有马的人借与人骑，今天没有（这种情况）了。"

【英译】

The Master said, "I still remember the time when I came upon vacancies in some historical documents, which is like lending a horse to others for riding. Such practice is no longer followed nowadays."

【辨正】

杨逢彬《论语今注今译》："吾犹及史之阙文也，有马者借人乘之"可以理解为"吾犹及史之阙文也，史之阙文，如有马者借人乘之"。

"史阙文"与"马借人"二事大小精粗实不相并，自汉及清，聚讼纷纭。

15·27　子曰："巧言乱德。小不忍，则乱大谋。"

【今译】

夫子说："花言巧语会败坏人的德行，小事情不忍耐，就会败坏大事情。"

【英译】

The Master said, "Clever talk ruins virtue. Lack of forbearance in small matters ruins great plans."

15·28　子曰："众恶之，必察焉；众好之，必察焉。"

【今译】

夫子说："大家都厌恶他，一定要考察考察；大家都喜欢他，（也）一定要考察考察。"

【英译】

The Master said, "When a man is disliked by all, be sure to look carefully into it. When a man is liked by all, also be sure to look carefully into it."

15·29　子曰："人能弘道，非道弘人。"

【今译】

夫子说："人能够使道发扬光大，不是道使人弘大。"

【英译】

The Master said, "It is man that can make the principles great; and not the principles that can make man great."

15·30　子曰：“过而不改，是谓过矣。”

【今译】

夫子说：“有了过错而不改正，这才叫过错呢。”

【英译】

The Master said, "To err and not reform it is indeed an error."

15·31　子曰：“吾尝终日不食，终夜不寝，以思，无益，不如学也。”

【今译】

夫子说：“我曾经整天不吃饭，彻夜不睡觉，一直思索，没有什么长进，不如去学习。”

【英译】

The Master said, "I once kept thinking all day without food and all night without sleep. It turned out to be useless. I should have spent the time learning."

15·32　子曰：“君子谋道不谋食。耕也，馁在其中矣；学也，禄在其中矣。君子忧道不忧贫。”

【今译】

夫子说：“君子志在求道，不在求食。耕种，其中有饥饿；学习，其中有食禄。君子担心道不能行，不担心贫穷。”

The Master said, "The gentleman devotes his mind to pursuing the truth rather than food. Farming may not guarantee you are free from hunger whereas learning may guarantee you a salary. The gentleman concerns himself about the truth rather than poverty.

15·33　子曰："知及之^①，仁不能守之，虽得之，必失之。知及之，仁能守之，不庄以涖^②之，则民不敬。知及之，仁能守之，庄以涖之，动之不以礼，未善也。"

【注释】

①知：同"智"。及：达到。之：指禄位或国家天下。

②涖（lì）：临，到。

【今译】

夫子说："（如果）凭聪明才智能得到的，但仁德不能守住它，即使得到，也一定会失去。凭聪明才智能得到它，仁德可以守住它，若不用严肃态度来对待它，那么百姓就会不尊重；凭聪明才智能得到它，仁德可以守住它，又能用严肃态度来对待，但不遵照礼的要求使用它，那也不尽善。"

【英译】

The Master said, "A man is bound to lose his power if he is intelligent enough to attain it, yet not benevolent enough to retain it. He will not be respected by his people if he is intelligent enough to attain it and benevolent enough to retain it, yet manages it without sobriety. He will still fall short of perfection if he is intelligent enough to attain it, benevolent enough to retain it and manages it without sobriety, yet does not wield it in accordance with the rites."

15 · 34　子曰："君子不可小知而可大受也，小人不可大受而可小知也。"

【今译】

夫子说："不可让君子去做细小事情，却可以让他们承担重大使命。小人不能承担重大的使命，但可以让他们做些细小事情。"

【英译】

The Master said, "The gentleman cannot be assigned to minor tasks but can be entrusted with grand missions; a petty man cannot be entrusted with grand missions but can be assigned to minor tasks."

15 · 35　子曰："民之于仁也，甚于水火。水火，吾见蹈而死者矣，未见蹈仁而死者也。"

【今译】

夫子说："百姓对仁，比对洪水烈火还畏惧。我见过人踏着水火而死的，却没有见过践仁而死的。"

【英译】

The Master said, "To the common people, benevolence is more fearful than water or fire. I have seen men die by treading on water or fire, but I have never seen any man die by practicing benevolence."

邢昺《论语注疏》里说:"此章劝人行仁道也。'子曰:民之于仁也,甚于水火'者,言水火饮食所由,仁者善行之长,皆民所仰而生者也。若较其三者所用,则仁最为甚也。'水火,吾见蹈而死者矣,未见蹈仁而死者也'者,此明仁甚于水火之事也。蹈犹履也。水火虽所以养人,若履蹈之,或时杀人。若履行仁道,未尝杀人也。王弼云:'民之远于仁,甚于水火,见有蹈水火者,未尝见蹈仁者也。'虽与马意不同,亦得为一义。"

邢昺这里说的"水火饮食所由,仁者善行之长,皆民所仰而生者",正是水火有益论的代表。黄怀信在《论语新校释》指出:"旧或释为民需要仁德急于需要水火,或释民生有赖于仁甚其有赖于水火,沿孟子'民非水火不生活'之说,以水火为人赖以为生之水火,皆不合人情,人岂有赖仁为生之理?"

夫子若果真谈水火益民,何以接下来不说如何益民,而说"蹈水火而死"?见蹈水火而死,不见蹈仁而死,并没有证明仁更重要,民更有赖仁。水火杀人,而仁未尝杀人,只能说明仁不如水火厉害,何以"明仁甚于水火"?何"甚"之有?

前一句"民之于仁也,甚于水火"与后一句"水火,吾见蹈而死者矣,未见蹈仁而死者也"之间也有语义上的转折。前一句是百姓对仁的看法,觉得仁比水火还厉害。后一句是夫子的反驳,说明仁没有水火厉害:水火能致人死而仁不。

15·36 子曰:"当仁,不让于师。"

【今译】

夫子说:"仁德当前,义无反顾,就是对老师,也不谦让。"

【英译】

The Master said, "When faced with the opportunity to practice benevolence, do not yield performance of it, even to your teacher."

15·37　子曰："君子贞而不谅①。"

【注释】

①谅：信，守信用，无原则地守信。刘宝楠《论语正义》："谅者，信而不通之谓。"

【今译】

夫子说："君子坚守正道，而不固执成见。"

【英译】

The Master said, "The gentleman is steadfast in purpose but not inflexible."

15·38　子曰："事君，敬其事而后其食。"

【今译】

夫子说："事奉君主，要认真办事而把俸禄的事放在后面。"

【英译】

The Master said, "In serving a lord, one should approach

one's duties with reverence before any thought of reward."

15·39　子曰："有教无类。"

【今译】

夫子说："人人我都教育，没有区别。"

【英译】

The Master said, "In teaching, I take disciples of all backgrounds without discrimination."

15·40　子曰："道不同，不相为谋。"

【今译】

夫子说："主张不同，无法一起谋事。"

【英译】

The Master said, "Those who have different beliefs cannot work together for the same goal."

15·41　子曰："辞达而已矣。"

【今译】

夫子说："言辞能表达意思就行了。"

【英译】

The Master said, "Words are good enough as long as they can get the point across."

15·42　"师冕见，及阶，子曰："阶也。"及席，子曰："席也。"皆坐，子告之曰："某在斯，某在斯。"

师冕出。子张问曰："与师言之道与？"子曰："然；固相师之道也。"

【今译】

乐师冕来见夫子，走近台阶，夫子说："这儿是台阶。"走到坐席旁，夫子说："这是坐席。"等大家都坐下来，夫子告诉他："某某在这里，某某在这里。"师冕走了以后，子张就问夫子："这就是与乐师谈话的方式吗？"夫子说："是啊，这本来就是帮助乐师的方式。"

【英译】

Mian, the blind Musician, called on the Master. When he reached the steps, the Master said, "You have reached the steps." And when he came to the mat, the Master said, "Here is the mat." When everyone was seated, the Master told him, "This is so-and-so here and that is so-and-so over there."

After Mian left, Zizhang asked, "Is that the way to talk to a musician?" The Master said, "Yes, that is the way to assist a musician."

季氏第十六

16·1　季氏将伐颛臾。冉有、季路见于孔子曰："季氏将有事①于颛臾。"

孔子曰："求！无乃尔是过与？夫颛臾，昔者先王以为东蒙主②，且在城邦之中矣，是社稷之臣也。何以伐为？"

冉有曰："夫子欲之，吾二臣者皆不欲也。"

孔子曰："求！周任③有言曰：'陈力就列④，不能者止。'危而不持，颠而不扶，则将焉用彼相⑤矣？且尔言过矣，虎兕⑥出于柙，龟玉毁于椟中，是谁之过与？"

冉有曰："今夫颛臾，固而近于费。今不取，后世必为子孙忧。"

孔子曰："求！君子疾夫舍曰欲之而必为之辞。丘也闻有国有家者，不患寡而患不均，不患贫而患不安。盖均无贫，和无寡，安无倾。夫如是，故远人不服，则修文德以来⑦之。既来之，则安之。今由与求也，相夫子，远人不服，而不能来也；邦分崩离析，而不能守也；而谋动干戈于邦内。吾恐季孙之忧，不在颛臾，而在萧墙⑧之内也。"

【注释】

①有事：指施加武力，采取军事行动。

②东蒙：蒙山。主：主持祭祀的人。

③周任：人名，周代史官。

④陈力就列：施展能力，担任官职。

⑤相：古代扶引盲人者叫相，这里是辅佐的意思。

⑥兕（sì）：雌性犀牛。

⑦来：通"徕"，招徕，吸引。

⑧萧墙：宫殿当门的小墙，或称"屏"。古代臣子进见国君，至屏而肃然起敬，故称"萧墙"。"萧""肃"古字通。这里指宫廷。

【今译】

季氏将要讨伐颛臾。冉有、子路去见孔子说："季氏快要攻打颛臾了。"孔子说："冉求，难道这不该责备你吗？颛臾，从前周天子让它主持东蒙祭祀，而且在鲁国的疆域之内。这种鲁国的重臣，为什么要讨伐他？"冉有说："夫子想去攻打，我们两个人都不愿意。"孔子说："冉求，周任有句话说：'有能力做就担任职务，没有能力就辞职。'有危险不去帮助，要跌倒不去搀扶，那还用你们的辅佐做什么？而且你说错了。老虎、犀牛从笼子里跑出来，龟甲、玉器毁坏在匣子里，这是谁的过错呢？"冉有说："现在颛臾城墙坚固，而且离费邑很近。现在不把它夺取过来，将来一定会成为子孙的忧患。"孔子说："冉求，君子痛恨那种不说想要又一定要找个借口的做法。我听说，对于诸侯和大夫，担心的不是贫穷，而是财富不均；不是人口少，而是不安定。因为财富平均，就无所谓贫穷了；大家和睦，就不会感到人少；社会安定，国家就没有倾覆的危险了。正因为这样，所以如果远方的人不归服，就提高道德教化招徕他们；把他们招徕来了，就使他们安心住下去。现在，仲由和冉求你们两个人辅助夫子，远方的人不归服，而不能招徕他们；国家分崩离析，而不能保全，反而打算在国内使用武力。我疑心季孙氏的忧患不在颛臾，而宫殿的门屏之内啊！"

The head of the Ji family was going to launch an attack on Zhuanyu. Ranyou and Jilu (Zilu), who were serving as stewards of the Ji family, went to see Confucius and said, "Our lord is going to take action against Zhuanyu."

Confucius said, "Qiu, aren't you to blame for that? Zhuanyu used to preside over Dong Meng Mountain, appointed by the King of Zhou, and his successor is now among the ministers of our state. Why do you attack it?"

Ranyou said, "It is what our lord wishes. Neither of us is in favour of it."

Confucius said, "Qiu, there is a saying of Zhou Ren's which goes: 'Hold an official post if you are capable, otherwise withdraw from it.' What's the use of your assistance if you do not offer any support when your lord is in danger, nor lend a hand when he is tripping over. Moreover, what you said is quite wrong. Whose fault is it when the tiger and the rhinoceros escape from their cages or when the tortoise shell and the jade are destroyed in their casket?"

Ranyou said, "But Zhuanyu is strongly fortified and close to Bi. If not taken now, it is sure to be a source of trouble for the descendants of our lord in the future."

Confucius said, "Qiu, the gentleman detests those who, instead of simply admitting that they want something, always invent excuses to justify their intent. I heard that the head of a state or a noble family worries not about poverty but about uneven distribution of wealth, not about underpopulation but about instability. For the fair distribution of wealth would, in a sense, eliminate poverty, harmony would ease the worry of underpopulation, and stability would assure the impossibility of subversion. It is for this reason that when distant subjects are compliant we should cultivates our moral quality to win them over, and once they have come round we should make them content. But (Zhong) You and Qiu, assistants as you are, failed to win over the distant subjects, nor can you preserve the state from disintegrating. Instead, you propose to resort to armed force within the state. I am afraid that Jisun's trouble lies not in Zhuanyu but within the palatial walls of Lu."

16·2　孔子曰："天下有道，则礼乐征伐自天子出；天下无道，则礼乐征伐自诸侯出。自诸侯出，盖十世希不失矣；自大夫出，五世希不失矣；陪臣执国命，三世希不失矣。天下有道，则政不在大夫。天下有道，则庶人不议。"

【今译】

孔子说："天下有道时，礼乐和征伐都由天子作决定；天下无道时，礼乐和征伐由诸侯作决定。由诸侯作决定，大概经过十代很少有不垮台的；由大夫决定，经过五代很少有不垮台的。由大夫的家臣把持国家政权，很少有经过三代不垮台的。天下有道，国政就不在大夫。天下有道，老百姓就不会议论了。"

【英译】

Confucius said, "When good government prevails in the Empire, the rites and music and punitive expeditions are initiated by the emperor. When ill government prevails in the Empire, they are initiated by the feudal lords. When they are initiated by the feudal lords, it is rare that they do not lose their power in ten generations' time. When they are initiated by the ministers, it is rare that they do not lose their power in five generations' time. When the assistants to the ministers get hold of the state power, it is rare that they do not lose their power in three generations' time. When good government prevails in the Empire, decision making does not rest with the ministers, nor do the common people ever comment on the government."

16·3　孔子曰："禄之去公室五世矣，政逮于大夫四世矣，故夫三桓之子孙微矣。"

【今译】

孔子说："鲁君失去政权已经有五代了，政权落在大夫之手已经四代了，所以三桓的子孙将要衰败了。"

【英译】

Confucius said, "It is five generations since royalty lost its power. It's four generations since the power fell into the hands of the three branches of the Huan. Thus, the descendants of the Huan are going downhill."

16·4　孔子曰："益者三友，损者三友。友直，友谅①，友多闻，益矣。友便辟②，友善柔③，友便佞④，损矣。"

【注释】

①谅：诚信。

②便辟（pián pì）：善于迎合。

③善柔：善于和颜悦色诱惑。

④便佞（pián nìng）：善于花言巧语讨好。

【今译】

孔子说："有益的交友有三种，有害的交友有三种。同正直的人交友，同诚信的人交友，同见闻广博的人交友，这是有益的。同谄媚逢迎的人交朋友，同善于阿谀奉承的人交朋友，同惯于花言巧语的人交朋友，这是有害的。"

【英译】

Confucius said, "Three sorts of friends are benefical and three sorts of friends are harmful. It is benefical to make friends with the straight, the trustworthy and the well- informed, while harmful to make friends with the ingratiating in action, the pleasant in appearance and the plausible in speech.

16·5　孔子曰："益者三乐①，损者三乐。乐节礼乐，乐道人之善，乐多贤友，益矣。乐骄乐，乐佚游，乐宴乐，损矣。"

【注释】

①乐（yào）：喜好。

【今译】

孔子说："有益的喜好有三种，有害的喜好有三种。喜好以礼乐调节自己，喜好称道别人的好处，喜好多交贤德之友，这是有益的。喜好骄纵，喜欢闲游，喜欢宴饮，这就是有害的。"

Confucius said, "Three sorts of pleasure are profitable while three sorts of pleasure are harmful. It is profitable to take pleasure in correcting oneself with rites and music, in singing the praises of other people's goodness and in making many virtuous friends. It is harmful to take pleasure in indulging oneself, in idling, and in carousing."

16·6 孔子曰："侍于君子有三愆①：言未及之而言谓之躁，言及之而不言谓之隐，未见颜色而言谓之瞽。"

【注释】

①愆（qiān）：过失。

【今译】

孔子说："侍奉在君子旁边，（说话）有三种过失：还不该他说就说话，这叫急躁；该他说时却不说，这叫隐瞒；不看君子的脸色而说话，这叫目盲。"

【英译】

Confucius said, "There are three mistakes one has to watch out when in attendance upon a gentleman. To speak before being spoken to is being rash; not to speak when spoken to is being evasive; to speak without observing the expression on the gentleman's face is being blind."

16·7　孔子曰："君子有三戒：少之时，血气未定，戒之在色；及其壮也，血气方刚，戒之在斗；及其老也，血气既衰，戒之在得。"

【今译】

孔子说："君子有三种事情应引以为戒：年少的时候，血气还不成熟，要戒除迷恋女色；到了壮年，血气方刚，要戒除争强好斗；到了老年，血气已经衰弱，要戒除贪得无厌。"

【英译】

Confucius said, "There are three things the gentleman should guard against. When young, while the vital spirits are not yet settled, he should guard against lust. In the prime of life, when the vital spirits are exuberant, he should guard against bellicosity. In old age, when the vital spirits are in decline, he should guard against greed."

16·8　孔子曰："君子有三畏：畏天命，畏大人，畏圣人之言。小人不知天命而不畏也，狎大人，侮圣人之言。"

【今译】

孔子说："君子有三件敬畏的事情：敬畏天命，敬畏地位高贵的人，敬畏圣人的话。小人不懂得天命，因而不敬畏，对待地位高贵的人举止轻佻，轻侮圣人的话。"

【英译】

Confucius said, "The gentleman holds these three in awe: destiny, the superior and the words of sages. The petty man, being ignorant of destiny, does not hold in awe of it. He despises the superior and disdains the words of the sages."

16·9　孔子曰："生而知之者，上也；学而知之者，次也；困而学之，又其次也；困而不学，民斯为下矣。"

【今译】

孔子说："生来就知道的人，是上等人；经过学习以后才知道的，是次一等的人；遇到困难再去学习的，是又次一等的人；遇到困难还不学习的人，这种人就是最下等的人了。"

【英译】

Confucius said, "Those who have innate knowledge are at the top of the scale. Those who attain knowledge through study come next. Those who study when faced with difficulties are lower still. Those who make no effort to study even when faced with difficulties are the lowest."

16·10　孔子曰："君子有九思①：视思明，听思聪，色思温，貌思恭，言思忠，事思敬，疑思问，忿思难②，见得思义。"

【注释】

①思：考虑，追求，用心做到的目标。邢昺《论语注疏》："此章言君子有九种之事当用心思虑，使合礼义也。"
②难（nàn）：祸患，发怒可能带来的灾难。

【今译】

孔子说："君子有九种情况下要用心思虑：看的时候，要注意看清楚；听的时候，要注意听清楚；自己的脸色，注意要温和；容貌，注意要谦恭；跟人说话，要注意忠诚；办事时，要注意认真严肃；遇到疑问，要注意向别人请教；怒时，要考虑结下怨仇；获取财利时，要考虑是否正当。"

【英译】

Confucius said, "There are nine things the gentleman should try to achieve: to see clearly when using his eyes; to hear distinctly when he uses his ears; to look gracious when it comes to his countenance; to be conscientious when speaking; to be reverent when he perfoms his duties; to seek advice when he is in doubt; to think of the consequences when he is enraged; and to think of what is right at the sight of gain."

16·11 子曰："见善如不及，见不善如探汤。吾闻其语矣，吾见其人矣。隐居以求其志，行义以达其道。吾闻其语矣，未见其人也。"

【今译】

夫子说："看到善的行为，就像追赶不上似地（追求），看到不善的行为，就像把手伸到开水中一样（赶快避开）。我听到过这样的话，也见到过这样的人。以隐居避世来保全自己的志向，依照义而贯彻自己的主张。我听到过这种话，却没有见到过这样的人。"

【英译】

Confucius said, "Seeing what is good, pursue it as if fear of missing it, and seeing what is evil, shrink from it as if from boiling water. I have heard this said and I have seen it practiced. Live in seclusion in order to attain his purpose and practice what is right in order to carry out his principles. I have heard such a claim, but I have never met such a man."

16·12 齐景公有马千驷①，死之日，民无德而称焉。伯夷叔齐饿死于首阳之下，民到于今称之。（《诗》云："诚不以富，亦只以异。"）②其斯之谓与？

【注释】
①驷：古代一辆车套四匹马，驷就是四匹马的统称。
②原在《论语·颜渊》12·10的结语，程颐认为应在此处。

【今译】
齐景公有马四千匹，死的时候，百姓觉得他没有什么德行可以称颂。伯夷、叔齐饿死在首阳山下，百姓到现在还在称颂他们。（《诗经》里说："确实不因为他富有，只是因为他不同。"）说的大概就是这种情况吧。

【英译】
Duke Jing of Qi had a thousand teams of horses, but upon his death the common people were unable to find anything to praise him for, whereas Bo Yi and Shu Qi starved to death at the foot of Mount Shou Yang and yet to this day, people still sing their praises.（A line from *The Book of Songs* says, "It is indeed not because of the wealth, but of different pursuit."）This is probably what is meant.

【辨正】

《论语·颜渊》12·10：子张问崇德辨惑。子曰："主忠信，徙义，崇德也。爱之欲其生，恶之欲其死。既欲其生，又欲其死，是惑也。'诚不以富，亦祇以异。'"

朱熹《论语集注》里说：胡氏曰："程子以为第十二篇错简'诚不以富，亦祇以异'，当在此章之首。今详文势，似当在此句之上。言人之所称，不在于富，而在于异也。"

错简这种推测是否合理，可以看看文章的字词与上下文是否妥帖，句意是否通顺连贯，文势是否和谐一致。

《论语·季氏》16·12中，"其斯之谓与"的"斯"字，在文中却无所指。"大概就是这个意思吧？"可"这个"又指什么呢？上文根本没有。因此，有人怀疑此处阙文。况且，齐景公与伯夷、叔齐的例子，正是对照人所称与财富之多寡无关，将"诚不以富，亦祇以异"放在这里，可以说文从字顺。

子张问崇德辨惑。孔子的回答先谈到崇德，又谈到惑，最后来一句"诚不以富，亦祇以异"，前面的"德""惑"如何与"富""异"联系上？

16·13　陈亢①问于伯鱼曰："子亦有异闻乎？"

对曰："未也。尝独立，鲤趋而过庭。曰：'学诗乎？'对曰：'未也。''不学诗，无以言。'鲤退而学诗。他日，又独立，鲤趋而过庭。曰：'学礼乎？'对曰：'未也。''不学礼，无以立。'鲤退而学礼。闻斯二者。"

陈亢退而喜曰："问一得三，闻诗，闻礼，又闻君子之远②其子也。"

【注释】

①陈亢（gāng）：即陈子禽。

②远（yuàn）：不亲近，不偏爱。

【今译】

陈亢问伯鱼："你在老师那里听到过什么特别的教诲吗？"伯鱼回答说："没有呀。有一次他独自站在堂上，我快步从院子里走过，他问我：'学《诗》了吗？'我回答说：'没有。'他说：'不学诗，就不懂得怎么说话。'我回去就学《诗》。又有一天，他又独自站在堂上，我快步从庭里走过，他问我：'学礼了吗？'我回答说：'没有。'他说：'不学礼就不懂得怎样立身。'我回去就学礼。我就听到过这两件事。"陈亢回去高兴地说："我提一个问题，得到三方面的收获，听了关于《诗》的道理，听了关于礼的道理，又听了君子不偏爱自己儿子的道理。"

【英译】

Chen Gang asked Boyu, "Have you received any special coaching from the Master?"

"No, I have not. One day, while my father was standing alone, I crossed the courtyard with quickened steps. He asked me, 'Have you studied *The Book of Songs*?' I answered, 'No.' He said, 'Unless you studied it you won't know how to speak properly.' I retired and studied *The Book of Songs*.

"Another day, my father was again standing by himself. As I crossed the courtyard with quickened steps, he asked me, 'Have you studied *The Book of Rites*? I answered, 'No.' He said, 'Unless you study *The Book of Rites*, you won't know how to behave properly.' I retired and studied *The Book of Rites*. I have heard only these two things."

Chen Gang retired and said happily, "I asked one thing and

learned three. I learned about *The Book of Songs*, I learned about *The Book of Rites*, and I learned that a gentleman keeps a distance from his son."

16·14　邦君之妻，君称之曰夫人，夫人自称曰小童；邦人称之曰君夫人，称诸异邦曰寡小君；异邦人称之亦曰君夫人。

【今译】

国君的妻子，国君称她为夫人，夫人自称为小童，国人称她为君夫人；对他国人则称她为寡小君，他国人也称她为君夫人。

【英译】

The wife of a lord is called by the lord "*Furen* （my lady）". She calls herself "*Xiaotong* （your little one）" when talking to the lord. She is called by the people of the state "*Jun Furen* （Lady of His Majesty）". When going abroad, the lord calls her "*Gua Xiaojun* （my little lord）". People of other states also use the term "*Jun Furen* （Lady of His Majesty）" when referring to her."

阳货第十七

17·1　阳货欲见孔子，孔子不见，归孔子豚①。

孔子时其亡也，而往拜之。

遇诸涂②。

谓孔子曰："来！予与尔言。"曰："怀其宝而迷其邦③，可谓仁乎？"曰："不可。"——"好从事而亟④失时，可谓知乎？"曰："不可。——日月逝矣，岁不我与⑤。"

孔子曰："诺，吾将仕矣。"

【注释】

①归（kuì）：通"馈"，赠送。

②遇诸涂：在路上遇到了他。涂，同"途"。

③迷其邦：听任国家迷乱，政局动荡不安。

④亟（qì）：屡次。

⑤与：等待。

【今译】

阳货想见孔子，孔子不见，他便赠送给孔子一只熟小猪，想要孔子去拜见他。孔子打听到阳货不在家时，往阳货家拜谢，却在半路上遇见了。阳货对孔子说："来，我有话要跟你说。"（孔子走过去。）阳货说："把自己的本领藏起来而听任国家迷乱，这可以叫做仁吗？"又说："不可以。"（阳货）说："喜欢参与政事而又屡次错过机会，这可以说是智吗？"又说：

"不可以。"（阳货）说："日子一天天过去了，年岁不等人啊。"孔子说："好吧，我将要去做官了。"

【英译】

Yang Huo wanted to see Confucius, and when Confucius refused to go and see him, he sent Confucius a present of a steamed piglet.

Knowing that Yang was not at home, Confucius then went to his house to pay a courtesy return call. On the way he happened to meet Yang Huo who said to him, "Come now. I have something to tell you." Then he went on, "Can a man be considered benevolent who, while hiding his talents, allows the state to go astray? No. Can a man be considered wise who, while eager to take part in government, constantly misses the opportunity? No." He then said: "Days and months rush by, and the years wait for no man."

Confucius then said, "All right. I shall take up office."

17·2　子曰："性相近也，习相远也。"

【今译】

夫子说："人的本性（本来都）很接近，生活习惯使它们有了差别。"

【英译】

The Master said, "Men are close to one another by nature. They drift apart through behaviour that is constantly repeated."

17·3　子曰："唯上知与下愚不移。"

【今译】

夫子说："只有上等人智慧与下等人愚笨是不变的。"

【英译】

The Master said, "What remained unchanged is the truth that the top class are intelligent and the bottom class are ignorant."

17·4　子之武城，闻弦歌之声。夫子莞尔而笑，曰："割鸡焉用牛刀？"

子游对曰："昔者偃也闻诸夫子曰：'君子学道则爱人，小人学道则易使也。'"

子曰："二三子！偃之言是也。前言戏之耳。"

【今译】

夫子到武城，听见弹琴唱歌的声音。夫子微笑着说："杀鸡何必用宰牛的刀呢？"子游回答说："以前我听先生说过，'君子学习了礼乐就能爱人，小人学习了礼乐就容易役使。'"夫子说："各位，言偃的话是对的。我刚才说的话，只是开个玩笑。"

【英译】

The Master went to Wucheng. There he heard the sound of stringed instruments and singing. The Master broke into a smile and said, "why kill a chicken with an ox-cleaver?"

Ziyou answered, "Some time ago, I heard it from you, Master, that a gentleman instructed in the right principles loves his fellow men and that the petty man instructed is easy to employ."

The Master said, "Ziyou is right, my friends. I was joking just now."

17·5　公山弗扰以费畔，召，子欲往。

子路不说，曰："末之也，已，何必公山氏之之也。"

子曰："夫召我者，而岂徒哉？如有用我者，吾其为东周乎？"

【今译】

公山弗扰据费邑反叛，来召夫子，夫子准备前去。子路不高兴地说："没有地方去就算了，为什么一定要去公山弗扰那里呢？"夫子说："他来召我，难道只是一句空话吗？如果有人用我，我会（把那里）搞成东周吗？"

【英译】

Gongshan Furao, taking Bi as a stronghold, staged a revolt. He summoned the Master to join him and the Master intended to do so.

Zilu was displeased and said, "We may have nowhere to go, but must we go and join Gongshan?"

The Master said, "Did he summon me for nothing? Will I create another East Zhou if I get a post there?"

17·6　子张问仁于孔子。孔子曰："能行五者于天下为仁矣。"

"请问之。"曰："恭、宽、信、敏、惠。恭则不侮，宽则得众，信则人任焉，敏则有功，惠则足以使人。"

【今译】

子张向孔子问仁。孔子说："能够处处实行五种品德，就是仁人了。"子张说："请问哪五种。"孔子说："庄重、宽厚、诚实、勤敏、慈惠。庄重就不致遭受侮辱，宽厚就会得到众人的拥护，诚信就能得到别人的信任，勤敏就会提高工作效率，慈惠就能够役使人。"

【英译】

Zizhang asked Confucius about benevolence. Confucius said, "Benevolent are those who can put the five virtues into practice in the world."

"May I ask what they are?"

"They are courtesy, tolerance, trustworthiness, agility and generosity. Courtesy frees you from insults, tolerance wins the hearts of the multitude, trustworthiness inspires the trust of others, agility ensures success, and generosity confers authority to employ others."

17·7　佛肸①召，子欲往。

子路曰：昔者由也闻诸夫子曰：'亲于其身为不善者，君子不入也。'佛肸以中牟②畔，子之往也，如之何？"

子曰："然，有是言也。不曰坚乎，磨而不磷③；不曰白乎，涅④而不缁⑤。吾岂匏瓜⑥也哉？焉能系⑦而不食？"

【注释】

①佛肸（bì xī）：晋国大夫范氏、中行（háng）氏家臣，中牟城地方官。

②中牟：地名，在晋国，约在今河北邢台与邯郸之间。

③磷：薄。

④涅：一种矿物质，可用作颜料染衣服。

⑤缁（zī）：黑色。

⑥匏（páo）瓜：葫芦中的一种，味苦不能吃。

⑦系（jì）：结，扣。

【今译】

佛肸召夫子去，夫子打算前往。子路说："从前我听先生说过：'本人亲身做坏事的，君子不去他那里。'现在佛肸据中牟反叛，你却要去，这如何解释呢？"夫子说："是的，有这话。不是说坚硬的东西磨也磨不坏吗？不是说洁白的东西染也染不黑吗？我难道是个葫芦吗？怎么能只挂在那里而不给人食用呢？"

【英译】

Bi Xi summoned the Master and the Master intended to go.

Zilu said, "Some time ago I heard it from you, Master, that a gentleman does not enter the domain of one who in his own person does what is not good. Now Bi Xi is using Zhongmou as a stronghold to stage a revolt. How can you justify going there?"

The Master said, "It is true, I did say that. But 'what is really hard can never be worn thin; what is pure white can never be dyed black.' Am I just a gourd good enough for decoration but is not edible?"

17·8 子曰:"由也,女闻六言六蔽①矣乎?"对曰:"未也。"

"居②!吾语女。好仁不好学,其蔽也愚;好知不好学,其蔽也荡③;好信不好学,其蔽也贼④;好直不好学,其蔽也绞⑤;好勇不好学,其蔽也乱;好刚不好学,其蔽也狂。"

【注释】

①言:字。蔽:毛病。六言六蔽:用六个字指六种毛病,即愚、荡、贼、绞、乱、狂。

②居:坐。

③荡:放纵。

④贼:害。

⑤绞:急切,偏激。

【今译】

夫子说:"由呀,你听说过六个字讲六种毛病吗?"子路回答说:"没有。"夫子说:"坐下,我告诉你。喜欢仁德而不喜欢学习,它的弊病是愚;喜欢智慧而不喜欢学习,它的弊病是荡;喜欢诚信而不喜欢学习,它的弊病是贼;喜欢直率却不喜欢学习,它的弊病是绞;喜欢勇敢却不喜欢学习,它的弊病是乱;喜欢刚强却不喜欢学习,它的弊病是狂。"

The Master asked Zhong You, "(Zhong) You, have you heard about the six qualities and the six attendant faults?"

"No, I have not." answered Zilu.

The Master said, "Be seated and I shall tell you. To love benevolence without loving learning may lead to foolishness. To love wisdom without loving learning may lead to indulging oneself. To love trustworthiness without loving learning may invite harm. To love forthrightness without loving learning may lead to being extreme. To love courage without loving learning may lead to insubordination. To love unbending strength without loving learning may lead to being arrogant."

17·9　子曰："小子何莫学夫《诗》?《诗》可以兴①,可以观,可以群②,可以怨③。迩之④事父,远之事君;多识于鸟兽草木之名。"

【注释】

①兴:兴起,发动。这里指激发人的意志和感情。

②群:合群。

③怨:讽谏上级,怨而不怒。

④迩(ěr):近。之:连词,相当于"则"。

【今译】

夫子说:"学生为什么不学习《诗》呢? 学《诗》可以激发想象,可以观察世俗兴衰,可以使人合群,可以学会讽喻。近可以用来事奉父母,远可以事奉君主;还可以多知道一些鸟兽草木的名字。"

【英译】

The Master said, "Why is it none of you, my young friends, study *The Book of Songs*? It can stimulate your imagination, widen your horizons, enable you to live in a community and teach you how to express grievances. It can help you serve your parents at home and serve your lord abroad. It can also help you get acquainted with the names of birds, beasts and plants."

17·10　子谓伯鱼曰："女为《周南》、《召南》①矣乎？人而不为《周南》、《召南》，其犹正墙面而立也与？"

【注释】

①《周南》、《召（shào）南》：《诗经·国风》中的第一、二两部分篇名。周南和召南本是地名，这两个地域收集在《诗经》中的民歌，就叫《周南》《召南》。

【今译】

夫子对伯鱼说："你学习《周南》、《召南》了吗？一个人如果不学习《周南》、《召南》，那就像面对墙壁站立着吧？"

【英译】

The Master said to Boyu, "Have you studied the *Zhou-nan* and *Shao-nan*? A man who does not study them is like one who stands squarely facing the wall."

17·11 子曰："礼云礼云，玉帛云乎哉？乐云乐云，钟鼓云乎哉？"

【今译】

夫子说："礼呀礼呀，难道仅仅是说玉帛之类的礼器吗？乐呀乐呀，难道仅仅是说钟鼓之类的乐器吗？"

【英译】

The Master said, "Do we merely mean jade and silk when we talk about the rites? Do we merely mean the bells and drums when we talk about music?"

17·12 子曰："色厉而内荏①，譬诸小人，其犹穿窬②之盗也与？"

【注释】

①厉：威严。荏：虚弱。色厉内荏：外表似乎刚强威严，而内心却柔弱怯惧。

②窬（yú）：同"踰"，越过。《字汇·穴部》："窬，踰墙为窬。"

【今译】

夫子说："外表严厉而内心怯懦，以小人作比喻，就像是挖洞穿墙的小偷吧？"

【英译】

A man who wears a stern look but is cowardly in his mind is, compared to the petty man, a thief who breaks in by making a hole in the wall.

17·13 子曰：“乡原，德之贼也。”

【今译】

夫子说：“没有原则的老好人，就是戕害道德的人。”

【英译】

The Master said, "The local hypocrite is the spoiler of virtue."

【辨正】

俞樾《群经平议》：“原当为愿。”愿：圆滑；随和。《说文·人部》：“愿，黠也。”乡愿，指乡里中貌似谨厚，而实与流俗合污的伪善者。《集注》：“盖其同流合污以媚于世，故在乡人之中独以愿称，夫子以其似德非德，而反乱乎德，故以为德之贼而深恶之。”

17·14 子曰：“道听而涂说，德之弃也。”

【今译】

夫子说：“在路上听到传言就到处去传播，这是道德所唾弃的。”

【英译】

The Master said, "The gossip-monger is the outcast of virtue."

17·15　子曰："鄙夫可与事君也与哉？其未得之也，患得之。既得之，患失之。苟患失之，无所不至矣。"

【今译】

夫子说："可以和一个鄙夫一起事奉君主吗？他在没有得到官位时，总为得到它而焦虑。已经得到了，又担心失去它。如果怕失掉官职，那他就什么事都干得出来了。"

【英译】

The Master said, "Is it possible to work side by side with a mean fellow in serving a lord? Before he gets the official post, he worries about how to get it. After he has got it, he worries that he might lose it. For fearing that he might lose his post, he would do anything possible to keep it."

【辨正】

古今很多学者认为"患得之"脱去一"不"字，应该为"患不得之"。《荀子·子道篇》："孔子曰：'……小人者，其得也，则忧不得；既已得之，又恐失之。'"王符《潜夫论·爱日》："孔子病夫未之得也，患不得之，既得之，患失之者。"沈作喆《寓简》："东坡解云：'患得之'当作'患不得之'。"

但是，杨逢彬《论语新注新译》有详细论证，支持"患得之"："1. 迄至战国晚期，文献中未见'不得之'。当'得'为'获得''取得'义时，'得之'的否定形式都是'不得'（或'弗得'），而且往往和'得之'对言。……不单动词'得'如此，还有一些动词，当宾语'之'不被强调时，其否定形式中'之'都不出现，如：'知之为知之，不知为不知，是知也。'……既然从战国末期后，原来整齐划一的'得之''不得'发生了变化而出现了若干'不得之',那么以后的'创作者'依据他自己的时代的语言表达习惯改写《论语》此章也就不足为奇了。何况,《荀子》《潜夫论》并非照录《论语》此章呢!

"2. 连词'既'两边的成分具有一致性。既然后句为'既得之',前句就不可能是'患不得之',而只能是'患得之'。换言之,如果前句为'患不得之',后句也必须为'既不得之'。连词'既'是由表示'已经'义的副词发展而来的,它仍然保留副词'既'的词义特征;因此,当'既'两边出现相同成分时,只能两边同为肯定,不能出现一边否定一边肯定的情形,如'……患不得之,既得之……'。"

17·16 子曰:"古者民有三疾,今也或是之亡也。古之狂也肆,今之狂也荡;古之矜也廉,今之矜也忿戾;古之愚也直,今之愚也诈而已矣。"

【今译】

夫子说:"古代人有三种毛病,现在恐怕连这三种毛病都没有了。古代的狂放者放纵,而现在的狂放者只是放荡;古代骄傲者正直,现在的骄傲者只是蛮横乖张;古代愚笨者耿直,现在的愚笨者只是欺诈而已。"

【英译】

The Master said, "In ancient times, the common people had three weaknesses, which cannot be found much unchanged in people today. In ancient times, people were wild in an unrestrained way; today, they were simply licentious. In ancient times, people were conceited in a self-restrained way; today, they are simply ill-tempered. In ancient times, people were foolish in a straight way; today, they are simply crafty."

17·17　子曰："巧言令色，鲜矣仁。"①

【注释】
①见《学而第一》1·3。

【今译】
夫子说："言语甜蜜动听，容色悦目谄媚，这种人很少有仁者。"

【英译】
The Master said, "Rarely is a man benevolent whose speech is cunning and whose countenance is ingratiating."

17·18　子曰："恶紫之夺朱①也，恶郑声之乱雅乐也，恶利口之覆邦家者。"

【注释】
①紫之夺朱：古代传统称朱为正色，而春秋时，一些诸侯喜欢着紫色衣，并有取代红色成为正色的趋势。

【今译】
夫子说："我厌恶用紫色取代红色，厌恶用郑国的声乐扰乱雅乐，厌恶用伶牙利齿而颠覆国家的人。"

The Master said, "I detest purple for displacing vermillion. I detest the tunes of the State of Zheng for corrupting classical music. I detest clever talkers who overturn a state or a noble family."

17·19　子曰："予欲无言。"子贡曰："子如不言，则小子何述焉？"子曰："天何言哉？四时行焉，百物生焉，天何言哉？"

【今译】

夫子说："我准备不再说话了。"子贡说："先生如果不说话，那么我们这些学生传述什么呢？"夫子说："天说了什么话呢？四季照常运行，百物照样生长。天说了什么话呢？"

【英译】

The Master said, "I am thinking of giving up speech." Zigong said, "If you did not speak, what would there be for us, your juniors, to transmit?" The Master said, "Does Heaven ever speak? Yet the four seasons keep going round and the plants and animals keep growing. Does Heaven ever speak?"

17·20　孺悲欲见孔子，孔子辞以疾。将命者出户，取瑟而歌，使之闻之。

【今译】

孺悲想见孔子，（派人来请，）孔子以有病为由推辞不见。传话的人刚出门，（孔子）便取来瑟边弹边唱，（有意）让他听到。

【英译】

Ru Bei wanted to see Confucius. Confucius declined to see him on the grounds of illness. As soon as the messenger stepped out of the door, Confucius took up his lute and began to sing, making sure that the messenger heard it.

17·21 宰我问："三年之丧，期已久矣。君子三年不为礼，礼必坏；三年不为乐，乐必崩。旧谷既没，新谷既升，钻燧改火①，期可已矣。"

子曰："食夫稻，衣夫锦，于女安乎？"

曰："安。"

"女安，则为之！夫君子之居丧，食旨②不甘，闻乐不乐，居处③不安，故不为也。今女安，则为之！"

宰我出。子曰："予之不仁也！子生三年，然后免于父母之怀。夫三年之丧，天下之通丧也，予也有三年之爱于其父母乎！"

【注释】

①钻燧改火：古人钻木取火，四季所用木头不同，一年轮用一遍，第二年按上年的次序依次取用，叫改火。钻燧改火，指过了一年。

②旨：甜美，指好吃的食物。

③居处：指住在平时所住的好房子里。古代守孝，应在父母坟墓附近搭一个临时的草棚，睡在草苫子上，以表示不忍心住在安适的屋子里。

宰我问："服丧三年，期限太长了。君子三年不行礼，礼一定败坏；三年不奏乐，乐一定荒废。旧谷吃完，新谷登场，钻燧取火改用新燧，一年就可止了。"

夫子说："（才一年的时间就）吃那大米，穿那锦缎，你心安吗？"

宰我说："我心安。"

夫子说："你心安，就那样去做吧！君子守丧，吃美味不觉香甜，听音乐不觉快乐，住在家里不觉舒服，所以不那样做。如今你既觉得心安，就那样去做吧！"

宰我出去后，夫子说："宰予真是不仁啊！孩子生下来，三年以后才能离开父母的怀抱。服丧三年，这是天下通行的丧礼。难道宰予没从他父母（怀抱里）得到过三年的爱吗？"

【英译】

Zaiwo said, "Three years is much too long for a man to be mourning his parents. If a gentleman does not practice the rites for three years, the rites will be desolated. If he does not play music, it will collapse. As the supply of old grain is exhausted and the new grain is in, and fire is renewed by fresh drilling, a full year's mourning is quite enough."

The Master said, "Would you, then, be able to enjoy eating your rice and wearing your finery?"

"Yes, I would."

The Master said, "If you are able to enjoy them, do so as you please. A gentleman in mourning finds no relish in good food, no pleasure in music, and no comforts in his own home. That is why he does not eat his rice and wear his finery. Since you are able to enjoy them, you might as well do as you please."

After Zaiwo had left, the Master said, "How unfeeling Yu is. It is three years' time before a child leaves the arms of his parents. So, three years' mourning is observed throughout the world. Didn't Yu enjoy three years of love and care from his parents?"

17·22　子曰："饱食终日，无所用心，难矣哉！不有博弈者乎？为之，犹贤乎已①。"

【注释】
①已：代词，相当于"此"。

【今译】
夫子说："整天吃饱了饭，什么心思也不用，真难办啊！不是有博彩下棋的游戏吗？做做这样的事，也比这样闲着好。"

【英译】
The Master said, "It is really intolerable that one eats his fill every day without applying his mind to anything else. Aren't there things like Go or other games to play? Even that is better than being idle."

17·23　子路曰："君子尚勇乎？"子曰："君子义以为上，君子有勇而无义为乱，小人有勇而无义为盗。"

【今译】
子路说："君子崇尚勇敢吗？"夫子说："君子以义作为最高

尚的品德。君子有勇无义就会作乱，小人有勇无义就会做强盗。"

【英译】

Zilu said, "Does a gentleman value courage?" The Master said, "A gentleman considers justice the supreme virtue. Being courageous without justice, a gentleman will become a rebel, and a petty man will become a bandit."

17·24　子贡曰："君子亦有恶乎？"子曰："有恶：恶称人之恶者，恶居下流而讪①上者，恶勇而无礼者，恶果敢而窒②者。"

曰："赐也亦有恶乎？""恶徼③以为知者，恶不孙④以为勇者，恶讦⑤以为直者。"

【注释】

①讪（shàn）：诽谤。
②窒：阻塞，不通事理，顽固不化。
③徼（jiǎo）：窃取，抄袭。
④孙：同"逊"。
⑤讦（jié）：攻击、揭发别人。

【今译】

子贡说："君子也有厌恶的事吗？"夫子说："有厌恶的事。君子厌恶宣扬别人坏处的人，厌恶身居下位而诽谤上司的人，厌恶勇敢而不懂礼节的人，厌恶固执而暴躁的人。"

夫子又说："赐，你也有厌恶的事吗？"

子贡说："我厌恶把窃取别人的东西当作聪明的人，厌恶把不谦虚当做勇敢的人，厌恶把揭发别人的隐私当作直率的人。"

Zigong said, "Does even a gentleman have his dislikes?" The Master said, "Yes. A gentleman has his dislikes. He dislikes those who go about publicizing the misdeeds of others. He dislikes those who, being in inferior positions, slander their superiors. He dislikes those who, while possessing courage, lack the spirit of the rites. He dislikes those whose resoluteness is not tempered by understanding."

The Master added, "Do you, Ci, have your dislikes as well?"

"I dislike those who consider themselves wise in plagiarizing others, courageous in being rude and forthright while exposing others' privacy."

17·25　子曰："唯女子与小人为难养也，近之则不孙，远之则怨。"

【今译】

夫子说："只有女子和小人是难以伺候的！亲近他们，他们就会对你不恭；疏远他们，他们就会抱怨。"

【英译】

The Master said, "Only women and the petty men are especially difficult to deal with. If you get too close to them, they will become insolent, but if you keep them at a distance, they will complain."

17·26 子曰："年四十而见恶焉，其终也已。"

【今译】

夫子说："到了四十岁的时候还被人厌恶，他这一生也就完了。"

【英译】

The Master said, "If by the age of forty a man is still disliked, there is no hope for him."

微子第十八

18·1　微子①去之，箕子②为之奴，比干③谏而死。孔子曰："殷有三仁焉。"

【注释】

①微子：殷纣王的同母兄长，见纣王无道，劝他不听，遂离开纣王。

②箕（jī）子：殷纣王的叔父。他多次劝说纣王，纣王不听，便披发装疯，被降为奴隶。

③比干：殷纣王的叔父，屡次强谏。"主过不谏，非忠也；畏死不言，非勇也；过则谏，不用则死，忠之至也。"纣王怒，说："吾闻圣人之心有七窍，信诸？"遂将比干剖胸挖心，残忍地杀死。

【今译】

微子离开了纣王，箕子做了他的奴隶，比干强谏而被杀。孔子说："这是殷朝的三位仁人啊！"

【英译】

The Viscount Wei left him; the Viscount Ji was imprisoned as a slave; and Bigan lost his life for remonstrating with him. Confucius commented, "There were three benevolent men in the Yin Dynasty."

18·2　柳下惠为士师①，三黜。人曰："子未可以去乎?"曰："直道而事人，焉往而不三黜? 枉道而事人，何必去父母之邦?"

【注释】
①士师：典狱官，掌管刑狱。

【今译】
柳下惠做典狱官，多次被罢免。有人说："你不可以离开鲁国吗?"柳下惠说："按正道事奉君主，到哪里不会被多次罢免呢? 如果不按正道事奉君主，何必要离开自己的祖国呢?"

【英译】
Liuxia Hui was dismissed three times when he was a judge. Someone said to him, "Why don't you leave this state?"

He answered, "If I serve others in an upright way, where can I go without meeting the same fate? If I serve others in a crooked way, what need is there to leave my motherland?"

18·3　齐景公待孔子曰："若季氏，则吾不能；以季、孟之间待之。"曰："吾老矣，不能用也。"孔子行。

【今译】
齐景公挽留孔子说："像鲁君对待季氏那样，我做不到；我用介于季氏孟氏之间的待遇对待他。"（不久，）又说："我老了，不能用了。"孔子离开了齐国。

【英译】
In receiving Confucius, Duke Jing of Qi said, "I am unable

to treat him the way the Ji family receives him. I will treat him like one between the Ji and the Meng." Later he said: "I am getting old, and I shall not be able to make use of his talent." Whereupon Confucius departed from Qi.

【辨正】

"吾老矣，不能用也"是齐景公说的，还是孔子说的？

司马迁《史记·孔子世家》："景公止孔子曰：'奉子以季氏，吾不能。'以季孟之间待之。齐大夫欲害孔子，孔子闻之。景公曰：'吾老矣，弗能用也。'孔子遂行，反乎鲁。"

杨逢彬《论语新注新译》："如果这话是孔子所说，根据《论语》文例，作为主语的'子'或'孔子'必须在'曰'前出现。此处没有出现，所以，'吾老矣，不能用也'只能是前文出现的主语'齐景公'说的。…… 2.'吾老矣，不能用也'的下文'孔子行'也说明这句话不是孔子说的，否则，依《论语》文例，'孔子'不必出现。…… 3. 与此相关，本章'曰'之前没有出现的主语若是孔子，依当时文法，应当不是'孔子行'，而是'遂行'或'乃行'。"

18·4　齐人归女乐，季桓子受之，三日不朝，孔子行。

【今译】

齐国人赠送了一些歌女给鲁国，季桓子接受了，三天不上朝。孔子就离开了鲁国。

【英译】

The State of Qi sent to the State of Lu a present of singing and dancing girls. Ji Huanzi accepted them and stayed away from court for three days. Whereupon Confucius departed from Lu.

18·5　楚狂接舆①歌而过孔子曰:"凤②兮凤兮! 何德之衰? 往者不可谏③，来者犹可追。已而，已而! 今之从政者殆而!"

孔子下，欲与之言。趋而辟④之，不得与之言。

【注释】

①接:迎。舆:车。迎面遇着孔子的车。这里因其事而呼其人为"接舆"。

②凤:凤凰。古时传说，世有道则凤鸟见，无道则隐。这里比喻孔子。接舆认为孔子世无道而不能隐，故说"德衰"。

③谏:劝而止。

④辟:同"避"。

【今译】

楚国的狂人接舆唱着歌从孔子的车旁走过，他唱道:"凤凰啊，凤凰啊，你的品德怎么这么衰败呢? 过去的已经无可挽回，未来的还来得及改正。停下吧，停下吧。今天的从政者危险了!"孔子下车，想同他谈谈，他却赶快避开，孔子没能和他交谈。

【英译】

Jieyu, the Madman of Chu, went past Confucius, singing,

"Phoenix, Oh phoenix!

How your virtue has waned!

The past is beyond retrieve,

The future has yet to come.

Give up, give up,

There is nothing but danger

For those in power today."

Confucius got down from his carriage with the intention of speaking with the "madman". But the man hurried off. In the end, Confucius never got to speak with him.

18·6　长沮、桀溺耦而耕，孔子过之，使子路问津焉。

长沮曰："夫执舆者为谁？"

子路曰："为孔丘。"

曰："是鲁孔丘与？"

曰："是也。"

曰："是知津矣。"问于桀溺。

桀溺曰："子为谁？"

曰："为仲由。"

曰："是孔丘之徒与？"

对曰："然。"

曰："滔滔者天下皆是也，而谁以易之？且而与其从辟人之士也，岂若从辟世之士哉？"耰①而不辍。

子路行以告。

夫子怃然曰："鸟兽不可与同群，吾非斯人之徒与而谁与？天下有道，丘不与易也。"

【注释】

①耰（yōu）：播种后平土覆盖种子。

【今译】

长沮、桀溺在一起耕种，孔子路过，让子路去寻问渡口在哪里。长沮问子路："那个拿着缰绳的是谁？"子路说："是孔丘。"长沮说;"是鲁国的孔丘吗?"子路说:"是的。"长沮说:"那他知道渡口的位置。"子路再去问桀溺。桀溺说:"你是谁?"子路说:"我是仲由。"桀溺说:"你是鲁国孔丘的门徒吗?"子路说:"是的。"桀溺说:"像洪水一般的坏东西到处都是,谁能改变它呢?而且你与其跟着躲避人的人,为什么不跟着我们这些躲避社会的人呢?"说完,仍旧不停地做田里的农活。子路回来后把情况报告给夫子。夫子很惆怅地说:"人是不能与飞禽走兽合群共处的,如果不与这样的人一道还与谁一道呢?如果天下太平,我就不会参与改变了。"

【英译】

Changju and Jieni were ploughing the field together. Confucius, passing by them, sent Zilu to ask where the ford was.

Changju said, "Who is the man driving the carriage?"

Zilu said, "It is Kong Qiu."

"Is it that Kong Qiu of Lu?"

"Yes."

"Then he should know where the ford is."

Zilu asked Jieni.

Jieni said, "Who are you?"

"I am Zhong You."

"Are you a disciple of Kong Qiu of Lu?

"Yes, I am," said Zilu.

"The whole world is now as turbulent as a river in spate. Who is there to change it? Moreover, would it be better if, instead of following a gentleman getting away from men, you follow one who tries to get away from the world altogether?" All the while he carried on harrowing without interruption.

Zilu went back and reported it to the Master, who was lost in thought for a while and said, "Men cannot be associated with birds and beasts. If I am not an associate of these men, whom should I associate with? If the world was governed on the right track, I would not have tried to change it."

18·7 子路从而后，遇丈人，以杖荷蓧①。

子路问曰："子见夫子乎？"

丈人曰："四体不勤，五谷不分。孰为夫子？"植②其杖而芸。

子路拱而立。

止子路宿，杀鸡为黍而食之，见其二子焉。

明日，子路行以告。

子曰："隐者也。"使子路反见之。至，则行矣。

子路曰："不仕无义。长幼之节，不可废也；君臣之义，如之何其废之？欲洁其身，而乱大伦。君子之仕也，行其义也。道之不行，已知之矣。"

【注释】

①蓧（diào）：古代用以除草的竹器。

②植：拄。

【今译】

子路跟随夫子出行，落在了后面，遇到一个老者，用拐杖掮着除草的工具。子路问道："你看到我的老师了吗？"老者说："四肢不劳动，五谷分不清，怎么当老师？"说完，便挂着拐杖去除草。子路拱着手恭敬地站在一旁。老者留子路到他家住宿，杀了鸡，做了小米饭给他吃，又叫两个儿子出来与子路见面。第二天，子路赶上夫子，把这件事向他作了报告。夫子说："这是个隐士啊。"叫子路回去再看看他。子路到了那里，老者已经走了。子路说："不做官是不对的。长幼间的关系既然不可废弃，君臣间的关系又怎么能废弃呢？想要洁身自好，却破坏了根本的君臣伦理关系。君子做官，只是为了行其大义。至于大道不得行，早就知道了。"

【英译】

Once Zilu fell behind his master on a trip, and happened to meet an elderly man carrying a weeding tool with a staff over his shoulder.

Zilu went up to him and asked, "Did you happen to see my Master?"

The old man said, "What kind of a master is he if he does not use his four limbs and cannot tell one kind of grain from another?" He then, leaning on his staff, started weeding.

Zilu stood, cupping one hand respectfully in the other.

The old man invited Zilu to stay for the night. He killed a chicken and prepared some millet for his guest, and presented his two sons to him.

The next day, Zilu caught up with Confucius and reported this conversation. The Master said, "He must be a recluse." He sent Zilu back to look for the old man. When he arrived, the old man had already left.

Zilu commented, "It is not right to refuse to take office. The proper regulation of old and young should not be abandoned. How, then, should the duty between ruler and subject be abandoned? It is not righteous to discard loyalty simply to keep one's virtue unsullied. A gentleman takes office in order to do his duty, even if he might have long foreseen that the right principles will not prevail."

【辨正】

白平《杨伯峻〈论语译注〉商榷》："原文这里的'子路曰'，其实当做'子曰'，在传抄的过程中多出了'路'字。下面一段文字所讲的道理显然是孔子的思想，子路并没有达到这种认识。如果他事先已有这种认识的话，在丈人批评孔子和使两个儿子来拜见他时，他就应该对丈人讲这番话了。孔子之所以派他返回去再见丈人，显然也是为了让他对丈人转达这番话。

"孔子认为，作为臣民，不能不承担起对君主应负的责任，对君主负责其实就是对社会负责。君臣之间的道义是人际间十分重要的伦理，仅次于父子之间的'孝'的讲究。君子出来做官，就是为了履行自己的这种责任，如果因为社会黑暗就拒绝做官，就是放弃了这种责任，是不道义的。隐士们洁身自好固然可敬，但却是一种因小失大的表现，是顾了自己而不顾社会，不能算是正确的选择。"

18·8 逸民：伯夷、叔齐、虞仲、夷逸、朱张、柳下惠、少连。子曰："不降其志，不辱其身，伯夷、叔齐与！"谓："柳下惠、少连，降志辱身矣，言中伦，行中虑，其斯而已矣。"谓："虞仲、夷逸，隐居放言，身中清，废中权。我则异于是，无可无不可。"

【今译】

古今隐逸不仕的有：伯夷、叔齐、虞仲、夷逸、朱张、柳下惠、少连。夫子说："不降低自己的意志，不屈辱自己的身分，这是伯夷和叔齐吧。"说柳下惠、少连是"被迫降低自己的意志，屈辱自己的身份，但说话合乎伦理，行为经过思虑。"说虞仲、夷逸"过着隐居的生活，说话畅言无忌，能洁身自爱，离开官位合乎权宜。"我却与这些人不同，没有什么可以的，也没有什么不可以的。"

【英译】

Men who withdrew from society: Bo Yi, Shu Qi, Yu Zhong, Yi Yi, Zhu Zhang, Liuxia Hui, Shao Lian. The Master commented, "Not to lower their purpose or to allow themselves to be humiliated describes, perhaps, Bo Yi and Shu Qi." Of Liuxia Hui and Shao Lian he said, "They, indeed, compromised their aspirations and suffered disgrace. But their words were consistent with their status and their behaviour prudent. That is all one can say about them." Of Yu Zhong and Yi Yi he said, "They lived as recluses and spoke their minds freely. They kept their character unsullied and showed sound judgment in accepting their dismissal. I, however, am different from them. I do not think there is any rigid rule as to what one should or should not do."

18·9　大师挚①适齐，亚饭干适楚，三饭缭适蔡，四饭缺适秦②，鼓方叔入于河，播鼗③武入于汉，少师④阳、击磬襄入于海。

【注释】

①大师挚："大"通"太"。太师是鲁国乐官之长，挚是人名。

②亚饭、三饭、四饭：都是乐官名。干、缭、缺是人名。

③鼗（táo）：小鼓。

④少师：乐官名，副乐师。

【今译】

太师挚到齐国去了，亚饭干到楚国去了，三饭缭到蔡国去了，四饭缺到秦国去了，打鼓的方叔到了黄河边，敲小鼓的武到了汉水边，少师阳和击磬的襄到了海滨。

【英译】

Zhi, the Grand Musician, left for Qi; Gan, musician for the second course, left for Chu; Liao, musician for the third course, left for Cai; Que, musician for the fourth course, left for Qin; Fang Shu, the drummer, went to live by the Yellow River; Wu, player of the hand drum, went to live by the Han River; Yang, the Grand Musician's deputy, and Xiang, who played the stone chimes, went to live by the sea.

18·10　周公谓鲁公曰："君子不施①其亲，不使大臣怨乎不以。故旧无大故，则不弃也。无求备于一人！"

【注释】

①施：通"弛"，怠慢、疏远。《坊记注》："弛，弃忘也。"

【今译】

周公对鲁公说："君子不疏远他的亲属，不使大臣抱怨不用他们。旧友老臣没有大的过失，就不要抛弃他们。不要对人求全责备。"

The Duke of Zhou told（his son）the Duke of Lu, "A gentleman does not neglect his relatives, nor would he cause his ministers to complain of not being trusted. Unless they make serious mistakes, those who have served for long years should not be dismissed. Do not demand perfection from any single individual."

18·11 周有八士：伯达、伯适、仲突、仲忽、叔夜、叔夏、季随、季骊。

【今译】

周代有八个士：伯达、伯适、仲突、仲忽、叔夜、叔夏、季随、季骊。

【英译】

There were eight great scholars in Zhou: Bo Da, Bo Kuo, Zhong Tu, Zhong Hu, Shu Ye, Shu Xia, Ji Sui and Ji Gua.

子张第十九

19·1　子张曰:"士见危致命,见得思义,祭思敬,丧思哀,其可已矣。"

【今译】

子张说:"士遇见危险时能舍命,在有利可得时能考虑是否该得,祭祀时能努力严肃恭敬,居丧时能努力悲痛哀伤,这样就可以了。"

【英译】

Zizhang said, "One can, perhaps, be satisfied with a scholar who is ready to lay down his life in the face of danger, who does not forget what is right at the sight of gain, and who shows reverence at a sacrificial ceremony and sorrow at mourning."

19·2　子张曰:"执德不弘,信道不笃,焉能为有? 焉能为亡?"

【今译】

子张说:"有德而不宏大,信道而不坚定,(这样)怎么能叫有,怎么能叫无?"

Zizhang said, "If the virtue a man holds is not grand, and the way he believes in right principles is not steadfast, can he be called virtuous? Can he be called villainous?"

19·3　子夏之门人问交于子张。子张曰："子夏云何?"
对曰："子夏曰:'可者与之，其不可者拒之。'"
子张曰："异乎吾所闻:君子尊贤而容众，嘉善而矜不能。我之大贤与，于人何所不容? 我之不贤与，人将拒我，如之何其拒人也?"

【今译】

子夏的学生向子张请教怎样结交朋友。子张说:"子夏怎么说?"答道:"子夏说:'可以相交的就交，不可交的就拒绝他。'"子张说:"我听到的和这些不一样:君子既尊重贤人，又能容纳众人;能够赞美善人，又能同情能力差的。如果我非常贤良，那我对别人有什么不能容纳的呢? 如果我不贤良，那别人就会拒绝我，我怎么会拒绝别人呢?"

【英译】

Zixia's disciples asked Zizhang about making friends.

Zizhang asked, "What did your master tell you?"

The student answered, "Zixia says, 'You should make friends with those who are worthy and spurn those who are not."

Zizhang said, "That is different from what I was taught. I was taught that a gentleman respects the virtuous while tolerating the ordinary, and praises the talented while sympathizing with the mediocre. If I am a truly virtuous man, what is it that I cannot tolerate? If I am not virtuous enough, the others will spurn me, then how can I spurn them?"

19·4　子夏曰："虽小道①，必有可观者焉；致远恐泥，是以君子不为也。"

【注释】
①小道：指各种农工商医卜之类的技艺。

【今译】
子夏说："即使是小技艺，也一定有可取的地方，但研究太深恐怕会陷在里面，所以君子不做这些小技艺。"

【英译】
Zixia said, "Even minor arts are sure to have their worthwhile aspects, but a gentleman does not take them up for fear of being bogged down when exploring deeply."

19·5　子夏曰："日知其所亡，月无忘其所能，可谓好学也已矣。"

【今译】
子夏说："每天学到一些他不知道的东西，每月不忘记他已掌握的东西，这就可以算是好学了。"

【英译】
Zixia said, "A man can, indeed, be said to be eager to learn who is aware of what he needs to learn every day and who will

review every month what he has mastered."

19·6　子夏曰;"博学而笃志，切问而近思，仁在其中矣。"

【今译】

子夏说："博览群书而坚守自己的志趣，急切地发问，思考身边的问题，仁就在其中了。"

【英译】

Zixia said, "Learn widely and hold fast to your purpose, inquire eagerly and reflect on what is at hand, as therein lies benevolence."

19·7　子夏曰："百工居肆以成其事，君子学以致其道。"

【今译】

子夏说："各行各业的工匠住在作坊里来完成自己的工作，君子通过学习来掌握真理。"

【英译】

Zixia said, "Artisans master their crafts by staying in their workshops; a gentleman masters the principles of the world through learning."

19·8　子夏说："小人之过也必文。"

【今译】

子夏说："小人犯了过错一定要掩饰。"

Zixia said, "When the petty man makes a mistake, he is sure to gloss it over."

19·9 子夏曰："君子有三变：望之俨然，即之也温，听其言也厉。"

【今译】

子夏说："君子有三变：远看他的样子庄重威严，走近了感觉温和可亲，听他说话又觉得义正辞严。"

【英译】

Zixia said, "A gentleman leaves people with three different impressions: From a distance, he looks solemn; when approached, he looks cordial; when he speaks, he sounds stern."

19·10 子夏曰："君子信而后劳其民；未信，则以为厉^①己也。信而后谏；未信，则以为谤己也。"

【注释】

①厉：祸害。

【今译】

子夏说："君子必须守信才能役使百姓；否则，百姓就会以为是你祸害他们。守信然后才能规劝；否则，（君主）就会以为你毁谤他。"

Zixia said, "A gentleman needs to be trustworthy before he can employ people. Otherwise, they will feel abused. He needs to be trustworthy before he can remonstrate. Otherwise, the lord would feel himself slandered."

19·11 子夏曰："大德①不逾闲②，小德出入可也。"

【注释】

①大德：与小德相对，犹言大节。

②闲：本义是阑，栅栏，引申为限制、规矩。这里指道德的规范。

【今译】

子夏说："大德不可超越界限，小德有些出入可以。"

【英译】

Zixia said, "On matters of principle no transgression should be made; in small matters, some deviation may be permissible."

19·12 子游曰："子夏之门人小子，当洒扫应对进退，则可矣，抑末也。本之则无，如之何？"

子夏闻之，曰："噫！言游过矣！君子之道，孰先传焉？孰后倦焉？譬诸草木，区以别矣。君子之道，焉可诬也？有始有卒者，其惟圣人乎？"

【今译】

子游说："子夏的学生，做些打扫、应对和迎来送往的事情可以，但这些是细枝末节，根本的东西却没有学到，这怎么行呢？"子夏听了，说："唉，言游错了。君子之道哪一样应先教，哪一样应后学，就像草木有种类的区别一样，都分得很清楚。君子之道怎么可以随意毁谤呢？能按次序有始有终地教授学生，大概只有圣人吧？"

【英译】

Ziyou said, "The disciples and younger followers of Zixia can certainly cope with the task of sweeping and cleaning, and escorting and seeing off guests, which are all trifling matters. When it comes to the basics, however, they have no idea. How can that be?"

When Zixia heard this, he said, "Alas, Ziyou has got it wrong! In the ways of a gentleman, what should be taught first and what comes afterwards? They are as clearly distinguished as grasses and trees. How can one defame the way of a gentleman? Is it the sage alone who can teach his disciples in the proper order from beginning to end?"

19·13 子夏曰："仕而优则学，学而优则仕。"

【今译】

子夏说："做官有馀力的人，就可以去学习，学习有馀力的人，就可以去做官。"

【英译】

Zixia said, "An official, after fully performing his duties, should devote his spare time or energy to learning; a learner, after fully completed his learning, should devote his time or energy to seeking to be an official."

19·14　子游曰："丧致乎哀而止。"

【今译】
子游说："居丧，能做到尽哀即止。"

【英译】
Ziyou said, "When in mourning, one should not go beyond expressing grief."

19·15　子游曰："吾友张也为难能也，然而未仁。"

【今译】
子游说："我的朋友子张可以说是难得的了，然而还没有做到仁。"

【英译】
Ziyou said, "My friend Zhang is a rare talent. Still, he has not yet attained benevolence."

19·16　曾子曰："堂堂乎张也，难与并为仁矣。"

【今译】
曾子说："子张外表堂堂，难以与他一起行仁。"

【英译】

Master Zeng said, "How superb Zhang looks. Yet, it is difficult to work with him to practice benevolence."

19·17　曾子曰："吾闻诸夫子：人未有自致^①者也，必也亲丧乎！"

【注释】

①致：穷其极。这里指充分表露自己的情感。父母之丧，哀痛之情，不待人勉而自尽其极。

【今译】

曾子说："我听老师说过，人没有竭尽自己情感的，（如果有，）一定是在父母离世时。"

【英译】

Master Zeng said, "I once heard the Master say that on no occasion does a man feel exhausted emotionally. If there is an exception, it must be the time when his parents depart the world."

19·18　曾子曰："吾闻诸夫子：孟庄子之孝也，其他可能也；其不改父之臣与父之政，是难能也。"

【今译】

曾子说："我听老师说过，孟庄子的孝，其他方面常人可以做到，但他不更换父亲的旧臣及其政治措施，这是常人难以做到的。"

Master Zeng said, "I once heard the Master say, other men can emulate everything Meng Zhuangzi did as a good son, but it will be difficult to follow his example of leaving unchanged both his father's officials and policies."

19·19　孟氏使阳肤为士师，问于曾子。曾子曰："上失其道，民散久矣。如得其情，则哀矜而勿喜！"

【今译】

孟氏任命阳肤做典狱官，阳肤向曾子请教。曾子说："在上位的人离开了正道，百姓不检束自己已经很久了。你如果能弄清他们的实情，就应当哀怜他们，而不要高兴。"

【英译】

The Meng family appointed Yang Fu as a judge and he sought the advice of Master Zeng. Master Zeng said, "Those in authority deviated from the right track and the common people have long been unrestrained. If you succeed in extracting the truth from criminals, you should have compassion on them instead of feeling pleased with yourself."

19·20　子贡曰："纣之不善，不如是之甚也。是以君子恶居下流，天下之恶皆归焉。"

【今译】

子贡说："纣王的坏，不像人说的这样厉害。所以君子憎恨处在下位，那样天下一切坏名声都归到他的身上。"

Zigong said, "King Zhou was not as wicked as all that. That is why a gentleman hates to dwell downstream for it is there that all that is sordid in the world finds its way."

19·21　子贡曰："君子之过也，如日月之食焉：过也，人皆见之；更也，人皆仰之。"

【今译】

子贡说："君子的过错好比日食月食。他犯过错，人人都看得见；他改正过错，人人都敬仰他。"

【英译】

Zigong said, "A gentleman's errors are like eclipses of the sun or the moon in that when he errs all men witness it; when he mends it, all men look up to him with admiration."

19·22　卫公孙朝问于子贡曰："仲尼焉学？"子贡曰："文武之道，未坠于地，在人。贤者识其大者，不贤者识其小者。莫不有文武之道焉。夫子焉不学？而亦何常师之有？"

【今译】

卫国的公孙朝问子贡说："仲尼（的学问）从哪里学来的？"子贡说："周文王、武王的道，并没有失传，还在人间。贤能的人记住它的根本，不贤的人记住它的末节，每个人都有一些文武之道。我们老师何处不学？又哪里有固定的老师呢？"

Gongsun Chao of Wei asked Zigong, "From whom did Zhongni learn?"

Zigong said, "The Way of King Wen and King Wu (of the Zhou Dynasty) never fell into oblivion. It remained alive among the people. The virtuous retained its essence while the mediocre retained a few details. Everyone had some elements of the Way of King Wen and King Wu. From whom, then, did our Master not learn? Yet, where was the need for him to have one fixed teacher?"

19·23　叔孙武叔语大夫于朝曰："子贡贤于仲尼。"子服景伯以告子贡。

子贡曰："譬之宫墙，赐之墙也及肩，窥见室家之好。夫子之墙数仞，不得其门而入，不见宗庙之美，百官之富。得其门者或寡矣。夫子之云，不亦宜乎！"

【今译】

叔孙武叔在朝廷上对大夫说："子贡比仲尼更贤。"子服景伯把这一番话告诉了子贡。子贡说："拿围墙来作比喻，我的围墙高度齐肩，人能从外面窥见房子漂亮。夫子的围墙高数仞，如果找不到门进去，就看不见里面宗庙华美，馆舍众多。能够找到门进去的人或许很少。叔孙武叔那么讲，不也是很正常吗？"

【英译】

Shusun Wushu said to the Counsellors at court, "Zigong is superior to Zhongni."

Zifu Jingbo reported that to Zigong.

Zigong said, "Let us take a boundary wall as an analogy.

My wall is at shoulder height, so that the fine architecture inside can be seen from outside. But the Master's walls are meters high. If one is unable to find the entrance, he cannot see the magnificence of the ancestral temples or the splendor of the mansions within. Since those who can find the entrance are, shall we say, few, is it not understandable that your master should have spoken so?"

19·24　叔孙武叔毁仲尼。子贡曰;"无以为也！仲尼不可毁也。他人之贤者，丘陵也，犹可逾也；仲尼，日月也，无得而逾焉。人虽欲自绝，其何伤于日月乎？多①见其不知量也。"

【注释】
①多：用作副词，只是，恰好是。

【今译】
叔孙武叔诽谤仲尼。子贡说："（这样做）是没有用的！仲尼是毁谤不了的。别人的贤德好比丘陵，还可超越过去；仲尼的贤德好比太阳月亮，是无法超越的。虽然有人要自绝于日月，对日月又有什么损害呢？只是表明他不自量。"

【英译】
Shusun Wushu made defamatory remarks about Zhongni. Zigong said, "It will make no difference. Zhongni cannot be defamed. Other virtuous men are like hills that can be surmounted. But Zhongni is like the sun or the moon that is insurmountable. Even if someone wanted to cut himself off from them, how could this detract from the sun and the moon? It would merely

serve to show that he did not know his own measure."

19 · 25　陈子禽谓子贡曰："子为恭也，仲尼岂贤于子乎？"

子贡曰："君子一言以为知，一言以为不知，言不可不慎也。夫子之不可及也，犹天之不可阶而升也。夫子之得邦家者，所谓立之斯立，道之斯行，绥之斯来，动之斯和。其生也荣，其死也哀，如之何其可及也？"

【今译】

陈子禽对子贡说："您是谦恭了，仲尼哪能比您更贤良呢？"子贡说："君子的一句话就显示出智慧，一句话就可以显示出无智，所以说话不可以不慎重啊！夫子的高不可及，就好比天是不能用梯子爬上去一样。夫子如果君临一方，就可以做到我们所说的'教百姓立于礼，百姓就会立于礼，引导百姓，百姓就会跟着走；安抚百姓，百姓就会归顺；役使百姓，百姓就会齐心协力。'（夫子）活着十分荣耀，（夫子）死了会让人悲哀。我怎么能赶得上他呢？"

【英译】

Chen Ziqin said to Zigong, "Surely you are being respectful to Confucius. How could Zhongni be superior to you?"

Zigong said, "A gentleman may be judged wise or foolish by a single utterance. That is why one cannot be too reckless with his words. The Master cannot be equalled just as the sky cannot be scaled with a ladder. Were the Master to become the head of a state or a noble family, he would be able to accomplish what is described in the saying: 'Make the people stand on their own（feet）and they will become well- established; lead them and they will follow him; appease them and they will be won ever; mobilize them and they will echo his call.' In life he is honoured and in death he will be mourned. How can he ever be equalled?"

尧曰第二十

20·1　尧曰："咨^①！尔舜！天之历数^②在尔躬，允执其中^③。四海困穷^④，天禄永终^⑤。"

舜亦以命禹。

曰："予小子履^⑥，敢用玄牡^⑦，敢昭告于皇皇后帝：有罪不敢赦，帝臣不蔽，简^⑧在帝心。朕^⑨躬有罪，无以万方；万方有罪，罪在朕躬。"

周有大赉^⑩，善人是富。"虽有周亲^⑪，不如仁人。百姓有过，在予一人。"

谨权量^⑫，审法度，修废官，四方之政行焉。兴灭国，继绝世，举逸民，天下之民归心焉。

所重：民、食、丧、祭。宽则得众，信则民任焉。敏则有功，公则说。

【注释】

①咨：即"啧"，感叹词，表示赞誉。

②历数：列次。这里指帝王相继的次序。

③允：诚信。执：保持。中：正，不偏不倚，不"过"也无"不及"。

④四海："八荒之内有四海，四海之内有九州。"四海之内，犹言天下。困：极。穷：尽。

⑤永终：永长。

⑥小子：祭天地时的自称。履：商汤的名字。

⑦玄：黑色。牡：公（牛）。

⑧简：察阅。这里是知道，明白，清楚。

⑨朕：我。古人自称。从秦始皇起，成为帝王专用的自称。

⑩赉（lài）：赏赐。

⑪周亲：至亲。

⑫权：秤锤，指计重量的标准。量：斗斛，指计容积的标准。

【今译】

尧说："啧啧！你这位舜！上天的大命已经落在你的身上。真诚地保持那中道吧！政通人和将遍及四海，天禄将永长。"

舜也用这话告诫禹。

（商汤）说："我小子履谨用黑色的公牛来祭祀，向伟大的天帝您祷告：有罪的人我不敢擅自赦免，作为天帝的臣仆我不敢掩蔽，（一切）都明察在天帝的心里。我本人若有罪，不要连累天下万方；天下万方若有罪，（罪责）都在我一个人身上。"

周朝有大封赏，要使善人都富起来。（周武王）说："我虽然有至亲，不如有仁德之人。百姓有过错，都在我一人身上。"

认真检验度量衡器，周密审定法令制度，修复废置的机构，国家的政令就会畅行无阻。恢复已被灭亡的国家，接续已经断绝了的家族，举用品行高尚的人，天下百姓就会真心归服。

所重视的四件事：人民、粮食、丧礼、祭祀。

宽厚就能得到众人的拥护，诚信就能得百姓的信任，勤敏就能取得成绩，公正就会使百姓高兴。

【英译】

Yao said,

"Oh, Shun!

The succession, ordained by Heaven, has fallen on thy person.

Holdst thou truly to the middle way.

Good government will cover every corner of the world,

The honors bestowed on thee by Heaven will forever last."

Shun spoke the same words to Yu when proclaiming him the successor.

(Shang Tang) said, "I, Lü, the little one, venture to offer a black bull and make this declaration to you, the great Lord of Heaven: I dare not pardon those who have transgressed. I, as your servant, shall hide nothing, as you have perceived everything in your heart. If I transgress, please do not impute it to my people, and if my people have committed any offence, let the punishment befall me alone.

In the Zhou Dynasty, a great number of people were made fiefs and the virtuous men were all made prosperous.

"I may have close relatives,

But better for me to have benevolent men.

If the people transgress

Let my person be punished."

Unify weights and measures, standardize laws and regulations, and re- establish official posts which have been abolished, then government orders will be carried out throughout the country. Restore states which have been destroyed, revive lineages of big families which have become extinct, promote talented people who have withdrawn from society, then you can win over the hearts of all the common people in the Empire.

What was considered of importance: people, food, mourning and sacrifice.

Leniency gains the support of the multitude. Sincerity wins the trust of the common people. Industriousness leads to success. Impartiality brings hearty admiration of the common people.

【辨正】

"四海困穷，天禄永终"是"天下陷入困顿，天赐禄位也会永远终止"，还是"德政遍及天下，天赐禄位永长不绝"？

《广雅·释古一》："困，极也。"《国语·越语下》："日困而还，月盈而匡。"韦昭注："困，穷也。"《说文·穴部》："穷，极也。"《书·微子之命》："作宾于王家，与国咸休，永世无穷。"孔传："为时王宾客与时皆美，长世无竟。""困"与"穷"，都有极、尽的含义。

毛奇龄《论语稽求篇》："盖'天禄永终'断无作永绝解者。潜丘尝谓汉魏以还，俱解永长；典午以后，始解永绝。此正古今升降之辨，如《金滕》'惟永终是图'，《周易·归妹》象词'君子以永终知敝'，则永终二字原非恶词。故汉魏用经语者，班彪《王命论》云：'福祚流于子孙，天禄其永终矣。'隽不疑谓暴胜之曰：'树功扬名，永终天禄。'《韦贤传》匡衡曰：'其道应天，故天禄永终。'灵帝立皇后诏曰：'无替朕命，永终天禄。'凡用些语者，无不以永长为辞。自新莽以后，魏晋五代皆用《尧曰》文作禅位之册，而策书引经前后顿异，此考之列史而昭然者。汉献禅位于魏，册曰：'允执其中，天禄永终。'魏使郑冲奉册于晋王曰：'允执其中，天禄永终。'汉武立子齐王闳策曰：'允执其中，天禄永终。'吴大帝告天文曰：'左右有吴，永终天禄。'皆作永长解。及三国以后，《魏志》：'山阳公深识天禄永终之运，禅位文皇帝。'又曰'山阳公昔知天命永终于己深观历数久在圣躬，因诏禅位于晋。'而嗣后宋、齐、梁、陈，其文一辙，皆曰：'敬禅神器，授帝位于尔躬。四海困穷，天禄永终。于戏！王其允执厥中，仪刑前典，以副昊天之望。'于是皆以'其中'为'厥中'，以'天禄永终'继'困穷'之后，为却位绝天之辞。而于是策书改，即《论语》亦俱改矣。此实经籍文体升降前后一大关节，而注其书者，安可姑置之不一察也！"

20·2　子张问孔子曰："何如斯①可以从政矣？"

子曰："尊五美，屏②四恶，斯可以从政矣。"

子张曰："何谓五美？"

子曰："君子惠而不费，劳而不怨，欲而不贪，泰而不骄，威而不猛。"

子张曰："何谓惠而不费？"

子曰："因民之所利而利之，斯不亦惠而不费乎？择可劳而劳之，又谁怨？欲仁而得仁，又焉贪？君子无众寡，无大小，无敢慢，斯不亦泰而不骄乎？君子正其衣冠，尊其瞻视，俨然人望而畏之，斯不亦威而不猛乎？"

子张曰："何谓四恶？"

子曰："不教而杀谓之虐；不戒视成谓之暴；慢令致期谓之贼③；犹之与人也，出纳④之吝谓之有司⑤。"

【注释】

①斯：则。

②屏（bǐng）：摒除。

③慢：懈怠，随便。致期：紧限日期。贼：祸害。

④出纳：财物的支出和收入。此处是偏义复合词组，只有"出"义。

⑤有司：本为官吏的统称。古代设官分职，各有专司，故称有司。这里指库吏。皇疏："有司，谓主典物者也，犹库吏之属也。库吏虽有官物，而不得自由，故物应出入者，必有所谘问，不敢擅易。人君若物与人而吝，即与库吏无异，故云'谓之有司'也。"

【今译】

子张问孔子说："怎么样才可以从政呢？"

孔子说："尊崇五种美德，摒除四种恶习，这样就可以从政了。"

子张问："五种美德是什么？"

孔子说："君子要给人恩惠却不浪费；使人劳作却不引人抱怨；有野心却不贪婪；庄重却不傲慢；威严却不凶猛。"

子张说："什么是给人恩惠却不浪费呢？"

孔子说："顺应百姓的利益去做对他们有利的事，这不就是给人恩惠却不浪费！选择可以役使的时间和事情让百姓去做，又会有谁抱怨呢？追求仁德便得到了仁德，有什么可贪的呢？君子待人，无论多少，不分大小，都不怠慢，这不就是庄重而不傲慢吗？君子衣冠整齐，目不邪视，使人见了就心生敬畏，这不就是威严而不凶猛吗？"

子张问："什么叫四种恶习呢？"

孔子说："不加教化而杀戮叫做虐；不加告诫而看成果叫做暴；下令缓慢而期限紧迫叫做贼；譬如给人财物，出手吝啬，叫做小气。"

Zizhang asked Confucius, "How does one qualify to govern?"

The Master said, "He should cultivate the five virtues and eschew the four evils."

Zizhang said, "What are the five virtues?"

The Master said, "A gentleman should be generous without being extravagant; employ the people without causing complaints; be ambitious without being greedy; be self-possessed without being arrogant; and be dignified without looking fierce."

Zizhang said, "What is meant by 'be generous without being extravagant'?"

The Master said, "If a man benefits the common people by taking advantage of the things that they find beneficial, is this not being generous without being extravagant? If a man chooses suitable time to employ the labor force, then who will complain? If, desiring benevolence, a man obtains it, and what need is there to be greedy? A gentleman treats people equally without slightness, irregardless of the number or age. Is this not being self-possessed without being arrogant? A gentleman dresses properly and looks dignified, thus people look at him with awe. Is this not being dignified without looking fierce?"

Zizhang said, "What is meant by the four evils?"

The Master said, "To impose the death penalty without first educating the people is called cruelty; to demand achievement without prior requirements is called tyranny; to impose a pressing deadline on a job when tardy in issuing orders is called circumvention; to give, for example, others things in a miserly way is called stinginess."

20·3　孔子曰:"不知命,无以为君子也;不知礼,无以立也;不知言,无以知人也。"

【今译】

孔子说:"不懂得天命,就不能做君子;不知道礼法,就不能立身处世;不能从言谈中了解真意,就不能真正了解他人。"

【英译】

Confucius said, "A man who does not know destiny will never become a gentleman. He who does not know the rites will never become established. He who cannot judge the words of others will never be able to really know the people who uttered them."